461-D-5

The Condition of Education in Rural Schools

Joyce D. Stern
Editor and Project Director

U.S. Department of Education
Office of Educational Research and Improvement
Programs for the Improvement of Practice

U.S. Department of Education
Richard W. Riley
Secretary

Office of Educational Research and Improvement
Sharon P. Robinson
Assistant Secretary

Programs for the Improvement of Practice
Eve M. Bither
Director

June 1994

Cover photo
End of the day at Solon Elementary School (enrollment:
145 students, grades K–8), Solon, Maine. **Photo by
Julie Searls**.

Inside front cover photo
Morning rush hour, country road, Cockeysville,
Maryland. **Photo by J. Norman Reid**, Falls Church,
Virginia.

For sale by the U.S. Government Printing Office
Superintendent of Documents, Mail Stop: SSOP, Washington, DC 20402-9328
ISBN 0-16-045034-9

Foreword

Publication of *The Condition of Education in Rural Schools* represents an important contribution to education policymaking in this country. To be effective, policy and practice must be informed by current and accurate information. Toward that end, the Office of Educational Research and Improvement (OERI) within the U.S. Department of Education (ED) has been charged with reporting on "the condition and progress of education" and diffusing information that will "promote the cause of education throughout the country."

Over the years, many OERI publications have taken note of education in rural areas of the nation, but only a few have been specifically dedicated to some aspect of rural schooling. And none has attempted to describe a full range of data on elementary and secondary education in rural schools. This report seeks to fill that gap. Indeed, the scope of the information gathered here about rural education may be unprecedented.

This report is well-timed. The nation has embarked on a strategic mission to upgrade the quality and outcomes of education throughout the country. The National Education Goals articulated in 1989 are beacons, not just for an elite but for every citizen. For its part, one of OERI's goals is to raise the achievement level of each child. The nation's investment in educational research has demonstrated student performance will improve under certain conditions, that is, when expectations are high and clear; when students and teachers are challenged and motivated through curricular demands that provide all students with opportunities to learn; and when parents are actively involved in supporting their children's academic progress.

OERI is not alone in this sense of mission. In January 1992, the report of the nonpartisan National Council on Education Standards and Testing gave voice to the growing consensus that all students should learn challenging subject matter to prepare them for citizenship in a democratic society, for further education, and for rewarding careers—regardless of race, sex, or social background.

Nor should location present a barrier to educational opportunity. Rural schools educate a large percentage of America's students under sometimes daunting conditions. At the same time, many of these institutions have had notable success in educating generations of students for productive lives and citizenship. Yet until now, information about school-age children and youth in Rural America, drawn as it has been from small studies and occasional state reports, has been sketchy. National education data could sometimes be found in the appendices of statistical reports and the occasional journal article that tapped into a national data base. But comparatively little was known on a broad scale about such basics as the number and location of rural schools, teachers, and students, or about the unique circumstances and outcomes of rural education. This information deficit has been unfortunate from the standpoint of policymaking.

A few years ago, when Congress charged OERI to carry out a rural education initiative through the federally funded regional educational laboratories, it requested preparation of a report on the condition of education in rural, small schools. OERI complied with a document composed of regional perspectives drafted by each laboratory. While useful for regional planning, such a document had obvious limitations for wider utility. Thus, OERI staff drew up plans for a more comprehensive report that would give an updated picture nationally about rural schooling.

The resulting report constitutes a source of information on education in rural communities that will be useful for education researchers, policymakers at the federal and state levels, as well as others concerned about issues in rural education. Specifically, we hope this report will increase federal policymakers' attention to rural education problems, promote improvements in rural schools, and stimulate further research on rural education.

The report offers significant amounts of information as well as a structure for considering the issues. It does not, however, prescribe how these issues should be addressed. Problems confronting rural education are many and complex, and rural settings are too diverse for simple or universal remedies. But this report should help insure that the rural perspective is not ignored as the nation goes about creating new approaches to education appropriate for the 21st century.

Sharon P. Robinson
Assistant Secretary
Office of Educational Research and Improvement
U.S. Department of Education

Contents

Foreword iii

1. Introduction 1

2. Context of Rural Education: The Economy and Population of Rural America 7

3. Location and Characteristics of Rural Schools and School Districts 13

4. The Rural School-Community Connection 21

5. Policies and Programs Benefiting Rural Education 27

6. Educators in Rural Schools 33

7. Effects of Education Reform in Rural Schools 41

8. Public School Finance Policies and Practices Affecting Rural Schools 47

9. Assessment of Student Performance in Rural Schools 53

10. Education and Work Experiences of Rural Youth 61

11. Looking Ahead 69

Figures

2–1.—Urban-rural difference in earnings, full-time workers aged 25–34: Males 8

2–2.—Urban-rural difference in earnings, full-time workers aged 25–34: Females 8

2–3.—Net migration of nonmetropolitan population aged 25–64: 1988–89 average 10

2–4.—Production sector job growth, by education level of job: 1980–88 10

3–1.—Regular public schools per 100 square miles, by division and region: 1991–92 13

3–2.—Percentage distribution of schools, by school enrollment size and locale: 1991–92 14

3–3.—Percentage distribution of students, by school enrollment size and locale: 1991–92 15

3–4.—ERS county types 17

3–5.—ERS nonmetropolitan socioeconomic county types 18

6–1.—Degree attainment of teachers, by setting and school level taught: 1987–88 33

6–2.—Average scheduled salary for rural and nonrural teachers 34

6–3.—Degree attainment of public school principals, by setting and sex: 1987–88 37

6–4.—Average annual salaries of rural and nonrural public school principals, by sex: 1987–88 38

6–5.—Percentage of rural and nonrural school principals receiving various benefits: 1987–88 38

8–1.—A state system of public school finance: A common example 47

8–2.—Characteristics of rural schools and rural school districts 48

8–3.—Current education expenditure, elementary and secondary education 49

9–1.—Percentage of rural eighth graders with various risk factors 55

10–1.—Postsecondary educational plans of 1980 seniors, by location 61

10–2.—High school program enrollment, by type and location 62

Appendices 75

A. Supporting Tables 77

Table 3–1.— Number and percentage of regular public schools, students, and average school
enrollment, by NCES locale code: 1991–92 77

Table 3–2.— Percentage distribution of regular public schools and students by school enrollment
size and type of school, by rural and urban locale: 1991–92 78

Table 3–3.— Student teacher ratios, by school type, size, and locale: 1991–92 78

Table 3–4.— Number and percentage distribution of rural schools and students, by
division and state: 1991–92 79

Table 3–5.— Number of rural schools and percentage, by enrollment size, by division
and state: 1991–92 80

Table 3–6.— Number and percentage distribution of school districts, by percentage of
students attending rural schools: 1991–92 81

Table 3–7.— Number and percentage distribution of districts, schools, students, and teachers,
by rural or urban type of district: 1991–92 81

Table 3–8.— Number of rural and urban school districts and percentage by enrollment size,
by division and state: 1991–92 82

Table 3–9.— Selected population indicators, by metropolitan and nonmetropolitan county type 84

Table 3–10.— Number and percentage of schools, rural schools, students, rural students, and density,
by metropolitan and nonmetropolitan county type: 1989–90 85

Table 3–11.— Number and percentage of schools by selected enrollment sizes, by metropolitan
and nonmetropolitan county type: 1989–90 86

Table 3–12.— Selected population and education statistics, by nonmetropolitan county policy
impact type 87

Table 5–1.— Tactical objectives of the 1983 U.S. Department of Education's Rural Education
and rural family education policy for the 1980s 88

Table 5–2.— Percentage of public and private school students receiving publicly funded ECIA
Chapter 1 services, by selected school characteristics: School year 1987–88 89

Table 5–3.— Ten largest providers of federal education funding for all levels of education:
Fiscal year 1992 90

Table 5–4.— Summary of basic strategies and tactics used by the states to enhance rural
education: 1990 91

Table 6–1a.— Percentage distribution of rural and nonrural public school teachers, by sex and age:
1987–1988 92

Table 6–1b.— Percentage distribution of rural and nonrural public school teachers, by years of
full-time teaching experience: 1987–88 92

Table 6–2.— Percentage distribution of rural and nonrural public school teachers, by highest earned
degree, sex, and level: 1987–88 93

Table 6–3.— Percentage of rural and nonrural public schools whose districts offered certain benefits
in teacher pay packages, by type of benefit: 1987–88 94

Table 6–4.— Percentage of rural and nonrural public school teachers who had nonschool employment, by time of year employed outside school: 1987–88 94

Table 6–5.— Percentage of rural and nonrural public schools whose districts used various criteria for teacher employment, by type of criteria: 1987–88 95

Table 6–6.— Percentage of rural and nonrural public school principals who used various strategies to compensate for unfilled vacancies: 1987–88 95

Table 6–7.— Percentage of rural and nonrural public school teachers who reported a high level of control over selected areas in their classrooms: 1987–88 96

Table 6–8.— Percentage of rural and nonrural public school teachers who reported having a great deal of influence over school policy in various areas, by level: 1987–88 97

Table 6–9.— Percentage of rural and nonrural public school teachers who were highly satisfied with various aspects of their working conditions, by level: 1987–88 98

Table 6–10.— Number of rural and nonrural public school principals, by sex and age: 1987–88 99

Table 6–11.— Percentage distribution of rural and nonrural public school principals, by sex and age: 1987–88 99

Table 6–12.— Percentage distribution of rural and nonrural public school principals, by race and ethnic origin: 1987–88 100

Table 6–13.— Percentage distribution of rural and nonrural public school principals, by highest degree earned, level, and sex: 1987–88 101

Table 6–14.— Average years of experience of rural and nonrural public school principals, by type of experience and sex: 1987–88 102

Table 6–15.— Average annual salary of rural and nonrural public school principals, by length of work year and sex: 1987–88 103

Table 6–16.— Percentage of rural and nonrural public school principals receiving various benefits: 1987–88 103

Table 6–17.— Percentage of rural and nonrural public school principals who reported that various groups had a great deal of influence on different activities, by level: 1987–88 104

Table 6–18.— Percentage of rural and nonrural public school principals who rated selected problems in their schools as "serious," by level: 1987–88 105

Table 8–1.— Classification of major state basic education aid programs, by state: 1986–87 106

Table 8–2.— Mean and percent variation in per pupil expenditure, by county type in order of decreasing variation, by state: 1982 107

Table 8–3.— Provisions in state funding formulas for additional revenue for rural school districts: 1989–90 108

Table 9–1.— NAEP reading assessment: national and extreme rural mean proficiency levels, by age and year of assessment 109

Table 9–2.— NAEP writing assessment: national and extreme rural mean proficiency levels, by grade and year of assessment 109

Table 9–3.— NAEP mathematics assessment: national and extreme rural mean proficiency levels, by age and year of assessment 110

Table 9–4.— NAEP science assessment: national and extreme rural mean proficiency levels, by age and year of assessment 110

Table 9–5.— Recent NAEP assessments: national and extreme rural mean proficiency levels for six subject areas, by grade and year of assessment 111

Table 9–6.— Recent NAEP assessments: disadvantaged urban and extreme rural mean proficiency levels for six subject areas, by grade and year of assessment 111

Table 9–7.— Recent NAEP assessments: advantaged urban and extreme rural mean proficiency levels for six subject areas, by grade and year of assessment 112

Table 9–8.— NELS:88 eighth-grade test scores in four subject areas, by urbanicity 112

Table 9–9.— Percentage of 1988 eighth graders with one or more risk factors, by urbanicity 113

Table 9–10.— Percentage of 1988 eighth graders with various risk factors, by urbanicity 114

Table 9–11a.— Percentage of schools offering levels of mathematics courses, by graduating class size: 1980 115

Table 9–11b.—Percentage of schools offering levels of science courses, by graduating class size: 1980 115

Table 9–11c.—Percentage of schools offering levels of foreign language courses, by graduating class size: 1980 116

Table 9–11d.—Percentage of schools offering different foreign language courses, by graduating class size: 1980 116

Table 9–12.— NELS:88 eighth-grade test scores in four subject areas, by school size 117

Table 10–1.— Jobs 1980 nonrural and rural high school seniors reported they expected to
have by age 30 117

Table 10–2.— Educational expectations of the high school class of 1980, by location 118

Table 10–3.— Lowest acceptable level of education expressed by the high school class of
1980, by location 119

Table 10–4.— Postsecondary educational plans of 1980 high school seniors, by SES quartile
and location 120

Table 10–5.— 1980 high school program type, by SES quartile and location 121

Table 10–6.— Parental expectations of children's post-high school experience as reported by
nonrural and rural students 122

Table 10–7.— Persistence in postsecondary education by members of the high school class of
1980 who had entered college between 1980 and 1984, by location 122

Table 10–8.— Education aspirations and attainment of rural, suburban, and urban youth: 1980–86 123

Table 10–9.— Percentage of adults who have completed 4 or more years of high school by year,
race, and community type 124

Table 10–10.—Percentage of adults who have completed fewer than 5 years of elementary school
by year, race, and community type 124

Table 10–11.—Status dropout rate ages 16–24, by region and metropolitan status: selected years,
October 1975 through October 1990 125

Table 10–12.—Educational attainment of 25–44-year-olds by county type, selected years 126

Table 10–13.— Share of counties with one or more colleges and universities: 1986 127

Table 10–14.—Educational attainment by rural youth in the high school class of 1980,
by census division: 1986 128

B. Statistical Data Sources and Methodology 129

Acknowledgments 139

1. Introduction

This comprehensive overview of the condition of education in Rural America today has been prepared to assist policymakers and practitioners by providing concise and current information on education for a major segment of America's population. That the nation, indeed, the world, has become an increasingly urban domain is beyond dispute. What, then, should prompt an interest in rural areas and in rural education in particular?

Importance of Rural America

All Americans have a stake in the health and well-being of Rural America. Taking first a completely utilitarian view of current circumstances, the importance of the countryside is evident. It is the source of the goods—food, fiber, minerals, timber, and their products—from which the United States has built its material wealth. Resources from rural areas not only provision the nation, but they also help provision the world through extensive trading networks.

But goods and materials are not the only products of Rural America, nor necessarily its most significant export. Since the 1920s, and especially after World War II, millions of Americans born in rural areas have migrated to urban centers, directing their intelligence and energy to build the nation's cities, factories, and offices and to construct communication and transportation arteries. Their investment in the nation's strength and fortune is incalculable. Those who stayed in the countryside also contributed to America's well-being, creating stable families and settlements, establishing small businesses,

staffing manufacturing plants, and laboring in fields, farms, mines, and forests. But the surge in emigration from the countryside in the last decade is a current and urgent reminder of the need to invest in Rural America, including its human resources, for the betterment of the country as a whole.

Less considered today, but of equal importance, is that Rural America has contributed ideas to the intellectual treasure of American thought. Thomas Jefferson, the agrarian philosopher and statesman, became the major architect of American democracy. And rural Americans like Henry David Thoreau, John Muir, and, in the 20th century, Wendell Berry, offer the vision of a positive connection between economics and nature. The American agrarian tradition articulated by these thinkers emphasizes diversification rather than specialization, cooperation rather than competition, conservation rather than blind efficiency, and reinvestment rather than sheer profit. These ideas provide a crucial link to a sustainable future. Indeed, the agrarian tradition in America suggests that " . . . care, commitment, stewardship, and husbandry are essential elements of the human experience[.]" (Theobald 1992). Thus, Rural America may be seen as offering one of the important spiritual and ethical anchors for the nation.

This legacy holds true as well in the field of education. Many so-called "innovations" being championed today were born of necessity long ago in the rural schoolhouse. Cooperative learning, multi-grade classrooms, intimate links between school and community, interdisciplinary studies, peer tutoring,

block scheduling, the community as the focus of study, older students teaching younger ones, site-based management, and close relationships between teachers and students—all characterize rural and small school practices. As the nation experiences its second decade of education reform, many feel the rural school still "has the potential to be a wonderful laboratory for educational innovation and improvement" (Sher 1991).

Focus of This Report

The health and prospects for the country's more isolated settlements and communities have been the subject of periodic study throughout this century, leading to major changes in state and national policy, including education policy. Today, concerns about the vitality of postmodern rural life are being voiced once again. One outcome of recent attention at the federal level has been a growing awareness of the need to better inform education policymaking through expanded research and improved data gathering. This report is a contribution to that end.[1]

The following are some of the questions posed as this project was undertaken:

Context

- From what range of employment activities do rural residents gain their livelihoods?

- What do economic and social indicators reveal about the health of Rural America today? What do they imply about educating rural residents for the future?

Rural Students, Schools, and Districts

- What are the numbers of rural students and schools, and where are they located geographically?

- Are rural schools and districts smaller than nonrural ones as has been claimed? What is the mix of rural and nonrural districts? To what extent are rural schools located in metropolitan counties?

- How is the concentration of rural schools and students distributed in counties defined by proximity to metropolitan centers or by primary economic activity?

Rural Communities and Schools

- Is there a unique interdependence between the school and the community in rural settings? How has the relationship evolved in recent years?

Rural Education Programs

- What programs and policies at the federal and state levels are designed to assist students who attend rural schools?

Teachers and Principals in Rural Schools

- How do school personnel in rural areas compare to those in nonrural areas in terms of education and experience?

- Are there significant differences in the pay and benefit packages for rural and nonrural school staff?

- Are there significant differences in the conditions of work in rural and nonrural schools?

Education Reform and Rural Schools

- Has reform impacted differentially on rural and nonrural schools?

- What innovations have been developed in rural settings?

Public Financing of Rural Schools

- What state financing policies exist that assist rural schools?

- What financing issues particularly confront rural schools?

Outcomes of Rural Schooling

- Are rural students receiving educational opportunities comparable to those of nonrural students?

- Are students in rural settings performing at levels comparable to their nonrural peers?

- How do the post-high school experiences of those educated in rural settings compare to those educated in nonrural settings?

Sources

Lack of adequate statistics has long hampered research in rural education. Yet this report is largely grounded in national data. Opportune timing made this possible. Results of an expanded set of surveys by the National Center for Education Statistics (NCES) were becoming available and were tapped to tell the rural education story with much greater precision than was possible before. Special analyses of other data sets were arranged and current research literature included. Appendix B identifies the major surveys cited. The acknowledgments section lists the authors of background essays used as primary re-

sources for the structure of and information in this document.

Absent a single large-scale study with a unitary definition of "rural," this report drew on many sources with different definitions, presenting obvious analytical challenges. For example, sometimes "rural" is conservatively defined as having no settlement with a population larger than 2,500. But when using sources grounded in metropolitan and nonmetropolitan contrasts, which are county-based terms, "rural" can expand to include small towns of considerable size. In other surveys, respondents were free to select a location category themselves, including "rural." The only practicable way to deal with this diversity of definitions was to be specific about the one(s) used in each chapter. Readers should be aware of these distinctions as they interpret discussions in this report.

Selected Findings

In addressing the goals set for this project, there have been several distinct achievements. Documented for the first time are the number of rural schools and districts, teachers and students, and where they are located—information critical for policy development. Likewise for the first time, this report compares rural and nonrural teachers and principals nationally for income, experience, training, and opinions.

The sensitive issue of rural school finance and previously unpublished information about the outcomes of rural schooling have also been brought together for the first time. This report presents such essential information in the context of the tension between funding constraints and the evolving agenda for education reform. It identifies how certain educational weaknesses (e.g., isolation, limited resources) may impede student progress, but how strengths of rural schools (e.g., small classes, community involvement) may serve to instruct the nation in ways to meet its goals for education. It considers the potential rural schools have for improving the economic and social conditions in their communities. Finally, it discloses gaps in what is known with confidence about the condition of education in rural settings.

This document presents the following information that is central to a basic understanding of rural education:

- Rural students are found in all parts of the country and in every state—often in large numbers. But the numbers and proportion that rural students are of a state's student population are independent of the state's geographic size. Locating rural students can serve to challenge popular conceptions. For example, a state with a predominately urban settlement pattern may still have a large number of rural residents, while a state with much land area, a condition suggestive of a rural settlement pattern, actually may have many or even most of its residents concentrated in a few urban centers.

- Many schools that meet the Census Bureau definition of "rural" are located in counties defined as metropolitan. They account for 12 percent of metropolitan county schools and a quarter of all rural schools, and they enroll nearly two out of five rural students.

Two major characteristics of rural schools were quantified as follows:

- Most rural schools and rural districts are small (district enrollments of less than 2,500), reflecting the low density of the populations they serve. The primary exception is in the Southeast where, depending on the state, from 25 to 62 percent of the local districts have enrollments exceeding 2,500.

- The number and proportion of rural schools and rural school districts vary widely among the states and different sections of the country.

The following information helps enlarge the picture:

- Rural America is economically diverse, but the shifting employment picture has caused significant levels of poverty, with many rural citizens ill-prepared to meet the challenges of the modern economy. Large segments of the older population remain comparatively poorly educated, while the departure of the young and the well-educated, drawn by higher wages and faster job growth elsewhere, is draining intellectual resources from the countryside.

- Rural residents contribute a greater percentage of their income for schooling, but hampered by the high cost of education in settings with low population density, they face major difficulties in meeting demands of the evolving federal and state reform agendas and in training students for the challenges of the information age. With the departure of their youth, rural communities additionally fail to get a return on their educational investment.

- A sizable number of rural programs may be identified at the state and federal levels. However, there is no federal policy on rural education, and state approaches are varied where they exist at all.

- Likewise, little information exists on rural school finance or on how rural schools are responding to reform measures. Analyses, however, suggest rural schools have limited fiscal resources to address the rising costs of education in general and of reform in particular. In spite of limitations that come with relatively sparse settlement, however, many rural schools participate hardly in reform initiatives. For example, the U.S. Department of Education reform strategy for achieving the National Education Goals is being embraced in many rural communities across the country.

- Teachers and principals in rural schools are generally younger, are less well educated, and receive lower pay and benefits than their nonrural counterparts. Evidence suggests many leave the countryside for better paying jobs elsewhere.

- In recent years, rural performance has risen on selected national assessments so it now approximates the national mean. Performance is below that of suburban students, but higher than that of urban students.

- Students in nonmetropolitan counties have less opportunity to continue their education. As a result, fewer dropouts return to complete high school, and fewer graduates aspire to and go on to higher education. Those who do, however, persist and perform as well as nonrural graduates.

- The high incidence of poverty is a controlling factor in much that is reported about rural education outcomes. When economically similar students are compared, there is little difference in academic performance.

Challenges to Understanding Rural Education

Rural education research. Impediments to a full understanding of rural education remain. The variables of small scale, isolation, and sparsity of population are still not considered important by many researchers, and most studies ignore them. Rural research, particularly education research, is undertaken by comparatively few scholars. To help correct this situation, in 1991, the U.S. Department of Education released a brochure entitled *An Agenda for Research and Development on Rural Education*, outlining the topics that representatives of the rural research community, education associations, and federal agencies deemed most pressing.

Limited awareness of rural diversity. Another problem concerns stereotypical images of rural life that inhibit understanding the wide diversity that exists not only across regions of the country but even within states. For example, the rural South and the Pacific region obviously have distinctive characteristics and needs, but varied terrain and resources may also dictate differences even within a state, (e.g., eastern and western North Dakota). In short, statements about the general rural situation may not match a particular rural circumstance.

Multiple definitions of rural. Few issues bedevil analysts and planners concerned with rural education more than the question of what actually constitutes "rural." This is of more than academic interest. Funding eligibility and policy issues are frequently linked to a school's or school district's rurality, usually measured in terms of sparse

settlement, isolation from a population center, or both.

Rurality as defined in state statutes, moreover, often varies depending on the program authorized. The definitions in federal statutes, regulations, and surveys also lack consistency. The differences between the two most common federal terms used—"rural" and "nonmetropolitan"—illustrate the problem:

(a) The Census Bureau in its decennial survey defines "rural" as a residual category of places "outside urbanized areas in open country, or in communities with less than 2,500 inhabitants," or where the population density is "less than 1,000 inhabitants per square mile."

(b) In monthly household sample surveys, the Census Bureau contrasts data in metropolitan and nonmetropolitan *counties*. It uses the term "nonmetropolitan" to describe counties outside of, or not integrated with, large population concentrations of 50,000 or more. "Nonmetropolitan" takes in larger areas than does the term "rural" and ones that are politically defined (i.e., *counties*, not just *places)*. In covering large geopolitical units, it thus encompasses larger populations.

Many major surveys and federal organizations follow the Census Bureau lead and contrast metropolitan and nonmetropolitan settings. Writers often consider "nonmetropolitan" to be roughly equivalent to and therefore a practical substitute for "rural." But the terms are not synonymous. The distinction between the decennial census and the monthly surveys may be illustrated by noting that areas meeting the definition of "rural" place may be found in metropolitan as well as nonmetropolitan counties. For example, New Jersey is the one state without a single nonmetropolitan *county*. Yet rural *places*

do exist in the Garden State where the size of the rural student population is significant.

Recent steps by NCES address these problems. Its forthcoming *School District Data Book* will offer the richest ever set of demographic data on school-age children and their households linked with descriptive data on school district personnel, operations, and finances. The data will be available on CD-ROM, a form that will make analysis possible for a greatly expanded number of potential users. In addition, this new resource will introduce parameters of the term "rural" including measures of population density and isolation that are both precise and flexible. This definitional breakthrough was arrived at jointly by the Office of Educational Research and Improvement (OERI) staff and the rural program directors at the regional educational laboratories.

The resulting wealth of data, ease of access, and inclusion of rural variables will be a boon to rural education researchers and policymakers alike. Not only will more finely tuned research be possible on the location and characteristics of rural districts, personnel, students, and households, but such research can be conducted easily and on site for state and local purposes. The potential at every level for improved analysis to inform policymaking is enormous. To ensure new data resources reach potential users as soon as possible, a series of training seminars for rural education researchers sponsored by OERI in collaboration with the regional educational laboratories were conducted in late 1993.

Conclusion

The cultural and social health of America's rural sector depends on how it participates in the national and global economy. At present, the terms of this participation are not clear, but education is key. The nation faces momentous choices. Policymakers could, for example, presume Rural America has few unique characteristics or particular dilemmas that distinguish it from the nation as a whole. But that would be a mistake. The information and analyses presented in the following pages demonstrate the desirability of devising targeted policies based on the distinct needs of rural students—wherever they may be located.

Offering rural students an equitable education can be met by a community of interests at the local, state, and federal levels. Clearer thinking about rural education, achieved by exploring its dimensions and establishing a better descriptive basis, can help policymak-ers devise more meaningful options and formulate better decisions.

Given the range of rural diversity and the scope of different needs, there are no simple solutions, just as there is no one best system of schooling. But by bringing to researchers and policymakers new knowledge about the condition of rural education and by describing an expanding variety of data bases that can be tapped in years to come to update this knowledge, this report should facilitate the task of improving the educational experiences of the millions of children who attend school in Rural America.

Notes

1. It should be seen in the wider context of previous departmental documents addressing rural education issues. For example, in 1975, the National Institute of Education (NIE) documented the education innova-tion process in 10 rural communities participating in its Experimental Schools program. In 1979, NIE co-sponsored a national seminar to consider federal policy options in rural education. A decade later, the Office of Educational Research and Improvement published *Rural Education: A Changing Landscape*, a collection of symposium papers, and in 1991 disseminated a rural education research agenda developed in collaboration with other agencies and associations. That year also, the National Advisory Council on Educational Research and Improvement drew attention to rural needs in its annual report.

References

Berry, W. 1990. *What are People For?* San Francisco: North Point Press.

Sher, J. 1991. "Common Problems, Uncommon Solutions." *Rural Education* 2:1.

Theobald, P. 1992. "Agrarian Visions." *Country Teacher* 15:9.

Food for America, a program of instruction for elementary school-age children conducted by students in the Future Farmers of America (FAA) program. **Photo from the National FFA Center, Alexandria, Virginia**.

2. Context of Rural Education: The Economy and Population of Rural America

"[In the 1980s], many rural Americans, unable to earn a decent living, left their communities. Businesses closed, entire towns died, and a valuable piece of American heritage was lost."

National Commission on Agriculture and Rural Development Policy, 1990

Rural America[1] has been buffeted by powerful economic and social forces during much of the last decade. These forces have shaped the experience of the country's rural population, bringing about significant demographic change. This change is a story of economic disruption, significant outmigration, and growing poverty— particularly affecting children. The education ramifications for school planners, practitioners, and policymakers are immense.

Location and Settlement Patterns

Rural America's defining features are its low population density and the great distances separating rural communities from one another and from urban centers of economic activity.

- On the whole, Rural America is sparsely populated, averaging fewer than 40 residents per square mile.

- Eighty percent of Rural America's nearly 2,400 counties have fewer than 40,000 residents, less than a moderate-sized city; half have populations smaller than 20,000.

- Half the nonmetropolitan population is located outside effective commuting range of a metropolitan area. Sparse settlement and isolation not only drive up the costs of providing public services, including education, but greatly hinder Rural America's ability to participate in the emerging national economy as well.

Employment Profile

Economic diversity. Although the popular perception equates rural areas with agriculture, the modern reality is quite different. The mechanization of farming released millions of rural workers, many of whom took jobs in manufacturing plants that had relocated to rural areas in the 1960s and 1970s. Farming now employs fewer than 1 in 10 rural workers. In fact, employment in all rural industries based on natural resources (e.g, mining, fishing) stands at less than 12 percent (Reid 1990a). Manufacturing employs one rural worker in six.

In fact, jobs that undergird the rural economy are surprisingly similar to those in urban areas. The largest rural industries are service producing. Retail and wholesale trade; hotel and tourist operations; and financial, health, legal, and government services together accounted for two-thirds of rural jobs by the end of the last decade (Butler 1991).

Regional variations. While the rural economy is diverse on a national scale, individual rural counties often depend on a limited range of industries (Reid and Frederick 1990). About 500 rural counties, mainly in the Great Plains region, remain highly dependent on farming. Another 500, concentrated in southeastern and eastern states, are closely tied to manufacturing. A smaller number—about 125 in Appalachia, the southern oil fields, and scattered areas of the West—depend on mining and energy extraction.

Current Economic Picture

Economic reversals in the 1980s. From 1979 to 1982, the nation suffered one of the worst recessionary periods in its history. While strong national growth followed, a number of circumstances conspired to keep the boom from reaching most nonmetropolitan counties.

- Early in the decade, a financial crisis in agriculture cost thousands of farmers their land and also produced a severe business downturn on the main streets of many farming communities.

- At the same time, rural communities that relied on manufacturing saw their employment base erode as many industries—faced with stiff foreign competition—substituted machines for jobs or moved away.

- In the aftermath of a sharp drop in energy prices, unemployment skyrocketed in areas dependent on oil drilling and mining. Not until the decade's end did rural job growth begin to catch up to urban area rates (Reid 1990a). But with the most recent recession, the rural economy stalled once again (Swaim 1991).

Emerging employment pattern. With the clarity of hindsight, it is now evident these events reflected much more than a temporary upset in fortunes; economic difficulties started well before the 1980s. Over a period spanning several economic cycles, Rural America lagged behind the rest of the nation in job and income growth (Reid 1990a). While traditional em-

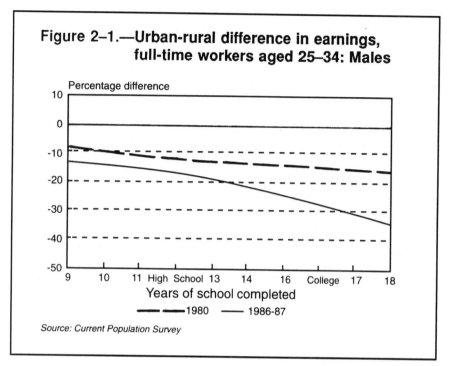

Figure 2–1.—Urban-rural difference in earnings, full-time workers aged 25–34: Males

Percentage difference

Years of school completed

—— ——1980   —— 1986-87

Source: Current Population Survey

ployment sources declined, reflecting both reduced demand for products and improved labor productivity, advanced services and manufacturing industries passed by the countryside to settle predominantly in the nation's cities and suburbs.

Urban counties increased their ratio of complex to routine manufacturing industries during the 1980s. Such change did not take place in rural areas. They lagged as well in the rate of growth in the faster growing and better paying producer services (Reid 1990a). The result of this economic restructuring was a growing urban-rural differential in wages for new entrants into the labor force, both male and female, particularly for the better educated (figures 2–1 and 2–2).

Unemployment. The major consequence of this restructuring has been growing unemployment. Before 1980, the jobless rate had been lower for nonmetropolitan than for metropolitan counties; since 1980, the reverse has been true (Rogers 1991). Moreover, the contrast worsened as the decade pro-

gressed. In 1980, the nonmetropolitan jobless rate was 7 percent higher than in metro counties; by 1988, it was 40 percent higher (Deavers 1989). The 1991 unemployment rate in nonmetropolitan counties, adjusted to reflect discouraged workers who have stopped job hunting and those who could only find part-time work, was 11.5 percent,

well in excess of the comparable metropolitan rate of 9.5 percent (Swaim 1991). Rising unemployment has meant, in the words of one rural scene observer, that ". . . in many rural areas, each job must now support more people" (Deavers 1989).

Low skills and low wages. The rural employment situation is compounded by a preponderance in the countryside of jobs that require few skills and pay poorly. But such jobs were not only those primarily available in the traditional, resource-dependent sectors. Service and manufacturing occupations also showed a clear pattern of locating low-paying production jobs in rural areas. Managerial and technical positions with better pay and career potential were found more often in cities (McGranahan and Ghelfi 1991).

Economic vulnerability. Rural areas are no longer insulated from current developments in the world economy. Foreign competition and fluctuations in demand, exchange rates, regulatory practices, or interest rates can have a

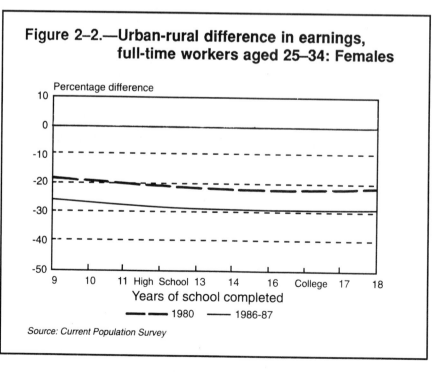

Figure 2–2.—Urban-rural difference in earnings, full-time workers aged 25–34: Females

Percentage difference

Years of school completed

—— —— 1980   —— 1986-87

Source: Current Population Survey

quick impact. In the 1980s, this effect was largely negative for Rural America. Reliance on one industry, moreover (e.g., timber or a single factory), severely constrained individual flexibility when changing conditions threatened that enterprise. As one analyst observed, "There is no local pool of employers in a small town" (McGranahan 1988).

Recent data from the Bureau of Labor Statistics suggest that because most rural jobs are among those most vulnerable to outside forces, the rate of rural employment growth will lag that of urban areas at least 15 years into the future (Hamrick 1991–92).

Consequences of a Distressed Economy

The major results of the upheavals in the rural economy have been a pervasive condition of poverty; outmigration, particularly of the better educated; and changes to the family structure.

Rural poverty. By almost every measure, rural residents are disadvantaged when compared with urban residents (Butler 1991).

- Incomes in nonmetropolitan counties were only about three-fourths those in metropolitan counties for most of the decade, a difference far in excess of the somewhat lower cost of living in rural areas.

- In every field, nonmetropolitan earnings in the 1980s were lower, with the gap widening to $6,270 by 1988, the worst since the 1980–82 recession.

- After narrowing during the late 1960s and early 1970s, the rural-urban gap in per capita income has widened steadily for the last 15 years.

- Rural poverty rates in the 1980s generally equalled or exceeded the rate in America's central cities (O'Hare 1988). And the rate of poverty has been worsening.

- Historically, poverty rates in non-metropolitan areas have exceeded those in more urbanized sections of the country. By 1990, the rural rate had increased to 16.3 percent, compared to 12.7 percent in metropolitan counties (U.S. Department of Commerce, Bureau of the Census, 1991).

- The percentage of rural residents below the poverty line increased during most of the last decade, rising from 13.5 percent in 1978 to 18.3 percent from 1983 to 1985; at the same time, rural residents living in poverty remained there for longer periods of time than before (O'Hare 1988; Reid 1990a).

Even more telling for the future is the impact of these problems on young families and children. As William P. O'Hare of the Population Reference Bureau observed, " . . . poverty among children has grown dramatically in the past decade, but it is not widely noted that this increase has hit rural children disproportionately" (O'Hare 1988). He reported that

- From 1979 to 1986, poverty increased twice as fast in rural areas as in urban areas, both among young adults (aged 18–44) and for children under 18.

- In 1986, one of every four children in Rural America was living in poverty.

A major reason for child poverty in Rural America has been the dramatic increase in the incidence of single-parent families, headed primarily by women. By 1987, 6 out of 10 rural families in which only the mother was present were poor (compared to 5 of 10 for such metropolitan families) (Rogers 1991).

While rural poverty exists in every region, it is most severe in the southern United States. Two-thirds of the nation's rural blacks and 95 percent of rural black children, as well as most of its growing rural Hispanic population, are concentrated there. The prevalence in rural areas of low incomes and poverty, as well as less educational attainment, is even greater among these population groups (U.S. Department of Commerce, Bureau of the Census 1991).

Population losses. A second major outcome of the economic situation has been a dramatic exodus from rural communities as breadwinners left in search of employment (Butler 1991).

- Between 1980 and 1990, one-half of the nonmetropolitan counties together lost 6.3 percent of their population, or 1.6 million persons. Predominately, these were counties dependent upon small manufacturing, agriculture, and mining and were not adjacent to metropolitan counties.

- While nationally the metropolitan population grew nearly 12 percent in the last decade, nonmetropolitan population growth was just 4 percent.[2]

- Large numbers of the more educated residents of working age departed Rural America in search of urban jobs to match their skills and training. Nearly 2.5 percent of those aged 25–64 who had 4 or more years of college left annually from 1986 to 1988. Those with some college education departed as well, but at a

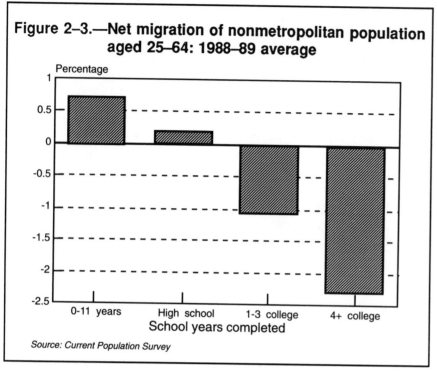

Figure 2–3.—Net migration of nonmetropolitan population aged 25–64: 1988–89 average

Percentage

School years completed

Source: Current Population Survey

much lower rate (Reid 1990b) (figure 2–3).

Changing family patterns. Proceeding from conditions of poverty and outmigration, other demographic consequences have particular relevance for rural schools.

- Nonmetropolitan real and projected birth rates no longer exceed those in metropolitan counties, a major historical shift (Beale and Fuguitt 1990).

- Most people leaving the countryside were younger adults of childbearing age. Consequently, the proportion of nonmetropolitan families with children remained constant at 44 percent, while the corresponding metropolitan rate rose to 48 percent (Swanson and Dacquel 1991).

- At the same time, the proportion of young rural families consisting of the traditional married couple with children dropped from 84 to 78 per-

cent between 1979 and 1990. For young children under 6 years of age, the percentage that lived in families headed by women rose from 11 to 17 percent; for black rural children, the increase during the period was 23 percentage points—to 58 percent (Swanson and Dacquel 1991).

- In 1988, 15 percent of nonmetropolitan births were to teen parents, and nearly one in four (23 percent) were to unmarried mothers. The shortage of accessible pre- and post-natal care makes this circumstance a serious threat to the welfare of young children in rural areas (Sherman 1992).[3]

Such developments not only affected the individuals involved, but also had repercussions for the larger rural society, as resources, including educational resources, evaporated along with employment opportunities.

Considering Education in Rural America

During the 1980s, education's importance to improved economic competitiveness grew. Both nationally and in rural areas, job growth has been strongest in industries and occupations demanding high levels of education and skills (Reid 1990b) (figure 2–4).

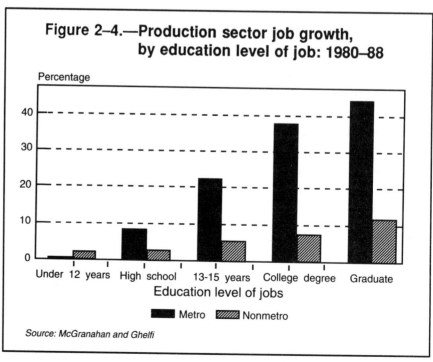

Figure 2–4.—Production sector job growth, by education level of job: 1980–88

Percentage

Education level of jobs

■ Metro ▨ Nonmetro

Source: McGranahan and Ghelfi

10

Education also is important to the development of new businesses. Research indicates the people who are most likely to start new rural businesses are those who already live in these areas. That start-up rates are highest in areas with higher average levels of education underscores the importance of skills and training to locally generated development as well.

Yet overall, economic restructuring meant that demand for workers of *any* skill level in rural areas was low during the 1980s (Reid 1990b) resulting in the increased levels of poverty and emigration just discussed. These developments presented grave dilemmas to rural communities in determining local education policies. But considering the course of rural education, they warrant wider attention beyond the affected community. For instance,

- Can rural schools serve both the national interest and the needs of local communities?

- Should state and federal involvement in plans for local economic development include a role for the rural school?

- What value can be placed on retaining small schools in rural areas that warrants the infusion of outside funding?

Such questions have no easy answers. But as long as rural out-migration remains high, the nation's response to the needs of rural education will have implications not only for the future of the rural communities that dot the landscape but for the country as a whole (Reid 1990b).

Summary

Sparse populations and distance from urban centers are the distinguishing characteristics of rural settlements. These features operated to Rural America's disadvantage in the economic restructuring of the last decade. Unemployment and underemployment led to increased poverty, emigration, and changing family patterns—developments that adversely affected all social institutions, including the schools. Because these conditions may be beyond the capacity of local communities to remedy, they pose policy challenges as well to state and federal governments and to other organizations concerned about the welfare of the rural student.

Notes

1. This chapter draws upon a data base that equates rural areas with nonmetropolitan counties (i.e., counties without a city of at least 50,000 or those lacking a commuting connection with such a county). Nonmetropolitan counties include both people living on the land and those residing in small towns and trade centers that service them. Of the 3,097 counties in the United States, 2,388, or 77 percent, are nonmetropolitan.

2. Despite advances in transportation and communications technology that make business activity feasible in all locations, recent trends point to distinct locational advantages for certain rural areas. In the 1980s, the most rapid rates of job and population growth occurred in areas within commuting range of major metropolitan areas and with climatic and scenic amenities attractive to retirees and businesses with no constraints on location. By contrast, more remote rural areas, suffering continued loss of employment in resource-based industries and unable to capitalize on spillovers from urban growth, experienced the greatest difficulties (Reid 1990a).

3. In rural areas, births to teens were more common, while births to unmarried mothers were slightly less common than in urban areas.

References

Beale, C., and G. Fuguitt. June–September 1990. "Decade of Pessimistic Nonmetro Population Trends End on Optimistic Note." *Rural Development Perspectives.* Washington, DC: U.S. Department of Agriculture, Economic Research Service.

Butler, M. Spring 1991. "Rural Population Growth Slows During 1980–90." *Rural Conditions and Trends* . Washington, DC: U.S. Department of Agriculture, Economic Research Service.

Deavers, K.L. 1989. "Economic and Social Trends in Rural America." Paper presented at the American Educational Research Association Conference, San Francisco, CA.

Ghelfi, L.M. Spring 1991. "Slight Decline Continues in Rural Earnings per Job." *Rural Conditions and Trends.* Washington, DC: U.S. Department of Agriculture, Economic Research Service.

Hamrick, K.S. Winter 1991–92. "Employment Mix Will Change by 2005." *Rural Conditions and Trends.* Washington, DC: U.S. Department of Agriculture, Economic Research Service.

McGranahan, D.A. 1988. "Rural Workers in the National Economy." *Rural Economic Development in the 1980s.* Rural Development Research Report No. 69. Washington, DC: U.S. Department of Agriculture, Economic Research Service.

McGranahan, D.A., and L.M. Ghelfi. 1991. "The Education Crisis and Rural Stagnation in the 1980s." *Education and Rural Economic Development: Strategies for the 1990s.* Washington, DC: U.S. Department of Agriculture, Economic Research Service.

O'Hare, W.P. 1988. *The Rise of Poverty in Rural America.* Population Trends and Public Policy Report No. 15. Washington, DC: Population Reference Bureau, Inc.

Reid, J.N. 1990a. "Economic Change in the Rural U.S.: A Search for Explanations."

Paper presented at the Seminar on Europe 1993: Implications for Rural Areas, The Arkleton Trust, Douneside, Tarland, Scotland.

Reid, J.N. 1990b. "Education and Rural Development: A Review of Recent Evidence." Paper presented at the American Educational Research Association Conference, Boston, Massachusetts.

Reid, J.N., and M. Frederick. August 1990. *Rural America: Economic Performance, 1989.* AIB–609. Washington, DC: U.S. Department of Agriculture, Economic Research Service.

Rogers, C.C. 1991. *The Economic Wellbeing of Nonmetro Children.* Washington, DC: U.S. Department of Agriculture, Economic Research Service.

Sherman, A. 1992. *Falling by the Wayside: Children in Rural America.* Washington, DC: The Children's Defense Fund.

Swaim, P. Fall 1991. "Rural Employment Down." *Rural Conditions and Trends.* Washington, DC: U.S. Department of Agriculture, Economic Research Service.

Swanson, L., and L. Dacquel. Spring 1991. "Rural Families Headed by Women are on the Rise." *Rural Conditions and Trends.* Washington, DC: U.S. Department of Agriculture, Economic Research Service.

U.S. Department of Commerce. Bureau of the Census. 1991. *Poverty in the United States: 1990.* Current Population Reports, Series P–60, No. 175. Washington, DC.

Audience at first grade graduation: Tornillo Independent School District, Tornillo, Texas (pop. 600). **Photo by Roz Alexander-Kasparik, Southwest Educational Development Laboratory (SEDL), Austin, Texas.**

3. Location and Characteristics of Rural Schools and School Districts

As noted in the Introduction, two sets of definitions are commonly used to analyze rural situations—one determined by *place* and one by *county*. The categories overlap so both urban and rural places may be found within both metropolitan and nonmetropolitan counties. The interrelationship between rural-urban and metropolitan-nonmetropolitan is not often explored. However, when schools are classified using both sets of Census definitions, a "rural" school can be precisely located. With this degree of accuracy, policy-makers can better target allocations and services for rural students.[1]

Rural Public Schools

According to the National Center for Education Statistics (NCES), in the 50 states and the District of Columbia, there were 79,876 regular public schools enrolling more than 41 million students during the 1991–92 school year. Population density influences both the location and the number of schools. As figure 3–1 shows, the number and concentration of schools differ quite a bit among regions of the United States. For example, there are more than twice as many schools per 100 square miles in the Mid-Atlantic states as in the South Atlantic states, and eight times as many as in the Pacific states.[2]

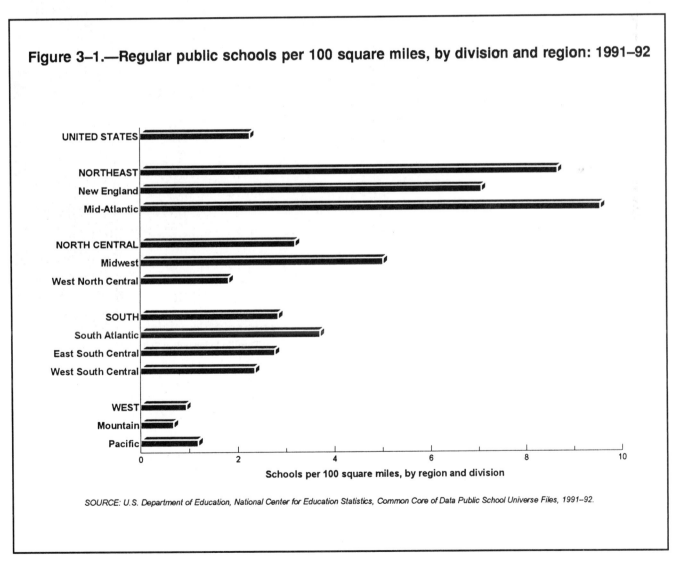

Figure 3–1.—Regular public schools per 100 square miles, by division and region: 1991–92

Schools per 100 square miles, by region and division

SOURCE: U.S. Department of Education, National Center for Education Statistics, Common Core of Data Public School Universe Files, 1991–92.

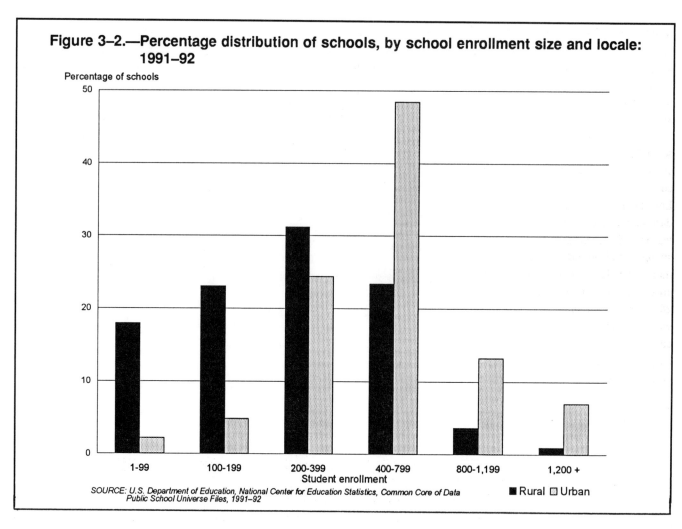

Figure 3–2.—Percentage distribution of schools, by school enrollment size and locale: 1991–92

Percentage of schools

SOURCE: U.S. Department of Education, National Center for Education Statistics, Common Core of Data Public School Universe Files, 1991–92

■ Rural □ Urban

Student enrollment

Table 3–1 summarizes the distribution of schools and students according to four major locales—*city, urban fringe, town,* and *rural.*[3]

• About 6.9 million students attend some 22,400 rural schools, accounting for 16.7 percent of regular public school students and 28 percent of regular public schools.

Rural schools and the students who attend them thus constitute a significant segment of U.S. public education.

Enrollment and locale. Figures 3–2 and 3–3 show the distribution of schools and students by enrollment and rural vs. urban locale. The remainder of this discussion contrasts rural and urban

schools, the latter encompassing the city, urban fringe, and town locales.

Generally, areas with large, densely settled populations have fewer, but larger schools; areas with sparser populations have more, but smaller schools. On average nationally, city and urban fringe schools are more than twice the size of rural schools (table 3–1).

For example, nearly three-quarters of all rural public elementary and secondary schools have fewer than 400 students (almost one out of five has fewer than 100 students). More than 40 percent (43.3) of all rural students are in buildings with enrollments under 400. In contrast, schools with fewer than 400 students comprise just about a third of urban schools and account for only

about 14 percent of all urban students. And comparing enrollments more than 800, just 4.5 percent of rural schools are that large and only enroll about 16 percent of rural students. In contrast, more than 20 percent of urban schools have enrollments more than 800, and they account for 40 percent of urban students.

Types of schools and school size. Whether primary, secondary, or combined, rural schools are small (Johnson 1989).[4] Table 3–2 shows the distribution of these three organizational groups by enrollment and locale.

It has been suggested secondary schools with enrollments of 400 or more are generally able to offer a reasonably comprehensive curriculum (Haller and

14

Monk 1988). Those with smaller enrollments may find it necessary to adopt innovative curriculum and instructional practices to make up for low enrollments and serve their students adequately. The challenge is acute in rural settings where 73 percent of rural secondary schools have fewer than 400 students and account for nearly 40 percent of all rural secondary students. Less than 17 percent of urban secondary schools are that small, attended by less than 5 percent of urban secondary students. Indeed, urban areas organize many very large schools, while rural areas organize very few large ones. The 26 percent of urban secondary schools with enrollments more than 1,200 account for nearly half of urban secondary students. By contrast, only 2 percent of rural schools have enroll-

ments exceeding 1,200, and these account for just 12 percent of all rural secondary students.

Small schools have lower student/teacher ratios than larger schools. This is true in both rural and urban settings, but rural school student/teacher ratios are lower. Schools that have exclusively secondary grades have lower ratios than schools with exclusively primary grades, and small, rural secondary schools have the lowest ratios of all (table 3–3).

Geographic diversity of rural school concentrations. The significance of rural schools and their populations may be determined by sheer numbers or by the proportion of rural schools and students to a state's

total. For example, Texas has the largest number of rural students (442,961) attending the largest number (1,376) of rural schools. But 35 other states have higher proportions of their schools in rural locales, and 40 have higher proportions of their students attending rural schools. And there is a wide range. For example, the percentage of a state's schools that are rural ranges from less than 5 percent in Rhode Island to more than 76 percent in South Dakota.

The different stories told by counts vs. percents may be illustrated by contrasting two states, one clearly perceived as urban and the other as rural: New Jersey and Montana. Actually, more students attend schools in the rural areas of New Jersey (68,209) than in the rural areas of Montana (54,230). But in New Jer-

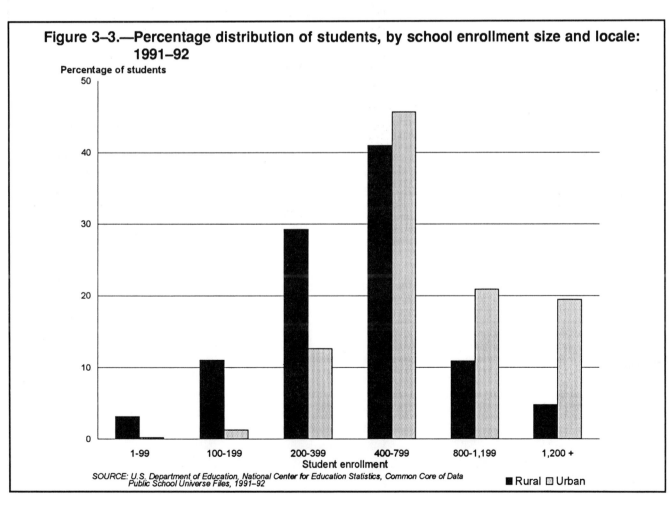

Figure 3–3.—Percentage distribution of students, by school enrollment size and locale: 1991–92

SOURCE: U.S. Department of Education, National Center for Education Statistics, Common Core of Data Public School Universe Files, 1991–92

15

sey, rural students constitute just 6 percent of all its public school students, while in Montana, the rural students constitute almost 35 percent. And the conditions for organizing schools in New Jersey with more than 146 students per square mile would be necessarily quite different from Montana with just 1 student per square mile.

This diversity may be illustrated further at the regional level. For example, the number of rural schools ranges from 864 in New England to just over 4,500 in the Midwest division. The West North Central division has the highest proportion of rural schools (56 percent) and also the highest proportion of students attending rural schools (35 percent). But because there are roughly 7.6 million students among Midwest states compared to 2.3 million in West North Central ones, the Midwest has nearly twice as many rural students (1.4 million) as does the West North Central regional division (803,000) (table 3–4).

Regions encompassing large areas have many relatively isolated rural schools, but because their populations are often concentrated in a few large urban centers, the overall percentage of students in rural schools may be relatively (and surprisingly) low. For example, in the spacious Mountain states where there are fewer than three students per square mile and less than one school per hundred square miles, only about 16 percent of the students attend rural schools. This compares to over 20 percent of students enrolled in rural schools among the South Atlantic states where there are more than 24 students per square mile and nearly four schools per 100 square miles.

Regional distribution of schools by locale and size. Almost 20 percent of the nation's 22,370 rural

schools have enrollments of fewer than 100 students. Among the states, the percent of rural schools with fewer than 100 students ranges from zero in Connecticut, Georgia, and Delaware, to nearly 73 percent in Montana. In 9 states, more than 30 percent of the rural schools have fewer than 100 students (table 3–5). Southern, Midwest, and Middle Atlantic states tend not to have many very small rural schools, but Plains states, Mountain states, and some New England and Pacific states do. As discussed below, these patterns reflect not only the rurality and isolation of various parts of the country, but also regional traditions in the organization and supervision of school districts. Clearly, with such diversity, school policies for bringing education to rural students can vary widely across the country, among regions, among the states—and even within states.

Rural School Districts

Defining rural districts. Different policy interests focus on different organizational features of the educational enterprise. For many issues, the individual *school* is the focus of attention (Timar and Kirp 1989). For other policy matters, such as governance, the *school district* is the primary unit of concern (Stephens 1988). Since district policies are shaped partly by the presence of rural or urban needs, it is important to identify the number and proportion of rural districts and the extent to which districts were mixed rural and urban.

Most school districts (88.3 percent) consist of either entirely rural or entirely urban schools.[5] Specifically, in 45 percent of the school districts (6,764), all students attend only rural schools; in 43.3 percent of the districts (6,503), all students attend only urban schools; and only 11.8 percent of the public school districts (1,762) administer schools lo-

cated in both rural and urban places (table 3–6). To compare rural and urban school districts, those districts with schools in both types of settings were first redefined as either rural or urban.[6] The resulting profile of rural school districts and comparison to urban districts follow.

Comparing rural and urban school districts. More than 46 percent (6,973) of school districts are predominantly rural, and 53.6 percent (8,056) are predominantly urban (table 3–7). Rural districts administer a total of 17,413 regular public schools enrolling nearly 4.8 million students; urban districts administer 62,463 schools enrolling more than 36.5 million students. Many rural schools are located in districts defined as urban. In fact, 23 percent of rural schools, 31 percent of students attending rural schools, and nearly 30 percent of the teachers working at rural schools are part of a predominantly urban district.[7]

Reflecting population concentrations, the number of schools in rural and urban districts presents a considerable contrast. While there is substantial range, on average fewer than three schools are in a rural district but almost eight in an urban one. Reflecting the small size of rural schools, rural districts also have smaller enrollments than urban ones. Districts with fewer than 300 students account for more than 41 percent of rural districts compared with nearly 11 percent among urban ones (table 3–8).

The nearly 3,000 smallest rural districts (fewer than 300 students) together contain more than 4,000 schools and enroll nearly 385,000 students. The more than 4,000 mid-size rural districts, those with between 300 and 2,500 students, include 10,700 schools and nearly 3.1 million students—about 64 percent of

Figure 3–4.—ERS county types

Code   Description

Metropolitan:

0   Central counties of metropolitan areas of 1 million population or more

1   Fringe counties of metropolitan areas of 1 million population or more

2   Counties in metropolitan areas of 250,000 to 1,000,000 population

3   Counties in metropolitan areas of less than 250,000 population

Nonmetropolitan:

4   Urban population of 20,000 or more, adjacent to a metropolitan area

5   Urban population of 20,000 or more, not adjacent to a metropolitan area

6   Urban population of 2,500 to 19,999, adjacent to a metropolitan area

7   Urban population of 2,500 to 19,999, not adjacent to a metropolitan area

8   Completely rural (no places of 2,500 or more population) adjacent to a metropolitan area

9   Completely rural, not adjacent to a metropolitan area

all students enrolled in rural districts. While districts with under 2,500 enrollment account for 59 percent of all urban districts, they account for 96 percent of all rural districts.

Geographic diversity among districts. While nearly all rural districts have fewer than 2,500 students, the pattern is diverse geographically. In New England and the Mountain states, nearly 70 percent of the rural districts have fewer than 300 students (table 3–8). In the Mid-Atlantic and Midwest, about 20 percent of the districts are that small; most have enrollments between 300 and 2,500. In the southern regions, where many states organize school districts along county boundaries, districts with under 300 students are rare. There, districts with 300 to 2,500 students are most common, and about one of three rural districts have enrollments exceeding 2,500 students.

Nonmetropolitan Diversity and Rural Education

The Economic Research Service (ERS) of the U.S. Department of Agriculture (USDA) has sought to quantify the diversity of rural areas by creating descriptive categories or typologies. The following analysis links rural school districts with two different ERS typologies to explore more fully the variety of settings in which rural schools operate.[8] This analysis found rural schools to be situated in very diverse circumstances both in terms of location—from remote villages to the fringes of large cities—and in terms of economic base—from farms to government-owned property.

Exploring the interrelationships between urban and rural and metropolitan and nonmetropolitan reveals information that could alter popular perceptions about where rural schools are and could have significant implications for a range of policy issues affecting schools, including how to define a school as rural.

1. Metropolitan adjacency. The first typology discussed groups counties according to metropolitan status, population size, and proximity to a metropolitan area (figure 3–4). The rurality types are directly related to both population density and per capita income. During the 1980s, population growth was concentrated in metropolitan county types. Apart from central cities that have high concentrations of young people, the proportion of the population under 18 years of age varies little among remaining county types (table 3–9).

Both rural and urban schools may be found in both metropolitan and nonmetropolitan counties. In nonmetropolitan counties, with 38 percent of all schools, just over half (more than 14,000) are actually rural schools; the remaining 45 percent (13,398) are in urban areas of these counties (table 3–10).

The ERS county types also show the relationships between population density, metropolitan adjacency, and school size. The size of rural schools is related directly to rurality (sparse population) and relative geographic isolation. The percent of rural schools with enrollments of less than 100 for the three adjacent nonmetropolitan county types is half that of the nonadjacent nonmetropolitan counties (table 3–11).

17

Metropolitan counties (ERS Codes 0, 1, 2, and 3). These counties contain 62 percent of all schools and 74 percent of all students. But nearly 12 percent of the schools (almost 5,800) in metropolitan counties are in rural places. These account for 26 percent of all rural schools and 38 percent of all rural students. The densities range from 2,100 students per 100 square miles to more than 14,000 per 100 square miles (table 3–10). They are the wealthiest and fastest growing counties.

Nonmetropolitan, large urban center counties (ERS Codes 4 and 5). These counties contain about 8,000 public schools—10 percent of the U.S. total. They enroll 3.4 million students—8.6 percent of the total. There are 2,800 rural schools in these counties, enrolling about 850,000 students. This accounts for 13 percent of all rural schools and 13 percent of all rural students. In the adjacent counties, there are nearly 1,300 students per 100 square miles, and about 10 percent of the rural schools enroll fewer than 100 students. In the nonadjacent group, there are about 650 students per 100 square miles, and about 19 percent of the rural schools enroll fewer than 100 students (table 3–10).

Nonmetropolitan, small urban center counties (ERS Codes 6 and 7). About 16,500 public schools are located in counties with a small urban center. They account for 21 percent of all public schools and 5.6 million students—14 percent of the U.S. total. There are 8,400 schools in the rural locales of these counties enrolling about 2.1 million students. This represents 38 percent of all rural schools and 32 percent of all rural public school students. In the adjacent counties there are 670 students per 100 square miles, and 14.5 percent of the rural schools

have fewer than 100 students. In the nonadjacent counties there are about 325 students per 100 square miles, and nearly 28 percent of the rural schools have fewer than 100 students (table 3–11). The adjacent counties have grown slightly in population and the nonadjacent group has, overall, remained stable.

Nonmetropolitan, completely rural counties (ERS Codes 8 and 9). About 5,300 regular public schools are located in these counties, representing 6.5 percent of all schools (table 3–10) and enrolling 1.2 million students (about 3 percent of the total). These counties account for 22 percent of all rural schools and 17.5 percent of rural students. In counties adjacent to metropolitan areas (Code 8) there are about 270 students per 100 square miles, and 17 percent of the rural schools have fewer than 100 students. But in counties not adjacent (Code 9), the number of students drops to just 133 per 100 square miles, and the percent of the rural schools with fewer than 100 students doubles to 35 percent. The adjacent counties increased in population

by 6.7 percent during the 1980s while the nonadjacent counties declined by about a percentage point. Together, these two types of rural counties share the lowest per capita incomes in the nation.

2. ERS socioeconomic types. Another ERS typology characterizes nonmetropolitan counties on the basis of their primary economic activity. Table 3–12 displays population, income, and school data for six of the ERS types. Figure 3–5 describes them.

The differences in the nature of the economic bases among these types of counties are also reflected in their population characteristics and organization of schools. Population in farm and mining-dependent counties declined by more than 4 percent during the 1980s, while the population in government-dependent counties increased by nearly 9 percent. Farm-dependent counties have the largest proportion of rural schools and the largest proportion of rural schools with fewer than 100 students. They also have the lowest density of students. While most of

---

Figure 3–5.— ERS nonmetropolitan socioeconomic county types

Farming-dependent—512 counties in which farming contributed 20 percent or more to total income.

Manufacturing-dependent—553 counties in which manufacturing contributed 30 percent to total income.

Mining-dependent—124 counties in which mining contributed 20 percent or more to total income.

Government-dependent—347 counties in which local, state and federal payrolls contributed 25 percent or more to total income.

Unclassified—712 counties in which no single industrial sector predominated.

Persistent poverty counties—239 counties ranking in the lowest quintile of per capita income for four decades.

these county types have similar per capita income levels, more than 700,000 nonmetropolitan students attending more than 1,200 schools reside in "persistent poverty" counties whose per capita income has ranked in the lowest quintile for four decades.

Summary

Rural schools and rural school districts are smaller than their urban counterparts, and their organization reflects the relative density and geographic isolation of the populations they serve. Diversity exists among them regionally and by the type of county they are in, whether that county typology is defined by distance from a metropolitan center or by economic base. This analysis quantifies on a national scale information generally understood from small or state studies. Noting the limitations of a single urban-rural or metropolitan-nonmetropolitan framework in rural research helps provide the groundwork for developing a better approach to defining rural communities.

Notes

1. The information in this chapter was developed using school and district data from the NCES Common Core of Data (CCD) and county descriptions from the Economic Research Service, U.S. Department of Agriculture. These data sources and methods of analysis are reviewed in appendix B.

For further discussion of the data see: Elder, E.L. Fall 1992. "The Use of Census Geography and County Typologies in the Construction of Classification Systems for Rural Schools and Districts." *Journal of Research in Rural Education* 8:3.

2. See appendix A for state groupings within the four regions and nine divisions of the United States.

3. Consolidating the seven NCES locale codes (Johnson 1989) to four, the locations are defined as follows: (a) City = central city of a Metropolitan Statistical Area (MSA); (b) Urban fringe = place within a MSA and defined as urban by the Census Bureau; (c) Town = town not within a MSA and with a population equal to or greater than 2,500 people; (d) Rural = a place with fewer than 2,500 people, or a place having a ZIP Code designated rural by the Census Bureau.

4. Schools with any enrollment in grades K–6 and none in grades 7–12 are "primary"; those with any enrollment in grades 7–12 and none in grades K–6 are "secondary"; and all others are "combined."

5. By aggregating the NCES file of regular public schools by local educational agency, a file was created of 15,029 school districts that administer regular public schools, and the percentage of each district's students who attended schools in rural areas was calculated.

6. Among these districts, about 12 percent (209) have more than three-quarters of their students attending rural schools. About half (913) are predominately urban, with fewer than a quarter of the students attending a rural school. More than two-thirds (640) have between 25 percent and 74 percent of their students attending a rural school. For purposes of this analysis, a mixed district was considered rural if 75 percent of students attended a rural school. This conservative definition resulted in putting most of the mixed districts into the urban category.

7. The proportion of rural schools in urban districts defined as urban may be slightly overstated because of the definition of rural districts adopted for this analysis.

8. At the time ERS and CCD data were merged, only 1989–90 CCD counts were available. Moreover, Alaska and Hawaii were excluded from this county-level analysis because their counties are so different from the other 48 states; consequently, the number of regular public schools in this part of the analysis was reduced to 78,624.

References

Haller, E.J., and D.H. Monk. April 1988. "New Reforms, Old Reforms, and the Consolidation of Small, Rural Schools." *Review of Educational Research* 17: 167–177.

Johnson, F. 1989. *Assigning Type of Locale Codes to the 1987–88 CCD Public School Universe.* Technical Report CS 89–194. Washington, DC: U. S. Department of Education, National Center for Education Statistics.

Stephens, E.R. 1988. *The Changing Context of Education in a Rural Setting.* Occasional Paper No. 26. Charleston, WV: Appalachia Educational Laboratory.

Timar, T., and D.L. Kirp. March 1989. "Education Reform in the 1980s: Lessons from the States." *Phi Delta Kappan*: 511.

U.S. Department of Commerce. Bureau of the Census. 1991. Census of Population and Housing. 1990: Summary Tape File 1 Technical Documentation. Washington, DC.

Rae Ellen McKee, National Teacher of the Year, 1991; remedial reading teacher, Slanesville Elementary School (enrollment: 189 students, grades K–6), Slanesville, West Virginia. Says Mrs. McKee, "The school cannot be the only agent responsible for developing the skills and character of young people. The community, too, must seek to educate." **Photo from the Council of Chief State School Officers, Washington, D.C**.

4. The Rural School-Community Connection

The key role of the school in rural communities, particularly the traditional ways in which the school and community have interacted, is important to understand. In recent years, many schools and communities have restructured their relationships both to improve student learning and to deal more effectively with economic and social change.

The School's Evolving Relationship With the Community

General statements about rural communities and their schools must be tempered by an awareness that a wide diversity of rural communities, schools, and mutual interactions exist in the countryside. Typologies have been created to illustrate community diversity (e.g., Gjelten 1982 and Nachtigal 1982) by making distinctions, for example, among isolated settlements, depressed areas losing population, and communities revitalized by an influx of immigrants from metropolitan areas. But regardless of setting, the school has served as the hub of the social structure.

The historical place of the school. The family, the church, and the school have been at the heart of rural communities since this country was settled. These three institutions have provided the standards of behavior, circles of personal interaction, and a variety of social activities that collectively shape community ethos and identity. Often, rural residents define their place of living by the church to which they belong or the school district in which they reside. Even with the on-going social and economic transformation of Rural America, these institutions still provide many rural Americans with their roots.

The local school's influence has been pervasive, often determining the vitality and character of a locality. For example, the school's athletic team and cultural activities create a gauge by which community comparisons are made (and often rivalries born). When the athletic team wins, the whole community wins.

The community-school tie is strong in other ways. The rural school was never just a place to receive instruction—central though that purpose was and is. School facilities—often the only public buildings in the area—serve in many capacities. Today a school may provide a polling place; the site for the annual farmers' organization banquet; the kitchen where meals-on-wheels for senior citizens are prepared; a meeting place for the 4–H clubs; classrooms for adult education programs; a stage for holiday programs; and a setting for band concerts and community picnics. Through these and similar activities, the rural school and its community are inextricably bound. So powerful is the interaction between community members and the school that rural residents often retain the feeling of belonging to the school, even into adulthood when they begin their own families.

Factors weakening community cohesion. In recent decades, powerful forces have been undermining this traditional sense of belonging. Because economic restructuring has led to a widespread deterioration in most traditional rural economies simultaneously, rural communities throughout the country find themselves in a precarious situation. Indeed, circumstances largely shaped by national and international forces have led to worse-than-average poverty, unemployment, underemployment, malnutrition, inadequate housing, inferior or nonexistent health care facilities, diminished social services, and emigration (Pulver 1988; Hobbs 1990; Sherman 1992). These had the effect of undermining the economic and social stability in much of Rural America, disrupting not only cohesiveness in many of its communities, but rural culture itself (e.g., Berry 1977). Another major consequence was diminished political influence at the state and local levels (Stephens 1988; Bailey et al. 1992).

These conditions affected education as well. Local communities rely heavily on the use of property taxes to fund education. As property values erode with the declining fortunes of rural communities in many states, there is generally less to spend (Jansen 1991). The result for much of Rural America is underfunded schools, declining enrollments, limited curricula, aging facilities, and persistent pockets of functional illiteracy (Stephens 1988; Bailey et al. 1992).

But loss of community cohesiveness may not necessarily be the result of anything so dramatic as closing a factory or mine. The network of state and interstate highways that effectively reduced geographic distances, a boon in many ways, weakened rural community ties. For example, the sense of community can dissipate as a town is overtaken by urban sprawl or as its citizens become employed outside the town and spend their earnings for sustenance and entertainment elsewhere (Miller 1991). The rapid advancement of modern telecommunication technologies is another factor. In dramatically reducing isolation, community values have become influenced by outside forces as much as by local mores. The causes are many, but the result is the same. In much of Rural America, " . . . functional rural communities are an endangered species" (Miller 1991).

In this context, the school has become an important symbol of community itself. This symbolism helps to explain the fierce resistance to school consolidation and school district reorganization where these state strategies for trying to improve curriculum and save money are being revived. Factors other than community identity enter into the equation as well. Rural schools and school districts often play an important role in the economic life of their communities and are thus not readily relinquished. This role can be significant, as the school is often one of the largest employers in the community. Resources devoted to education are often the largest single expenditure of locally generated tax revenues (Mulkey and Raftery 1990). Through the employment of administrators, faculty, and staff, the local economy benefits directly, with the multiplier effect extending far beyond the schoolhouse. Buildings and equipment also manifest the community's commitment to itself.

But not all rural communities benefit economically from having a school. Highways may permit staff and faculty to be part of the larger, commuter culture, and they may choose to live in larger towns, cities, or another rural settlement and travel daily to work at the school. As a consequence, the rural community generates the payroll dollars, but the neighboring location or a nearby mall reaps the economic benefit. A commuting faculty, particularly

if turnover is extensive, also can have a depressing effect by undermining a community's sense of its long-term viability.

On the other hand, commuters who live in rural areas and work elsewhere may more often use the services and activities of the city where they work but *do not* pay taxes. If these commuters have no children, or if their children have completed school, they may resist higher property taxes to finance local schools.

The graying of Rural America is another phenomenon affecting rural schools. Indeed, rural communities have a higher concentration of older people than do urban communities, a situation often associated with the exodus of many younger people to urban areas (Hobbs 1990). In some areas, an influx of retirees intensifies this general trend. Retirement counties—defined as those with at least 15 percent net in-migration of the elderly—made up fewer than a fourth of all nonmetropolitan counties, yet they account for more than half of all nonmetropolitan population growth from 1980 to 1986.

Retirees bring employment growth, generate a larger tax base, and have a moderately successful record for raising income levels in many counties (Reeder and Glasgow 1990). However, like commuters who work outside the community, retired people who own property may have no families in the area, and seeing no benefit to themselves, are reluctant to support higher property taxes. According to a 1985 Advisory Commission on Intergovernmental Relations study, the elderly are twice as likely to oppose education funding as people under 35; indeed, retirement counties were found to spend 10 percent less per resident than other nonmetropolitan counties on education.

In summary, while the school still provides an anchor for most rural communities and many citizens will resist any move to deprive them of their local school, traditional assumptions regarding the rural school's role may no longer be fully operational. Dramatic and continuing changes in the world economy threaten the viability of many rural communities throughout America, undermining their capacity to support local services, including schools. At the same time, the nation's extensive transportation and communications networks have dramatically lessened community isolation and with that change, community cohesiveness has also diminished. As a result, the school may be underfunded as much through lack of will as through lack of resources. How some communities and schools have formed new alliances to face this changing world is discussed in the next section.

Responding to the Modern Challenge

In the last decade of this century, many rural communities and schools will struggle for physical survival and psychological health. Many will founder. But some schools and communities are finding new ways to work together to provide mutually rewarding experiences. Examples involve updates of traditional community interaction, community-based curricula, and student entrepreneurship.

The school in the community. The modern approach to traditional rural school-community relations is characterized by more sustained interactions and involvement of the community in defining its needs. The emphasis is on establishing links through social services and continuing education activities, so standard definitions of "student" and "client" become blurred. An example of one small K–12 rural school's service element enabled young students to benefit from an adopt-a-grandparent program at the local nursing home, while older students could qualify as on-call ambulance drivers for the hospital. Lifelong-learning strategies include offering community college-level evening courses open to both adults and teenagers, using qualified members of the community as instructors, and sharing the cost of resources (e.g., computers or physical fitness courses) to be used both by the school and the wider community (Rural Adult Education FORUM 1990).

The rural community as a curriculum resource.

Over the past quarter century, rural schools have been confronted with curricula that have an urban orientation. Some believe this situation may work to the rural communities' disadvantage since material is often not culturally relevant (Eller 1989). And by directing attention and values away from the local community, it encourages youths to leave the home community (Miller 1991). To counter outside influences perceived as negative and also provide students with a full array of skills, some schools have looked to their own communities for subject content and with it, a restoration of a given community's history and collective memory (Hobbs 1990). A primary example is the system of nine Foxfire Teacher Networks across the country that promote approaching the community as a classroom to develop courses covering music, literature, folklore, and environmental studies. The overarching purpose is to " . . . advocate the need for an understanding of and pride in the parent culture and a concomitant respect for and interest in the cultures of others" (Wigginton 1985). The Mid-

continent Regional Educational Laboratory has launched a related endeavor in six South Dakota schools. There, traditional courses are enriched by using the community as a resource. In many courses, students' products are of direct use to the community (e.g., a demographic report to guide long-range planning by community officials).

Using the community as a focus of study is consistent with current thinking about how learning can be facilitated. Educational research suggests the potential to learn is enhanced when students cooperate on a task, when the instructional process meaningfully involves decisionmaking and problem solving, when it is oriented to an outcome or product, and when activities are interdisciplinary and connected to real-world objects, events, and situations. Because of their size and because the communities they serve provide accessible and safe learning environments, rural schools are uniquely positioned to provide such learning opportunities.

School-business cooperatives.

Another approach involves rural schools playing a larger role in local job development. Examples include school-business arrangements whereby vocational courses at the school are specifically tailored to the local business (e.g., a metal building manufacturing company and a meat packing plant). In a colorful example, what began as a cooperative arrangement between a high school and the state game commission has become a boon to community employment through the development of a trout farming enterprise (Rural Adult Education FORUM 1990). These are only a few of the innovative ways schools and their communities can adopt strategies that are mutually strengthening.

School-based businesses. A related approach encourages high school youths to be principal operators of school-based businesses while involving them in the kinds of activities needed in the new economy (REAL 1990). Following a concept Jonathan Sher formulated some 15 years ago and that was developed by Sher and Paul DeLargy at the University of Georgia, REAL Enterprises (Rural Education through Action Learning) now has some 36 projects in North Carolina, South Carolina, and Georgia. The businesses have become vehicles for providing entrepreneurial training, academic development, vocational education, youth employment, and community service. The Ford Foundation is helping to expand the approach to other sites and a national federation of state REAL Enterprises is envisioned.

The Future Farmers of America (FFA), 4–H, and Junior Achievement have offered entrepreneurial experiences for youth in both rural and urban schools for many years. But these programs are usually either individual projects, in the case of 4–H and FFA, or short-term business experiences in the case of Junior Achievement. By contrast, REAL and similar ventures aim to have students create permanent local businesses. REAL Enterprises have included a day care center, a feeder hog operation, ice cream parlors, a graphic arts service, a shoe repair shop, and a miniature golf business. And in contributing to the community by filling a niche, students also consider remaining and helping revitalize it over the long term.

In Rothsay, a Minnesota town of 500, high school students discovered two niches—a grocery and a hardware store—that had recently closed. With students, faculty, school board members, and local business leaders working together, both businesses reopened as student-led operations. Thus, felt needs in the community are being met, students are receiving on-the-job training for the modern business world, and the town has renewed optimism (North Central Regional Educational Laboratory 1992).

Efforts like Rothsay's and REAL's dovetail with current reform measures around the country. These are the innovations that depart from curriculum uniformity, redefine the learning environment, identify others in the community as "teachers," and set new standards for evaluating student learning. School-based enterprises also recognize most new employment in the United States is generated by small firms and that entrepreneurial training of students can mean opportunities for economic gains (Hobbs, Heffernan, and Tweeten 1988). Historically, such skills were taught in the rural high schools through vocational and agricultural programs like the FFA. While FFA remains strong in many rural high schools today, rural youth have few alternative routes to obtain entrepreneurial training. The vocational education programs established 25 years ago are also being challenged to keep pace with emerging demands for training as work skills needed rapidly change (Hobbs 1990).

However, school-based enterprise practices are as yet not widespread; schools still are rarely collaborative partners with their communities (Miller 1991). Indeed, a vision of how schools and communities can respond to the demands of the emerging information age is in the very early stages of formulation everywhere (McCune 1988). And barriers to collaboration exist in many rural places. For example, regu-

lations governing school building operations may inhibit using schools for entrepreneurial activities or for social and recreational functions involving the wider community. And in some communities, local control translates into resistance to change. The concerted efforts of schools and their rural communities together with assistance from outside agencies, such as the Cooperative Extension Service, the regional educational laboratories, and others, are necessary to overcome such barriers and transform these examples into the norm.

Education and Rural Economic Development

During the last few years, a strong rural community development movement re-emerged. It is marked, however, by intense debates about what to emphasize in this effort—building a physical infrastructure and job creation or promoting a social and cultural infrastructure designed to improve the capacity of people (i.e., education). For example, many communities whose youth left in search of economic opportunities reduced their investments in education and instead supported something like a local industrial park (Hobbs, Heffernan, and Tweeten 1988).

Yet an understanding of the correlation between education and rural community development is growing (Reid 1991). The importance of a well-educated work force to enhance rural economic development objectives is increasingly accepted, though this principle has yet to be widely incorporated into policy. But communities with an inadequately trained work force are unattractive to expanding manufacturing and service industries

(Mulkey and Raftery 1990). And poorly educated rural residents are unable to compete for knowledge-oriented jobs (McGranahan and Ghelfi 1991). As has been observed, "Without a quality basic education, students will be hampered in whatever they do and wherever they go—including remaining in the locality" (Hobbs 1990).

Because the economy of Rural America in general is no longer dominated by farm employment, rural policy can no longer be equated with farm policy. Thus, in fashioning strategies for rural development, many circumstances must be considered. Over the last 5 years, the following events designed to help shape these strategies have occurred and most highlighted the importance of education:

- Four regional workshops were held in 1988 (Focus on the Future 1988) to develop a consensus on priorities for rural development. Sponsors were the Extension Service of the U.S. Department of Agriculture; the U.S. Department of Labor; the Farm Foundation; the Aspen Institute; and the Economic Development Administration. Participants included rural leaders, local and regional development organizations, state officials, staff from several federal agencies, including the U.S. Department of Education, and rural specialists from several of the regional educational laboratories. As a rural development strategy, education ranked at the top of the list of needs compiled in each region. The goals identified were to have rural schools offer the same level of education as urban schools so students would have equal opportunity in competing for jobs and to eliminate rural illiteracy so that the flexibility of the rural labor force could be enhanced.

- The President's Initiative on Rural America, launched in January 1990, is a multi-faceted undertaking that promotes economic development. State Rural Development Councils are key. Their mission is to improve rural employment opportunities by coordinating the delivery of federal and state programs that can respond to local rural economic development needs. As of spring 1993, Councils were fully operational in 8 states and an additional 28 states were in the process of establishing them.

- In late 1990, a major national commission called for improved education in rural areas. Strategies proposed included distance learning, school-based entrepreneurship, and job training to ease forced career changes. It also stressed the need to integrate these programs into a wider rural development effort (National Commission on Agriculture and Rural Development Policy 1990).

- In June, 1992, the General Accounting Office (GAO) held a symposium on rural development to respond to a congressional request to "identify the challenges Rural America faces in dealing with current economic realities." Its published report identified education as central to rural revitalization (U.S. GAO 1992).

Summary

Rural areas have always depended upon their schools to be the focus of community life. Yet that relationship has undergone significant change in recent decades. To the perennial problems of isolation, low population density, and limited fiscal resources have been added economic dislocation, easier access to the wider world, and the graying of the population—resulting both from youth emigration and, in some places, from an influx of retirees from metropolitan areas. Under these circumstances, maintaining community cohesion and fashioning a vision of the future have become particularly challenging. Certainly the school is now expected to prepare students for a society very different from that known by previous generations of rural Americans. Whether innovative community arrangements that strengthen the historical tie with the school become widespread and in turn contribute to revitalizing communities and whether recent high level policy recommendations result in enhanced educational opportunities and in expanded rural employment opportunities remains to be seen.

References

Bailey, G., P. Daisey, S. M. Maes, and J. D. Spears. 1992. *Literacy in Rural America: A Study of Current Needs and Practices*. Manhattan, KS: Rural Clearinghouse on Lifelong Education and Development.

Berry, W. 1977. *The Unsettling of America: Culture and Agriculture*. New York: Avon Books.

Eller, R. 1989. "Integrating the Local Community into Rural School Curriculum." *The Role of Rural Schools in Community Development: Proceedings*. S. Raftery and D. Mulkey (Eds.). Mississippi State, MS: Southern Rural Development Center.

Focus on the Future: Options in Developing a New National Rural Policy. Proceedings of Four Regional Rural Development Policy Workshops. May 1988. S.H. Jones (Ed.). College Station, TX: Texas Agricultural Extension Service, Texas A&M University.

Gjelten, T. May 3–5, 1982. "A Typology of Rural School Settings." Paper presented at the Rural Education Seminar, Washington, DC: U.S. Department of Education.

Hobbs, D. 1990. "School-based Community Development: Making Connections for Improved Learning." *The Role of Rural Schools in Community Development: Proceedings*. S. Raftery and D. Mulkey (Eds.). Mississippi State, MS: Southern Rural Development Center.

Hobbs, D., W. Heffernan, and L. Tweeten. May 1988. "Education, Retraining, and Relocation Policy." *Focus on the Future: Options in Developing a New National Rural Policy. Proceedings of Four Regional Rural Development Policy Workshops*. May, 1989. S. H. Jones (Ed.). College Station, TX: Texas Agricultural Extension Service, Texas A&M University.

Jansen, A. October 1990–January 1991. "Rural Counties Lead Urban in Education Spending, But Is That Enough?" *Rural Development Perspectives*. Washington, DC: U.S. Department of Agriculture, Economic Research Service.

McCune, S.D. Fall 1988. "Schools and Restructuring." *Policy Notes*. Aurora, CO: Mid-continent Regional Educational Laboratory.

McGranahan, D.A., and L.M. Ghelfi. 1991. "The Education Crisis and Rural Stagnation in the 1980s." *Education and Rural Economic Development: Strategies for the 1990s*. Washington, DC: U.S. Department of Agriculture, Economic Research Service.

Miller, Bruce. September 1991. "Rural Distress and Survival: The School and the Importance of Community." *The Northwest Regional Educational Laboratory Program Report*. Portland, OR: The Northwest Regional Educational Laboratory.

Mulkey, D., and S. Raftery. 1990. *School-Community Relationships Within a Community Development Framework*. Occasional paper. Research Triangle Park, NC: Southeastern Educational Improvement Laboratory.

Nachtigal, P.M. 1982. *Rural Education: In Search of a Better Way.* Boulder Co: Westview Press, Inc.

National Commission on Agriculture and Rural Development Policy. 1990. *Future Directions in Rural Development Policy.* Washington, DC: U.S. Department of Agriculture.

North Central Regional Educational Laboratory. 1992. "School-Based Enterprise: Expanding the Walls of the School to Prepare Students for Real Life." *Rural Audio Journal* 1:1.

Pulver, G.C. 1988. "The Changing Economic Scene in Rural America." *The Journal of State Government* 61:1.

REAL Enterprises, Inc. Spring/Summer 1990. Vol. 1. *The REAL Story.* Chapel Hill, NC.

Reeder, R.J., and N. Glasgow. February 1990. "Nonmetro Retirement Counties' Strengths and Weaknesses." *Rural Development Perspectives.* Washington, DC: U.S. Department of Agriculture, Economic Research Service.

Rural Adult Education FORUM. January 1990. G. Bailey (Ed.). Manhattan, KS: Rural Clearinghouse for Lifelong Education and Development.

Sherman, A. 1992. *Falling by the Wayside: Children in Rural America.* Washington, DC: The Children's Defense Fund.

Stephens, E.R. 1988. *The Changing Context of Education in a Rural Setting.* Occasional Paper 26. Charleston, WV: Appalachia Educational Laboratory.

U.S. General Accounting Office. November 1992. *Rural Development: Rural America Faces Many Challenges.* GAO/RCED–93–35. Washington, DC.

Wiggenton, E. 1985. *Sometimes a Shining Moment: The Foxfire Experience.* Garden City, NY: Anchor Press/Doubleday.

Language arts class, Yap State, Federated States of Micronesia. In the Pacific region, school may mean a modern, well-equipped building or it may mean a wooden platform with a thatched roof and no electricity. **Photo from the Pacific Region Educational Laboratory (PREL), Honolulu, Hawaii.**

5. Policies and Programs Benefiting Rural Education

Until fairly recently, the circumstances surrounding rural education have largely been ignored in most policy circles. Rather, throughout most of this century, the trend has been to have rural schools become more like urban schools in size and curriculum. In recent years, however, the special needs of the nation's rural, small schools have gained the attention of Congress, a number of federal departments and independent agencies, some state governments, the courts, and several postsecondary institutions, professional associations, and foundations. Some programs that promote equity and quality in rural schools predate this current interest; many others have been established recently. In the absence of a special survey on the topic, the following information resulted from examining existing sources.

Federal Government

While there is no overarching federal policy on rural education, programs exist that either directly or indirectly benefit rural schools and their students.

U.S. Department of Education.
Some of the U.S. Department of Education's (ED) administrative strategies and authorized programs focus attention on rural education and have assisted rural students either directly or incidentally.

Administrative action. The U.S. Department of Education Authorization Act of 1979 (Public Law 96–88, Section 214) directed ED to establish a new organizational commitment to the nation's rural schools and placed responsibility for carrying this out in the Office of Vocational and Adult Education (OVAE). The initial response was to create a committee chaired by the Assistant Secretary, OVAE, with representatives from all the major ED offices. Of the many goals it articulated, the committee over time focused on achieving two: articulating a Departmental policy on rural education and developing a rural education research agenda.

Policy: In 1983, then Secretary T.H. Bell responded to the congressional directive by issuing the "Rural Education and Rural Family Education Policy for the 1980s," which was specific in its intent: "Rural education shall receive an equitable share of the information, services, assistance, and funds available from and through the U.S. Department of Education and its programs."

The statement was accompanied by an array of activities ED would undertake to fulfill this policy, subject to the availability of resources (table 5–1). OVAE monitored compliance with this policy for some years and produced annual status reports to the Secretary.

Research: In 1989, the Federal Interagency Committee on Education (FICE) endorsed a research agenda developed by the rural education committee with advice from specialists from other federal agencies and from other researchers and practitioners.[1] The priorities covered overall rural school effectiveness; curricular provisions; school and community partnerships; human resources; use of technology; and financial support and governance. FICE formally expressed its desire to have the agenda made "broadly available . . . so that educators in Rural America can be given greater help in their efforts to improve educational outcomes for rural learners of all ages."

Consequently, the Office of Educational Research and Improvement (OERI) widely disseminated a brochure containing the agenda. The need for research in this area is great. One study (Barker and Beckner 1987) reported that few established scholars—just 2 percent of 14,000 higher education faculty members surveyed—concentrate on rural issues.

The rural education committee (and a FICE subcommittee on rural education) were deactivated in 1990. Attention to rural education concerns, meanwhile, advanced in other Departmental units.

The *National Center for Education Statistics* collects data by community type in its longitudinal survey instruments (e.g., NELS:88), teacher and administrator samples (Schools and Staffing Survey), and the National Assessment of Educational Progress (NAEP). Its periodic reports increasingly include distinctions by setting, though definitions of "rural" currently differ among these surveys. Of significance is that NCES has constructed a new typology assigning all schools to mutually exclusive locales, including a rural category (Johnson 1989). This typology is now used in the Common Core of Data, which is the NCES annual universe survey of public schools, and is influencing other data gathering in the Center as well. As a result of a joint project with the Census Bureau on the 1990 Census, rural schools will be defined with even greater precision, allowing more sophisticated analyses. The development of software and targeted training programs for rural researchers will make the data widely accessible, permitting direct analysis by state and local officials.

Another example of ED's administrative targeting is OERI's *Blue Ribbon Schools Program* that recognizes exemplary schools annually. Because initial rural school representation was low, program staff actively encouraged rural participation, but it has still fluctuated. For example, 33 of the 226 elementary schools recognized in 1991 were located in small, mostly rural communities.

Discretionary and targeted programs. Of ED's approximately 140 elementary and secondary assistance programs, 12 specifically target or include rural schools, either by statute or agency regulation. Five selected for discussion follow:

Chapter 1 Rural Technical Assistance Centers. Authorized in 1988 to improve the quality of education provided to educationally disadvantaged children who reside in rural areas or attend small schools, these 10 regional centers have a special mission to help rural districts that have declining enrollments (Request for Proposals, RFP 89–054, May 1989).

Rural Education Initiative. This activity began in fiscal year 1987 with a modest congressional set-aside for contracts OERI awarded to the regional educational laboratories. Beginning with the new 5-year contract in fiscal year 1991, OERI required each laboratory to certify that at least 25 percent of its annual award supported activities serving rural schools (Request for Proposals, RFP 91–002, April 1990). Annual Congressional allocations of around $10 million have met or exceeded that minimum each year since. As a result of this program, numerous intervention strategies uniquely suited to rural schools have been identified or developed by the laboratories and widely disseminated. Moreover, research on rural schools has been significantly expanded through the support and concentration at the laboratories of a cadre of researchers and development experts in rural education issues.

ERIC Clearinghouse on Rural Education and Small Schools (ERIC/CRESS). The Educational Resources Information Center (ERIC) system is comprised of 16 centers on different topics. Rural education has been an ERIC component since the inception of this major education information network in the late 1960s. Presently housed in Charleston, West Virginia, ERIC/CRESS collects and disseminates educational research information covering economic, cultural, social, or other factors related to education programs and practices for rural residents.

The Star Schools Demonstration Project. Designed to employ telecommunications to improve the quality of school program offerings and overcome the disadvantages of isolation, this program was authorized in 1988 (Education for Economic Security Act of 1988, Title D, Section 905 (c)(1)). Instructional programs are delivered by satellite to rural communities and underserved metropolitan areas with scarce resources and limited access to courses in mathematics, science, and foreign languages. Some 6,000 schools in 49 states, the District of Columbia, and Puerto Rico participate. In addition to high school- and middle school-level courses, some college and graduate courses are offered for staff development.

Library Research, Demonstration and Training Programs. Under Title II of the Higher Education Act (P.L. 89–329), these programs have included a number of grants benefiting rural areas. For example, the Center for the Study of Rural Librarianship was funded to conduct a national survey to determine adult use of rural public libraries.

The remaining ED discretionary programs that include a rural specification include: early childhood experimental, demonstration, and outreach projects (Education of the Handicapped Act (EHA), sec. 623 9 (a)); projects for the severely handicapped (EHA, sec. 624 (c)); Even Start (Elementary and Secondary Education Act (ESEA)); dropout prevention demonstrations; basic skills demonstration projects (ESEA); and rehabilitation research and information dissemination by the National Institute on Disability and Rehabilitation Research (NIDRR). (Note: The Office of Special Education Programs included among its grant priorities between 1985 and 1990 training rural special educators. Fifty-three projects were funded and about 600 teachers prepared for rural placement. While this is no longer a special emphasis, projects to train teachers to work in rural areas continue to be funded.)

Formula grant programs. Rural schools also share in the several multi-million dollar state formula programs administered by ED that assist special populations, for example, students who are disadvantaged, handicapped, or engaged in vocational training. Laws establish requirements for fund distribution, and these may include a rural provision. One example is the *Eisenhower Mathematics and Science Education State Grant Program* (P.L. 100–297). Designed to improve the quality of elementary and secondary school mathematics and science instruction, it requires states to take into consideration the needs of students in "sparsely populated areas." Moreover, the provision in most ED formula grant programs for benefiting children in low-income families or living in areas with high concentrations of low-income families, would bring funds to the many high poverty rural areas.

The primary federal program directing funds to disadvantaged children is *Chapter 1 of Title I, Elementary and Secondary Education Act (ESEA)*. Table 5–2 shows the percentage of students receiving services under this program by school location. *Chapter 2 of Title I, ESEA*, allocates funds according to student enrollments. The legislation permits states to provide higher allocations to districts having the greatest number and percentage of children living in sparsely populated areas, and most rural states do include a sparsity factor in their calculations.

Generally, however, the extent to which rural areas attract ED formula funds is difficult to assess, in part because the authorizations do not target funds by location, rural, or otherwise. Nor do the operating units of ED employ standard definitions of community types. In addition, states employ their own formulas for distributing funds. For example, definitions of sparsity used under Chapter 2 vary by state.

Three other formula programs have potential to help rural areas. One is *Impact-Aid* (P.L. 81–874) that provides entitlements for operating expenses and construction directly to school districts. Funding is based on need generated by government activities as in the acquisition of land for federal purposes such as a military installation, a national park, or an Indian reservation and which thus diminish the base on which local taxes for schools would be assessed. The program does not define districts by rurality, but given the remote location of many such federal operations, a large proportion of appropriated funds bene-

fit predominately rural districts, including Indian reservations.

The second is the *Migrant Education Program*. Under this portion of the Chapter 1, ESEA formula grant program, funding is directed to state education agencies to provide instructional support for the children of migrant workers. Most projects are in rural areas.

The third is the *Library Services and Construction Act* (P.L.101–254). Originally established 38 years ago to help develop rural libraries, all libraries are now eligible to apply for assistance under formula grants to states. Also, eligible Indian tribes, most of which are located in rural areas, and Hawaiian native organizations can receive grants for public library services. Discretionary grants focus on literacy programs and foreign language materials, and many rural public libraries have benefited.

Some federal and state programs require that for a school to be eligible for funds, a minimum number of students must be served. Given their often small enrollments, many rural schools view this as a discriminatory policy since it renders them ineligible despite having children in need. The Eisenhower program addresses this issue by requiring that any school district whose entitlement is less than $6,000 must enter into a consortium with other districts so collectively they receive at least $6,000.

Few national studies have attempted to ascertain fund distribution by location, and because of the circumstances just noted above, those that did had difficulty. For example, a 1989 General Accounting Office report noted that "[t]he rural percent of the relatively massive vocational education program—Basic Grants to the States (CFDA #84.048) could not be estab-

lished, nor could [that for] several of the smaller scale vocational education programs." How much rural students benefit from the Department's formula programs, then, remains uncertain.

Other Major Federal Programs. In fiscal year 1991, an estimated 61.4 billion federal dollars went toward education (Hoffman 1993). Of that total, 43.3 percent came from ED (table 5–3). Only two other departments—Agriculture and Interior (with its Bureau of Indian Affairs schools)—and the Appalachian Regional Commission specifically targeted rural education. However, as with ED entitlements, broad mandates do encompass rural locations. The following are the major federal responses affecting rural elementary and secondary level students.

U.S. Department of Agriculture. A number of programs and units in the U.S. Department of Agriculture (USDA) impact rural education directly or indirectly.

The *Child Nutrition Program* administers food programs that address the nutritional needs of America's school-age children and youth. It is the single largest federal program for elementary and secondary schools. Most schools, including rural schools, offer free and reduced-priced lunches through this program.

The *Economic Research Service* carries out analyses and issues major documents for policymakers on the economic and social trends in nonmetropolitan counties, including discussion of rural education's role in rural economic development.

The *Cooperative Extension System* is a decentralized educational network that functions as a partnership involving USDA, state land-grant universities, and county governments. It includes initiatives for youth-at-risk and family well-being that impact children from the pre-school years to the late teens and also sponsors the National 4–H program of informal education for youth age 9–19. In 1988, the Extension Service joined the U.S. Department of Labor, the Southwest Educational Development Laboratory (SEDL), and many other public and private organizations to sponsor four regional workshops to assess the role of education in rural economic development.

The *National Agriculture Library* administers the Rural Information Center, an information and referral service for rural local government, and the Youth Development Information Center, a similar service for professionals who work with rural youth.

U.S. Department of Health and Human Services.

This Department operates *Head Start*, which provides comprehensive health, educational, nutritional, social, and other services to preschool children who are economically disadvantaged. The program's formula portion is based on poverty measures, while the discretionary portion is focused on Indian tribes, territories, migrants, and the handicapped. Under both portions, funds would reach rural children.

U.S. Department of Labor.

This agency administers the *Job Training Partnership Act* and the *Job Corps* programs that provide employment and training to economically disadvantaged youth. While there are no rural set-asides, allocation formulas targeting areas of unemployment enable rural youth to benefit as well.

Appalachian Regional Commission.

This independent agency follows a relatively ambitious agenda to address equity and quality issues in rural, small school districts in the Ap-palachian area of the country. Involving counties in 13 states, it strongly supports vocational education and conducts special studies on such topics as adult literacy, high school dropouts, and the impact of reform on schools in its region.

State Policies and Programs

Many state governments have long engaged in special efforts to promote equity and quality in rural, small school districts. One can classify these efforts into five broad categories (table 5–4).

Structural strategies. The approach most widely implemented involves mandating the reorganization of neighboring districts with small enrollments into new, larger administrative units, a practice known as consolidation. This practice, used extensively and with dramatic effects in earlier decades, is still actively under consideration in many states, (e.g., Oregon, North Carolina, Iowa, and Minnesota). A number of states now use fiscal incentives to promote voluntary consolidation. Still other states (e.g., West Virginia) promote merging small enrollment schools with larger schools in the same district. Some states also have established special-purpose regional schools (e.g., special education or vocational-technical) or comprehensive regional secondary schools.

Service delivery strategies. A wide variety of mechanisms are used in virtually all states primarily to assist rural districts. They make available specialized programs and services usually beyond the means of systems having small enrollments (e.g., cooperative purchasing, staff development, curriculum development or management support, and special education services). Common structures are state-operated, single-purpose, or comprehensive educational service agencies; regional branches of the state education agency; multidistrict sharing of whole grades (usually at the secondary level) or the joint employment of staff; distance-learning for course delivery and staff training; and instructional programs operated by the state.

School choice options. Many advocacy groups now support interdistrict school choice. But its early supporters were rural parents in areas of limited possibilities who sought richer educational experiences for their children. This practice is now permissible in Arkansas, Iowa, Minnesota, Nebraska, Ohio, and Wisconsin.

Revenue enhancement. Several mechanisms have been designed to augment support for revenue-poor, primarily rural, schools. The most common practice is state-aid formulas that include a sparsity factor to account for districts with thin populations.

Administrative tactics. Rural interests are represented through the presence of policy or planning positions at the state level in a number of cases.

Other Initiatives

Several public and private agencies, organizations, and institutions have undertaken many voluntary actions to enhance the programs of rural, small school districts. They are grouped into four categories.

University-based programs. Programs to train new rural teachers and administrators exist in some dozen colleges and universities. Examples include Western Montana College's policy of a half-year student teaching assignment in a rural district, and an interdisciplinary graduate seminar at the University of Vermont for aspiring and experienced school administrators and other human service professionals who work in rural areas. Also, many postsecondary institutions located in nonmetropolitan areas have for many years provided in-service training for school teachers and administrators. In addition, the state of Washington provides incentives for teacher candidates to do student teaching in rural districts.

Some postsecondary institutions have established rural school research and technical assistance centers, while a limited number offer high school and advanced placement courses via telecommunications. Kansas State University, Manhattan, is home to the Rural Clearinghouse for Lifelong Education and Development, which recently developed a telecourse on change in rural communities available through the PBS Adult Training Service. In still a different example of postsecondary involvement in rural education, the University of Maine, Orono, for the last decade has published a journal dedicated to research on rural education.

Professional associations and organizations. Several entities exist to promote rural education concerns. The oldest continuing organization dedicated to this purpose is the National Rural Education Association (NREA) founded in 1907. Among its publications is a quarterly journal, *The Country Teacher.* NREA recently endorsed three postsecondary institution-based research centers, attesting to their quality and investment in rural studies. They are the Center for the Study of Small/Rural Schools at the University of Oklahoma, Norman; the Rural Education Research and Service Consortium, Tennessee Tech University, Cookeville; and the Center for Rural Education and Small Schools, Kansas State University, Manhattan.

Other examples of rural education organizations are the American Council on Rural Special Education, the Southern Rural Education Association, and the Future Farmers of America. The latter is a school-based, federally chartered national organization of students preparing for a range of careers in agriculture.

In addition, rural interest units have been established within associations that have a wider focus, for example, the National School Boards Association (NSBA) and the American Association of School Administrators (AASA). In 1989, an umbrella group, Organizations Concerned About Rural Education (OCRE), was formed in Washington, D.C. to bring together those interested in rural education issues. OCRE membership includes NREA, NSBA, AASA, the National Education Association (NEA), the American Federation of Teachers (AFT), the National Grange, the Triangle Coalition, U.S. West, and the Council for Education Development and Research (CEDaR).

A major compilation of state and national organizations having a rural interest may be found in the *Rural Education Directory: Organizations and Resources,* a joint publication of the ERIC Clearinghouse on Rural Education and Small Schools and the NREA.

State-level rural education interest groups. Voluntary state organizations have sprung up in more than a dozen states, including Missouri, Nebraska, Pennsylvania, and Utah. Many have been instrumental in challenging existing school finance formulas in their respective states.

Foundations. The Annenberg, Ford, Kellogg, and Charles Stewart Mott Foundations, and the Lilly Endowment, Inc., among others, support a wide range of activities to assist rural schools and communities. Examples include support for research analysis, grants to targeted schools, and funds for expanding school-business enterprises.

Summary

Institutional activities on behalf of rural education present a mixed picture. On the one hand, a number of initiatives have been designed to address the needs of rural schools and their students. On the other hand, these needs, especially in circumstances of poverty, can be extreme. Lack of adequate research and impact evaluations, together with definitional inconsistencies severely limit policymakers' ability to know either the effect of federal, state, and local programs on rural schools or whether rural interests are being equitably addressed. Until this deficiency is corrected, policymaking on behalf of rural students will be impeded.

Notes

1. Operated by Executive Order in the 1960s, but established by statute in 1979, FICE provides the Secretary of Education with a mechanism to coordinate the Department's education activities with those of other federal units.

References

Barker, B.O., and W.E. Beckner. 1987. "Preservice Training for Rural Teachers: A Survey." *Rural Educator* 8:3.

General Accounting Office. 1989. *Rural Development: Federal Programs That Focus on Rural America and its Economic Development.* Washington, DC.

Hoffman, C.M. 1993. *Federal Support for Education: Fiscal Years 1980 to 1992.* Washington, DC: U.S. Department of Education, National Center for Education Statistics.

Johnson, F. 1989. *Assigning Type of Locale Codes to the 1987–88 CCD Public School Universe*. Technical Report CS 89–194. Washington, DC: U.S. Department of Education, National Center for Education Statistics.

Rural Education Directory: Organizations and Resources. 1993. Charleston, WV: ERIC Clearinghouse on Rural Education and Small Schools and the National Rural Education Association.

U.S. Department of Education. 1983. *Rural Education and Rural Family Education Policy for the '80s*. Administrative Document. Washington, DC.

U.S. Department of Education, Office of Educational Research and Improvement. 1990. *An Agenda for Research and Development on Rural Education*. Washington, DC.

U.S. Department of Education, Office of Educational Research and Improvement. *May 1989. Request for Proposals*. RFP 89–054, Appendix A. Washington, DC.

U.S. Department of Education, Office of Educational Research and Improvement. *April 1990. Request for Proposals*. RFP 91–002, Attachment A. Washington, DC.

FAA local chapter officers, Turner Ashby High School (enrollment 869, grades 9-12), Bridgewater, Virginia. **Photo by Andrew Markwart, for the National FFA Center, Alexandria, Virginia.**

6. Educators in Rural Schools

For the past decade, the role of America's educators in achieving school improvement has received considerable attention. Yet little notice has been taken of those in rural schools, partly because of inadequate statistical information. Recently analyzed data from the Schools and Staffing Survey (SASS) conducted by the National Center for Education Statistics (NCES) help remedy this situation. Basic demographic characteristics (including education and work experiences), compensation, recruitment, and working conditions of rural public school teachers and principals are now available. Except where noted otherwise, all information reported comes from original analyses of these new data. In making comparisons with nonrural educators, some conceptions about education in Rural America have been confirmed, while others have not.[1]

Rural Teachers

It has been observed that, "Attracting and keeping competent individuals to teach the 'three R's' in rural schools is largely a function of the 'three C's,' characteristics, conditions, and compensation" (Sher 1983). These aspects are presented in the following paragraphs:

Demographic characteristics. Some 560,000 elementary and secondary teachers, or about 24 percent of America's more than two million public school teachers, were employed in a rural setting in school year 1987–88.[2]

Sex and race-ethnicity. The proportion of male and female teachers in rural and nonrural elementary schools had virtually no differences of consequence—females outnumbered males

about 7 to 1. At the secondary level, there was greater sex parity. Only 6 percent of rural school teachers were members of minority groups compared to 12 percent in nonrural schools. This partly reflects the lower proportion of minority groups in Rural America where 87 percent of the student population is white. However, there are large concentrations of rural black, Hispanic, Pacific Islander, and Indian students in certain regions of the country.

Age and experience. As suspected from previous research, rural teachers were found to be younger than nonrural teachers (table 6–1a), with somewhat more under the age of 30 (16

vs. 12 percent) and with considerably fewer over the age of 40 (44 vs. 53 percent). Reflecting these age differences, proportionately more rural teachers had less than 10 years of experience, while fewer (17 vs. 23 percent) had more than 20 years experience (table 6–1b).

Training. In the context of education reform, many have expressed concern about the quality of teachers in rural schools. One index of quality is amount of preparation. As widely believed, the survey confirmed rural teachers generally have less professional preparation (figure 6–1 and table 6–2). The difference was most dramatic at the secon-

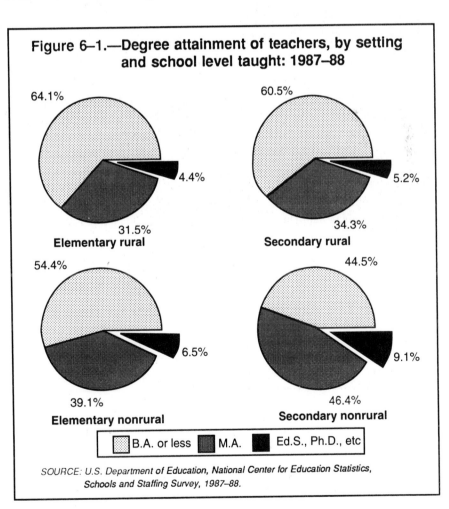

Figure 6–1.—Degree attainment of teachers, by setting and school level taught: 1987–88

64.1%
4.4%
31.5%
Elementary rural

60.5%
5.2%
34.3%
Secondary rural

54.4%
6.5%
39.1%
Elementary nonrural

44.5%
9.1%
46.4%
Secondary nonrural

B.A. or less   M.A.   Ed.S., Ph.D., etc

SOURCE: U.S. Department of Education, National Center for Education Statistics, Schools and Staffing Survey, 1987–88.

dary school level where 34 percent of rural teachers had at least a master's degree compared to 46 percent for nonrural teachers. Part of the difference may be attributable to the rural teachers' relative youth. Another contributing factor may be the limited access rural teachers in more isolated settings have to continuing education and professional development opportunities.

Moreover, many teachers had not majored in the subject they were teaching. About one out of five teachers in both rural and nonrural settings was responsible for subjects for which they were not academically prepared or certified. In rural areas, the mismatch was greatest for two subjects at the secondary level: 27 percent of special education teachers and 24 percent of science teachers lacked academic majors or certification compared to 18 percent of the teachers for these two subjects in nonrural settings.

This information on experience and training is underscored by recent findings from a sample survey carried out for the National Science Foundation (Carlsen and Monk 1992). Rural science teachers in middle and secondary schools not only averaged 3.1 years less experience teaching science, but they reported taking significantly fewer undergraduate science courses or even science methods courses. Moreover, fewer than half (48 percent) of rural science teachers compared to 65 percent nonrural science teachers had advanced degrees.

Compensation. The common perception that teachers' salaries are less in rural schools than in nonrural schools was borne out by the SASS survey. Rural teachers' base salary, defined as the average of all teacher salaries exclusive of any contracted supplements, was $22,600 in 1988, approximately $4,800 less than that earned by nonrural teachers.[3]

Another comparison is that of officially scheduled salaries. Figure 6–2 compares the average scheduled salary of rural and nonrural districts by teachers' academic preparation and experience. Rural school districts offered teachers with a bachelor's degree and no experience approximately $1,600 less on the average than did nonrural districts, a 10 percent differential. More noteworthy, however, is that rural teachers with a master's degree and 20 years on the job earned an average of $5,000 less, widening the disparity to more than three times that experienced by beginning teachers. Such an income shortfall could be a factor causing many rural teachers to leave for jobs outside rural areas, and for those who remain, could serve as a disincentive for obtaining an advanced degree.

In addition to lower salaries, rural school districts tended to offer fewer benefits to their teachers than did nonrural districts. They paid less frequently for teachers' general medical, dental, and life insurance, and proportionately fewer of them contributed to a pension fund for teachers (table 6–3).

Possibly as a result of these discrepancies in compensation, rural teachers engaged in supplemental school employment somewhat more than did nonrural teachers (38 vs. 33 percent). But they did not moonlight more, that is, hold jobs outside school. However, nearly one-quarter of all teachers, regardless of setting, took such jobs at some time during the calendar year (table 6–4), suggesting possible general teacher dissatisfaction with income levels, though the desire to fill time usefully during the long summer vacation may be a factor as well.

Recruitment and retention of qualified teachers. The supply of qualified teachers for rural schools has been a concern for some time. Upon examination, many factors are found to affect the issues of teacher selection, supply, demand, and shortage in rural schools.

Teacher selection criteria. Policymakers debate considerably what qualifications should govern teacher hiring. While most schools employed traditional criteria, somewhat more rural than nonrural schools reported them being used in their districts (table 6–5). Examples are: a major or minor in the field for which a teacher was being considered (68 vs. 61 percent), completion of an approved teacher education program (72 vs. 65 percent), and state certification (81 vs. 77 percent).

However, despite the widely publicized national move during the early 1980s to promote using standardized tests for

Figure 6–2.— Average scheduled salary for rural and nonrural teachers			
Setting	No experience	No experience	20 years experience
	B.A.	**M.A.**	**M.A.**
Rural	$16,973	$18,519	$27,245
Nonrural	$18,610	$20,303	$32,194

teacher candidates before they could enter the classroom, only a minority of rural districts used each type (table 6–5). A little more than one out of four rural districts employed the National Teachers Examination and just over one-third used a state test (37 percent), proportions that were slightly less than that of nonrural districts. Only a few used a district examination (3 vs. 11 percent). (Note: These data should not be added; a district may employ more than one test in its process.)

Recruitment. In school year 1987–88, about 12 percent of principals in rural schools reported having difficulty recruiting teachers, while one out of four said recruitment was hard only for selected subjects. However, contrary to expectations based on limited research (Harris 1989; Hatton et al. 1991), it did not appear to be more difficult, on average, to recruit teachers for rural schools than for nonrural schools.

When rural principals were unable to find qualified teachers, they acted somewhat differently than nonrural principals. While use of substitutes was the dominant solution, rural school principals employed them less often (26 vs. 40 percent)—possibly because substitutes were unavailable in relatively sparsely settled areas. As a result, they tended somewhat more to cancel a course or to reassign teachers, with nearly one out of five using the latter solution (table 6–6).

Retention. Attrition is a major issue in all education settings because stability of personnel is necessary for schools to be effective (Purkey and Smith 1983). Between the 1986–87 and 1987–88 academic years, the attrition rate in rural and nonrural schools was 9 percent. Schools with enrollment under 150, however, had attrition rates

as high as 13 percent, a relevant finding for many rural communities where small schools predominate.

Moreover, the proportion of teachers leaving a school for a given reason varied by setting. For those leaving the profession, retirement was the primary reason, although consistent with data on age and work experience, proportionately fewer rural teachers reported this choice (27 vs. 36 percent). Significantly, former rural teachers were more likely to have taken a job outside of education than were those who left nonrural schools (21 vs. 15 percent). That one out of five rural teachers left the profession for reasons other than retirement is consistent with widespread reports of teacher turnover in rural areas.

But not all departing teachers are lost to the profession (Rollefson 1990). In fact, over 50 percent of the attrition is accounted for by those who transfer to other schools. The scant research that exists indicates rural teachers move to obtain better salaries and benefits (Matthes and Carlson 1986) or to teach in a larger community (Harris 1989; and Hatton et al. 1991).

Working conditions. Recent studies (Chubb and Moe 1990; Corcoran et al. 1988; Rosenholtz 1989) have raised the issue of the school as work place, though none addressed rural settings. This perspective reflects an assertion made at the beginning of the current school reform era that the most important public policy for effecting reform should be to transform "schools into 'good work' places . . ." (Sykes 1983). NCES data revealed rural teachers experienced both advantages and disadvantages relative to their nonrural peers in conditions they face daily.

Workload. While rural teachers were found to have smaller classes, the average class size difference of two fewer students at both the elementary and secondary levels was not as great as would have been expected from the research literature. However, the data confirmed findings from earlier studies that secondary-level subject area teachers in rural schools teach more subjects, requiring more preparations. They were nearly twice as likely as nonrural teachers to be responsible for three or more subjects daily—31 percent as opposed to 17 percent. Looked at from another way, just over a third of the rural secondary school teachers taught just one subject daily compared to half of the nonrural teachers.

Spheres of influence—the classroom. The data also bore out the common belief that rural teachers exercised considerable control over the instructional process in their classrooms. Larger proportions of rural teachers reported they had a high level of control over five classroom processes: determining the amount of homework to be assigned (90 percent); selecting teaching techniques (88 percent); disciplining students (74 percent); selecting content, topics, and skills to be taught (67 percent); and selecting textbooks and other instructional materials (65 percent). The rural advantage was particularly marked in the last two categories (table 6–7).

Spheres of influence—the school. By contrast, smaller proportions of rural teachers indicated having "a great deal of influence" over various aspects of school policy (range=20 to 46 percent) that included discipline, inservice training, ability grouping, and curriculum (table 6-8). The dominant distinction was level, rather than setting: for three of the four areas, more elementary than secondary school teachers reported influence. And only for discipline at the secondary level (28 vs. 23.5 percent) and in curriculum at both levels (40 percent) did a significantly larger percentage of rural teachers than nonrural teachers report a great deal of influence.

Satisfaction. Of special concern, however, is the low level of satisfaction teachers had with their working conditions—regardless of setting. A minority of teachers were "highly satisfied" with the key areas of "support and administrative leadership" (22 percent) and "buffering and rule enforcement" (33 percent), and an even smaller proportion had that view regarding "cooperation among staff" (9 percent) and "adequacy of resources" (2 percent) (table 6–9). Reflecting these expressions of dissatisfaction, 24 percent of the rural teachers indicated they would not choose to teach again. Two out of three, however, said they would remain in the profession as long as possible. Significantly, there were no appreciable differences between rural and nonrural teachers on any of these measures.

Rural School Principals

That the principal is central to a school's effectiveness has been documented in numerous studies over the last two decades. Indeed, much of the hoped-for success of the latest reform strategies hinges on the school building administrator's skill. Yet little has been written about the rural school principal. Fortunately, the Schools and Staffing Survey makes it possible to gain information about those who bear so much responsibility for educating the next generation under what may often be trying circumstances. (Note: These data are only on building principals and not on other types of administrators,

since other administrators were not surveyed.)

Demographic characteristics. About one-third of America's 78,000 public school principals said they worked in rural communities (table 6–10).

Sex and race-ethnicity. Of these rural principals, about 83 percent were male (21,000 compared to 4,300 females); in nonrural areas, 72 percent of the principals were male (table 6–11). As with teachers, just 6 percent of rural school principals are Native American, Asian, black, or Hispanic, compared to 13 percent in nonrural schools (table 6–12).

Age and experience. It has been suggested (Jacobson 1988) that school administrators often begin their careers in rural areas, only to move on to nonrural areas or out of the profession. The survey attests to the rural school principals' comparative youth. One quarter of rural principals are under age 40, compared to 15 percent of nonrural principals. Moreover, only 3 out of 10 rural principals are 50 years of age and older, compared to 4 of 10 for nonrural principals (table 6–11).

Training. As for education levels (figure 6–3 and table 6-13), just as many rural principals had master's degrees as did nonrural principals (over half); the same is true for those holding education specialist degrees (over one-third). But there were significant differences at either end of the education spectrum. Less than half as many rural principals held a Ph.D. or similar advanced degree (5 percent vs. 11 percent). Correspondingly, about 5 percent had just a B.A. or less, while this was true of only 1 percent of nonrural principals. The relative youth of

principals at rural schools may be part of the explanation for both phenomena.

Stark differences in educational attainment emerged when rural principals were compared by sex and when women principals in the two settings were contrasted. Rural female principals were three times as likely not to have advanced beyond the B.A. (12 vs. 4 percent). Moreover, rural female principals were considerably outpaced by women in nonrural settings. They were six times as likely to hold just a B.A. (12 vs. 2 percent) while the rate at which they had advanced beyond the master's degree was half that of nonrural females (6 vs. 13 percent). Similar discrepancies characterized males in both settings, but they were not as extreme.

Contrasts also appeared when comparing the work histories of principals (table 6–14). The most striking difference was by sex, with rural male principals having been in the profession considerably longer than their female counterparts (10.4 vs. 5.7 years). A similar contrast existed in nonrural settings. In addition, rural male principals had worked in that role for 10.4 years compared to 11.8 years for nonrural males. The difference between female principals in the two settings was smaller (5.7 vs. 6.3 years). In addition, women in both settings had entered the profession later, averaging 3 years more working outside the principalship, primarily as a result of spending more time as teachers than men did—about 12 vs. 9 years.

Compensation. As shown in figure 6–4, rural principals received substantially less pay than nonrural principals (table 6–15). The average salary for a principal of a rural school was about $36,000 compared to nearly $45,000 for a nonrural school principal. In addition to the basic economic difficulties that restrain rural salaries, some part of this difference may be due to the relatively small size of rural schools. Larger, usually urban, schools have the capacity to attract personnel with more credentials and experience and to pay them accordingly.

Male rural principals earned more than female rural principals by about $4,600. The male pay advantage in rural areas was nearly three times the advantage of male principals in nonrural areas (an 11 vs. 4 percent differential compared to female principals). Even greater was the pay disparity between women in the two settings—$11,000, or 25 percent. A major

contributing factor may be that a large proportion of rural female principals had not attained the academic credentials of their nonrural counterparts.

Compensation disadvantages for rural principals extended to the benefits available in their pay packages (table 6–16). As shown in figure 6–5, significantly fewer rural principals received benefits such as medical insurance, life insurance, and pensions. Moreover, rural principals were twice as likely to receive no benefits at all (7.7 vs. 3.3 percent).

Working conditions. Large proportions of rural school principals exercise considerable control over key adminis-

trative areas (table 6–17). Both rural and nonrural principals reported having considerable influence over teacher hiring and school discipline policy, with slightly more rural principals saying this was the case. But rural principals were far more likely to say they also had a great deal of influence in curriculum development (64 percent rural vs. 49.5 percent nonrural). The complement to more local control is less outside control. Thus proportionately fewer rural principals reported their district offices had "a great deal of influence" on curriculum (43 percent vs. 60 percent).

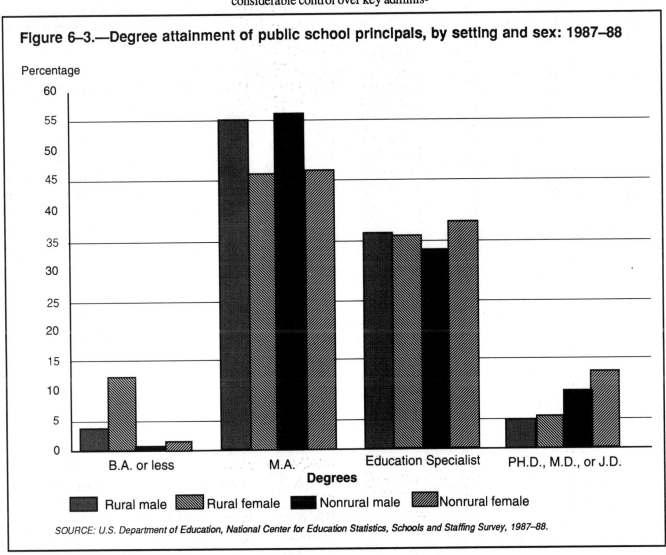

Figure 6–3.—Degree attainment of public school principals, by setting and sex: 1987–88

SOURCE: U.S. Department of Education, National Center for Education Statistics, Schools and Staffing Survey, 1987–88.

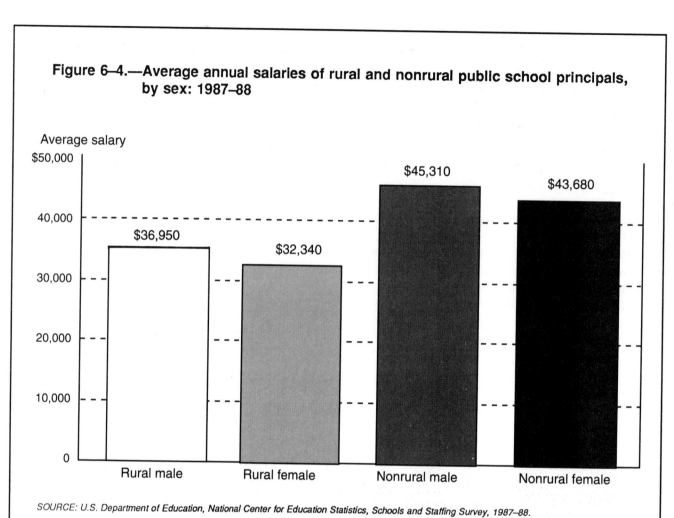

Figure 6–4.—Average annual salaries of rural and nonrural public school principals, by sex: 1987–88

SOURCE: U.S. Department of Education, National Center for Education Statistics, Schools and Staffing Survey, 1987–88.

Figure 6–5.— Percentage of rural and non-rural school principals receiving various benefits: 1987-88

Benefits	Total	Rural	Nonrural
Housing	1.0	2.7	0.2
Meals	1.8	3.5	0.9
Tuition	9.4	9.8	9.2
General medical insurance	85.3	80.5	88.0
Dental insurance	60.4	47.5	67.1
Group life insurance	66.6	54.3	73.1
Transportation	35.0	35.9	35.1
Pension contributions	58.5	51.7	61.5
Receiving none of these	4.9	7.7	3.3

Yet while many rural principals aspire to be instructional leaders, many wear several hats. They may be principals whose contracts require them to teach, coach, or perform the duties of business manager, personnel director, and transportation coordinator, or principals who also serve as superintendents (Tift 1990). And of course, because of the lack of support staff, considerable time is spent on day-to-day management, student discipline, and interactions with parents (Chance and Lingren 1989).

Rural areas are not immune to societal ills that affect schools in more densely settled areas. When asked to identify serious problems in their schools, both rural and nonrural secondary level principals responded similarly (table 6–18). But while the problem named by the largest proportion of nonrural principals was absenteeism (18 percent), the most frequently identified problem in rural schools was alcohol use, cited by 15 percent of secondary school principals.

Despite difficulties that equal or exceed those of nonrural principals, job satisfaction on most indices (e.g. professional life, working conditions) remained as high or higher than that of nonrural principals (Feistritzer 1988). The major exception concerned income. Only 64 percent of rural principals expressed satisfaction with their present salaries. Except for principals in very large cities where 60 percent expressed satisfaction, 72 percent or more of principals in other community types said they were satisfied with their salaries.

Summary

Teachers in rural schools were found to be younger, less experienced, and less likely to have completed advanced degrees than those in nonrural schools. Their salaries and benefits were less, with the salary differential worsening over time. They reported somewhat smaller classes and significantly more control over the classroom than nonrural teachers. A minority of teachers indicated a great deal of influence over school policies, and there were only a few areas in which a proportionately larger group of rural than nonrural teachers made this claim. In addition, rural teachers were far more likely to be confronted with multiple subject preparations. Moreover, the rate of teaching some subjects for which one was not trained or certified exceeded the national average of 20 percent. Satisfaction levels reported by rural teachers were as low as elsewhere in the country, and their attrition rates were just as high.

Rural principals were found to be younger than nonrural principals. But in terms of credentials, they differed from nonrural principals only at the extremes of the spectrum, with more having only a B.A. or less and fewer having attained a degree above the M.A. They received considerably less pay and fewer benefits than nonrural principals. Rural female principals, unlike nonrural female principals, had less education and received considerably less pay than males. Larger proportions of rural principals indicated having considerable control over key administrative areas. But high percentages of secondary level principals also reported significant problems like those that plague schools elsewhere. Yet, except for pay, overall satisfaction levels were high. Possibly, the qualities of many rural schools, such as small size, homogeneity, and links to the community serve to satisfy a large proportion of the principals. And yet their relative youth suggests many move on, possibly attracted by the higher salaries in larger communities and a perception of greater professional visibility and opportunity.

Notes

1. "Rural" was self-determined by respondents who selected from among 10 community types. Choices of *rural or farming community* and *Indian reservation* represent "rural" in this chapter. The remaining options constitute "nonrural." Appendix B lists all 10 community types.

2. Unless otherwise stated, data cited are from tabulations of the SASS base-year survey that were specially commissioned for this report. However, because of space limitations, only a few of the more than 65 tabulations are produced in this volume. A complete set may be obtained by writing the editor.

3. There is no way to determine how much of this contrast is attributable to cost of living. Findings from a study in one state suggest that location accounts for less than half the differences in income (Ghelfi 1988). If this were true elsewhere, then salary differences discussed here and elsewhere in this chapter would be substantial even after adjusting for cost differences due to location.

References

Carlsen, W.S., and D.H. Monk 1992. "Rural/Nonrural Differences Among Secondary Science Teachers: Evidence from the Longitudinal Study of American Youth." Paper presented at the American Educational Research Association Conference, San Francisco, CA.

Chance, E., and C. Lingren. 1989. "The Great Plains Rural Secondary Principal: Aspirations and Reality." *Research in Rural Education* 6:1.

Chubb, J.E., and T.M. Moe. 1990. *Politics, Markets, and America's Schools.* Washington, DC: Brookings Institution.

Corcoran, T.B., L.J. Walker, and J.L. White. 1988. *Working in Urban Schools.* Washington, DC: Institute for Educational Leadership.

Feistritzer, C.E. 1988. *Profile of School Administrators in the U.S.* Washington, DC: National Center for Education Information.

Ghelfi, L.M. October 1988. "About That Lower Cost of Living in Non-Metropolitan Areas." *Rural Development Perspectives* 5:1. Washington, DC: U.S. Department of Agriculture, Economic Research Service.

Harris, M. October 1989. "First Year Teachers in North Dakota." Paper presented at the National Rural Education Association Research Forum, Reno, NV.

Hatton, N.G., et al. 1991. "School Staffing and the Quality of Education, Teacher Stability, and Mobility." *Teaching and Teacher Education* 7:3.

Jacobson, S.L. 1988. "The Rural Superintendency: Reconsidering the Administrative Farm System." *Research in Rural Education* 5:2.

Matthes, W.A., and R.V. Carlson. 1986. "Conditions for Practice: the Reasons Teachers Selected Rural Schools." *Journal of Rural and Small Schools* 1:1.

Purkey, S.C., and M.S. Smith. 1983. "Effective Schools: A Review." *Elementary School Journal* 83:4.

Rollefson, M. April 1990. "Patterns of Entry to and Exit from Teaching." Paper presented at the American Educational Research Association Conference, Boston, MA.

Rosenholtz, S.J. 1989. *Teachers' Workplace.* New York: Longman.

Sher, J. 1983. "Education's Ugly Duckling: Rural Schools in Urban Nations." *Phi Delta Kappan* 65:4.

Sykes, G. 1983. "Teacher Preparation and Teacher Workforce: Problems and Prospects for the 80s." *American Education* 19:2.

Tift, C. 1990. *Rural Administrative Leadership Handbook.* Portland OR: Northwest Regional Educational Laboratory.

Students at the Dubois, Wyoming Middle School (enrollment: 85) plant trees in preparing an outdoor classroom for Fremont County School District #2. **Photo by Larry Lewis.**

7. Effects of Education Reform in Rural Schools

The education reforms that swept the country in the 1980s redefined the balance of authority between state governments and local school districts, although considerable room for flexibility and local activism remained (Fuhrman and Elmore 1990). In the absence of national data on the impact of reform in rural areas, this chapter reports several rural responses to specific reform initiatives, identifies alternatives to school consolidation, and describes implications of school finance litigation.

Reform Mandates and Rural Schools

Probably at no time since successive state drives to consolidate schools and school districts in earlier decades has so much been demanded of rural schools. Factors such as size, geographic location, isolation, culture and language, economic status, and legislative contexts have all influenced the ways educational reform has been implemented in rural settings (Forbes 1989). The issue today, as it has been throughout this century, is how to respond to state-mandated initiatives while at the same time retaining local control and creating an education system that serves community needs (DeYoung 1990).

The ongoing reform movement has presented unique opportunities for rural schools—and great difficulties. For example, many observers have noted that the structure and characteristics of many rural schools create an atmosphere conducive to school improvement. These include low student-teacher ratios, individualized instruction and attention, cooperative learning opportunities, close relationships and ties to the community, and strong staff commitment (DeYoung 1987; Stephens 1988; Hobbs 1990; McREL 1990). At the same time, the scarcity of human and fiscal resources and the accelerated pace of change have further strained the capacities of many rural school districts, especially those already impoverished. This is particularly the case with more complex and comprehensive reforms that require significant time and resources to be incorporated fully into district procedures (State Research Associates 1988).

Key Areas of Reform

Following the publication of *A Nation at Risk* in 1983, governors and state legislatures targeted several key areas for reform: high school course requirements, staff training, special needs students, and school organization. Rural areas have responded in a variety of ways.

Expanding academic course requirements. State reform measures defined more rigorous academic standards for secondary students, increased the number of courses required for high school graduation (Center for Policy Research in Education 1990), and instituted state assessment programs (National Governors' Association 1989). Faced with perennial budgetary difficulties, rural districts used numerous strategies to expand the number of academic courses offered to high school students. They shared teachers and facilities, employed a variety of modern technologies, and added extra class periods when they could afford to (State Research Associates 1988).

But districts with fewer resources were forced to combine basic and advanced classes or move teachers from one curriculum area to another to comply with state mandates. The new requirements also aggravated a shortage of science laboratory facilities, a problem not readily amenable to personnel adjustments or telecommunications (State Research Associates 1988). Furthermore, increased academic requirements have led to a decrease in the number of vocational courses and electives offered by rural schools, matched by a decline in vocational education enrollment in many rural areas (Firestone, Fuhrman, and Kirst 1989; General Accounting Office 1989). Concerns have been expressed that constraining options for the rural noncollege bound will leave them unprepared for a productive future (William T. Grant Foundation 1988; State Research Associates 1988). Such issues present serious challenges to education policymakers.

Improving teachers and school leadership. As noted in chapter 6, recruitment and retention of qualified teachers, especially teachers certified in mathematics and science, are among the most pressing problems facing rural administrators (General Accounting Office 1989). A number of states such as New Jersey and Texas responded by enacting alternative teacher education programs to provide enough teachers for rural (and urban) areas and for critical-shortage subjects at both the elementary and secondary levels. Just as with student courses, some rural areas used nontraditional delivery systems to provide course work and other staff-development activities. Some examples follow (Office of Technology Assessment 1989):

- Colleges in such diverse locations as Maine (Community College of Maine) and Mississippi (Mississippi State University) used telecommunications technology to provide inservice or graduate courses to teachers in their rural areas.

- North Carolina inaugurated a statewide telecommunications system to deliver teacher training, including short and full courses, to all sections of the state.

- Western Montana College created a computer network linking teachers in one-room schools, librarians, and others throughout the state to enable them to share ideas, request software and books, and take classes.

An additional example is provided by the North Central Regional Educational Laboratory, which helped to develop and widely disseminate a reading curriculum training program specifically designed for rural schools (Lewis 1992). Key to the success of the Wisconsin Rural Reading Improvement Project has been a range of technologies for teacher training, including videotapes, audiotapes, teleconferencing, and an on-line and audio-video system. These technologies enable participating schools to communicate with each other, the laboratory, and other experts in the field.

Programs for special populations. New and expanded initiatives in the late 1980s focused on at-risk youth, early childhood and preschool readiness programs, homeless children, and special education students. Large proportions of children with special needs are found in rural areas. Some school officials report that many education-

ally disadvantaged students are experiencing achievement gains because reforms have allowed access to remedial instruction and special programs (General Accounting Office 1989).

However, reports by the National Rural Development Institute (Helge 1990) and the Charles Stewart Mott Foundation (MDC, Inc. 1988) indicate that programs and services for rural children considered at-risk—including minority, teenage parent, poor, and handicapped students—are often not available or may not offer a full array of education and health services when they are available. The plight of someone in need may be aggravated by distance to services, barriers of topography found in certain locations, turnover of trained staff, or even impediments of language or local attitudes (Helge 1991). At the same time, many rural schools successfully integrate handicapped students into mainstream classes even when faced with lack of specialty personnel or professional services.

Little is known on a national level of the extent to which rural students are being reached by state initiatives for special student populations. But illustrations of efforts being made on their behalf do exist.

- Indiana, Iowa, Vermont, and Virginia are among the states with large rural populations that have developed or expanded their programs to target preschools serving at-risk students (National Governors' Association 1989).

- The Bloomfield School District in rural New Mexico served grades K–2 in an early-prevention-of-school-failure program, provided an alternative secondary program, and offered a program for teen parents and their offspring (New Mexico

State Department of Education 1988).

- The Bureau of Indian Affairs and the State of Alaska, through participation in the federal Star Schools program, used distance learning to reach underserved populations on Native American reservations and in remote Native Alaskan villages (Office of Technology Assessment 1989).

- The Texas Education Agency funded dropout prevention programs for migrant secondary students to enable them to take and pass exit-level graduation examinations and tests for admission to college (Texas Education Agency Dropout Information Clearinghouse 1990).

School organization and accountability. In recent years, school reformers have promoted the idea of "restructuring," a term for redesigning the entire public school system, proposed as the only realistic way to improve student learning outcomes significantly while holding educators accountable. A key goal is to decentralize authority and decisionmaking through site-based management and participatory leadership. The purpose is to achieve dramatic changes in curriculum and instruction to promote student acquisition of higher order thinking skills and create new staff roles, different outcomes measures, and eventually a comprehensive service system based at school sites (National Governors' Association 1991a.)

A majority of states have adopted or are adopting state-level initiatives to promote school or district restructuring (Council of Chief State School Officers 1989). These include deregulation and course requirement waivers for schools (National Governors' Association 1991b). Many rural districts have an uncomplicated bureaucratic structure that makes it easier to institute change. Where there is the capacity to do so, therefore, a number of rural schools and districts are attempting flexibility in school design and decisionmaking. For example,

- Course requirement waivers permitted a school-within-a-school program at the Central High School in Springdale, Arkansas, funded with assistance from the Winthrop Rockefeller Foundation. Students take four interdisciplinary classes that promote skills in critical thinking, problem solving, and communication (Paulu 1988).

- The Southwest Educational Development Laboratory identified exemplary rural school programs that featured key elements of the restructuring process. For example, the Little Axe Public School District, a small, rural district outside of Norman, Oklahoma, employed districtwide goal setting, school-based management, and participatory decisionmaking to design and implement its school improvement programs (Vaughan 1990).

- Research for Better Schools, the regional educational laboratory for the Mid-Atlantic, is developing an extensive school redesign strategy involving several rural schools in that region. Restructuring guidelines, frameworks, and models are being developed for rural educators to facilitate planning and implement reform on a continuing basis (Grove 1992).

The Issue of School Consolidation

No discussion of reforms impacting rural schools, and school organization in particular, would be complete without mentioning consolidation. This has been the single policy option used throughout the 20th century to try and achieve cost savings and improve education in rural districts (Stephens 1988). Opponents of consolidation argue that it is difficult to place a simple monetary value on such strengths of rural schools as the involvement and support of parents and the community, individualized instruction, and widespread student participation in school activities made possible by small school and class size. These benefits are often lost when schools are eliminated and districts enlarged. A growing body of research is challenging the assumptions of consolidation, and many observers recommend that each case be judged on its individual merits (Fox 1981; Butler and Monk 1985; Sher 1986; Stephens 1991).

Alternatives to Consolidation

Although full consolidation is seen as a viable option for many rural districts, some local planners have adopted other innovative strategies to cope with sparse settlement and limited budgets. They include what has variably been termed "partial reorganization" (Monk 1991) or "clusters" (Nachtigal and Parker 1990), and telecommunications.

Partial reorganization. Like consolidation, clustering increases the size of the population served, but each administrative unit continues to exist and retain autonomy. Communities thus can be strengthened through cooperation. Banding together in rural areas is not new and has been compared to the tradition of barn-raising and harvesting crews (Nachtigal 1984). Partial reorganization strategies are varied, but they generally involve either two or more districts or local districts and other institutions.

Local district cooperation can simply serve to reduce per unit cost purchasing or to obtain the services of specialists too costly for any one district to employ. Some districts even share superintendents (Sederberg 1985). More complex program objectives usually yield formal cooperatives. Purposes have ranged from enhancing secondary school offerings to expanding extracurricular activities (Ditzler 1984). One example is the South Dakota Small School Cluster, operational since 1981 (Jensen and Widvey 1986). It involves seven small school districts, the South Dakota State University, and the Mid-continent Regional Educational Laboratory. Begun when a joint inservice day was organized, participants now share teachers and specialists and have expanded into adult and community education programming.

The long-established practice of having central high school districts and regional vocational-technical schools is a more elaborate form of interdistrict sharing. Central high schools make possible comprehensive secondary programs while allowing elementary schools to remain under individual community control. This approach also avoids long bus rides for young children (Sher 1988). Regional vocational-technical schools, many of which are state established, allow small districts to share vocational education expenses while maintaining their own academic programs.

Districts may seek assistance from regional education service agencies in 35 states that serve schools in the majority of school districts (Sederberg 1985; Hillman 1991; Stephens and Turner 1991). Examples of the largest are the Boards of Cooperative Education in New York State and the Education Service Centers of Texas. Some provide regional vocational programs; others offer library resources, business administration assistance, or inservice teacher education.

Cooperatives also exist between local rural districts and institutions of higher education, community and health services, and the business community (Dale 1986; DeYoung 1987; Stephens 1988; State Research Associates 1988; Phelps and Prock 1991). Such cooperative efforts are still relatively new. Some colleges and universities assist rural schools with teacher training and school management, or conduct educational research in rural sites. The potential remains for colleges to offer vocational-technical programs and advanced placement courses to rural high school students (Stephens 1991).

The ease or difficulty of sharing services depends upon the following key conditions: stability among teaching and administrative staff; consensus among those involved about the purpose of sharing services; benefits to all collaborating districts; agreement on governance of the shared operation; and recognition that sharing services requires operating costs (Berliner 1990).

Telecommunications. Rural, small schools have been in the forefront of developing innovative uses of instruc-

tional technology. Indeed, the last half of the 1980s saw a tremendous surge of distance-learning activity whereby rural schools provided a wide variety of course work and enrichment materials for students and administrators (Office of Technology Assessment 1989). Distance-learning projects, including those supported by the federal Star Schools program, made available hundreds of courses to remote sites or locations that could not otherwise afford the necessary specialists. Included was instruction in business and economics, foreign languages, mathematics, science, and vocational education.

The three most popular delivery systems are satellite, audiographics, and two-way TV. Each has advantages and disadvantages that help determine which one a district should choose (Barker 1992). In satellite systems, the teacher is seen by students in multiple receiving site classrooms, but two-way communication, when available, is by telephone hook-up. Satellite dishes were rarely seen on school campuses just 10 years ago. But today, 21 percent of districts having fewer than 1,000 students use them (Kober 1990). The largest provider of interactive broadcasts, the TI–IN Telecommunications Network, based in San Antonio, alone serves 6,000 students in 30 states.

But more modest approaches are available too. Audiographic teleteaching requires just a small network of compatible personal computers and can be quickly created and disbanded as need dictates. Unlike satellite transmission purchased from a provider frequently many states away, this approach allows considerable control over course content and may be preferred by some districts. Students cannot, however, see the teacher. The most costly, for equipment and maintenance, is two-way TV that allows for

totally interactive communication. Such communication has the advantage of visually linking teacher and students. Such linkage can be particularly effective with younger and less motivated students.

Some observers believe telecommunication course delivery has the potential to neutralize arguments for consolidation. There are two basic reasons for this view. Courses a given school could not offer can be accessed, and cooperative ventures that share costs and teaching expertise among school districts can be fostered. The state may also play a role. For example, Oklahoma has offered grants to small school cooperatives to encourage innovation and broaden the application of distance-learning technologies (Office of Technology Assessment 1989).

School Reform and Litigation

Reforms usually involve additional expenditures, and many rural school districts confronting fiscal difficulties are hard pressed to fund new initiatives. Objections to the disparities in school district wealth preceded the reform era. Since the 1960s, challenges to state-approved methods of school financing, often initiated by rural school districts, forced many states to re-examine the issue of resources necessary to operate schools in an effective manner. The matter goes well beyond an ability to implement state-mandated reforms to the broader issue of constitutional assurances of education equity.

Nowhere is this seen more clearly and dramatically than in Kentucky. Educational leaders in 66 poor, rural districts united to challenge the state's funding formula in 1989 (*Rose v. Council for Better Education*). The unexpected and unprecedented result was that the Kentucky supreme court declared the entire state system of education unconstitutional (Coe and Kannapel 1991). The 1990 measure constituting the governor's and legislature's response to that landmark decision addressed not only finance, but also curriculum, professional development, at-risk students, and governance as well.

Nothing less than a complete overhaul of the state's approach to education is underway. Rural communities stand to gain substantially as new systems of family service centers, early childhood education, and school-based management are implemented over the next several years (Coe and Kannapel 1991). Undoubtedly education reform in Kentucky will have significance for rural communities everywhere and for education throughout the country. But their reorganization will not be a simple formula that can be adopted elsewhere. Wherever change occurs, "Rural school improvement initiatives must be diverse and reflect the different values and socioeconomic characteristics of the rural communities they serve" (Stephens 1988).

Summary

Little is known on any scale about the effects of education reform in rural areas. In the absence of summative evaluation data, this chapter addressed key issues of interest to policymakers and practitioners by using illustrations. Examples of successful approaches to reform in rural areas were provided, but it is not known how widespread they are. Effective alternatives to school consolidation reflect a keen interest in retaining local autonomy at the district level, while school finance litigation, often brought by rural districts, has broad implications for education reform generally. Clearly, considerably more needs to be known about the var-

ied capacities of rural schools to cope with reform demands and the extent to which the proposed or mandated reforms actually reach rural students.

References

Barker, B.O. 1992. *The Distance Education Handbook: An Administrator's Guide for Rural and Remote Schools.* Charleston, WV: ERIC Clearinghouse on Rural Education and Small Schools.

Berliner, B. 1990. "Alternatives to School District Consolidation." *Knowledge Brief.* San Francisco, CA: Far West Laboratory.

Butler, R.J., and D.H. Monk. "The Cost of Public Schooling in New York State: The Role of Scale and Efficiency in 1978–79." *Journal of Human Resources* 20:3.

Center for Policy Research in Education. May 1990. "Decentralization and Policy Design." *CPRE Policy Briefs* RB–05–590. New Brunswick, NJ: State University of New Jersey at Rutgers.

Coe, P., and P. Kannapel. June 1991. *Systemic Reform in Six Rural Districts: A Case Study of First Reactions to the Kentucky Education Reform Act of 1990.* Charleston, WV: Appalachia Educational Laboratory, State Policy Program, and ERIC Clearinghouse on Rural Education and Small Schools.

Council of Chief State School Officers. 1989. *Success for All in a New Century.* Washington, DC.

Dale, D., and K.H. McKinley. 1986. *Alternative Instructional Delivery Systems for Rural and Small Schools.* (ERIC Document Reproduction Service No. ED 315 260).

DeYoung, A.J. 1987. "The Status of American Education Research: An Integrated Review and Commentary." *Review of Educational Research* 57:2.

DeYoung, A.J. 1990. *Community Schools in the National Context: The Social and Cultural Impact of Educational Reform*

Movement on American Rural Schools. Greensboro, NC: Southeastern Educational Improvement Laboratory.

Ditzler, L. June 1984. "These Small Schools Pooled Resources to Beef Up Bare-bones Curriculums." *American School Boards Journal* 171:6.

Firestone, W.A., S.H. Fuhrman, and M.W. Kirst. 1989. *The Progress of Reform: An Appraisal of State Education Initiatives.* New Brunswick, NJ: Center for Policy Research in Education, The State University of New Jersey at Rutgers.

Forbes, Roy H. 1989. "Rural Education and the Reform Movement." *Rural Education: A Changing Landscape.* Washington, DC: U.S. Department of Education, Office of Educational Research and Improvement.

Fox, W.F. 1981. "Reviewing Economies of Size in Education." *Journal of Education Finance* 6:3.

Fuhrman, S.H., and R.F. Elmore. 1990. "Understanding Local Control in the Wake of Education Reform." *Educational Evaluation and Policy Analysis* 12:1.

General Accounting Office. 1989. *Education Reform: Initial Effects in Four School Districts.* GAO/PEMD–89–28. Washington, DC.

Grove, R. December 1992. "A Conceptual Framework for Redesigning Rural Schools." *RBS Report.* Philadelphia, PA: Research for Better Schools.

Helge, D. 1990. *A National Study Regarding At-risk Students.* Bellingham, WA: National Rural Development Institute, Western Washington University. (ERIC Document Reproduction Service, No. ED 324 178).

Helge, D. 1991. "At-risk Students: A National View of Problems and Service Delivery Strategies." *Rural Special Education Quarterly* 10:4.

Hillman, A. 1991. *There are No Subways in Lickingville.* Shippenville, PA: Riverview Intermediate Unit.

Hobbs, D. 1990. "An Overview of Rural America." *Rural Revitalization Through Education* 1:1.

Jensen, D., and L. Widvey. 1986. "The South Dakota Small School Cluster." *The Rural Educator* 8:1.

Kober, N. 1990. "Think Rural Means Isolated? Not When Distance Learning Reaches Into Schools." *The School Administrator* 47:10.

Lewis, A.C. 1992. *Rural Schools on the Road to Reform.* Washington, DC: Council for Educational Development and Research and the Regional Educational Laboratories.

MDC, Inc. 1988. *America's Shame, America's Hope: Twelve Million Youth at Risk* (Prepared for the Charles Stewart Mott Foundation). Chapel Hill, NC.

Mid-continent Regional Educational Laboratory, Rural Institute. 1990. "Rural Schools and Education Reform: They May be Closer than You Think." *The Rural Report.* Aurora, CO.

Monk, D.H. 1991. "The Organization and Reorganization of Small Rural Schools." *Rural Education: Issues and Practice.* Alan J. DeYoung (Ed.). New York: Garland Publishing, Inc.

Nachtigal, P. 1984. *Clustering for Rural School Improvement.* Aurora, CO: Mid-continent Regional Educational Laboratory.

Nachtigal, P., and S.D. Parker. 1990. *Clustering: Working Together for Better Schools.* Aurora, CO: Mid-continent Regional Educational Laboratory.

National Commission on Excellence in Education. 1983. *A Nation at Risk.* Washington, DC: U.S. Department of Education.

National Governors' Association. 1989. *Results in Education: 1988.* Washington, DC.

National Governors' Association. 1991a. *From Rhetoric to Action: State Progress in Restructuring the Education System.* Washington, DC.

National Governors' Association. 1991b. *State Actions to Restructure Schools: First Steps.* Washington, DC.

New Mexico State Department of Education. 1988. *At-risk Youth: A Call for Action.* Santa Fe, NM.

Office of Technology Assessment. 1989. *Linking for Learning: A New Course for Education.* (OTA–SET–430). Washington, DC: Government Printing Office.

Paulu, N. 1988. *Experiences in School Improvement: The Story of 16 American Districts.* Washington, DC: U.S. Department of Education, Office of Educational Research and Improvement.

Phelps, M.S., and G.A. Prock. 1991. "Equality of Educational Opportunity in Rural America." *Rural Education: Issues and Practice.* Alan J. DeYoung (Ed.). New York: Garland Publishing, Inc.

Sederberg, C.H. 1985. "Multiple District Administration in Small Rural Schools." *The Rural Educator* 7:1.

Sher, J.P. 1986. *Heavy Meddle: A Critique of the North Carolina Department of Public Instruction's Plan to Mandate School District Mergers Throughout the State.* North Carolina's School Boards Association.

Sher, J.P. 1988. *Class Dismissed: Examining Nebraska's Rural Education Debate.* Chapel Hill, NC: Rural Education and Development, Inc. (ERIC Document Reproduction Service No. ED 305 194).

State Research Associates. 1988. *Education Reform in Rural Appalachia, 1982–87.* Washington, DC: Appalachian Regional Commission.

Stephens, E.R. December 1988. "Implications of Economic, Social, and Educational Developments in Rural America for Rural School Systems." Paper presented at the Appalachia Educational Laboratory's Third Annual State Educational Policy Symposium, Lexington, KY.

Stephens, E.R. 1991. *A Framework for Evaluating State Policy Options for the Reorganization of Rural, Small School Districts.* Charleston, WV: Appalachia Educational Laboratory and ERIC Clearinghouse on Rural Education and Small Schools.

Stephens, E.R., and W.G. Turner. 1991. *Approaching the Next Millennium: Education Service Agencies in the 1990s.* Arlington, VA: American Association of Educational Service Agencies, American Association of School Administrators.

Texas Education Agency Dropout Information Clearinghouse. 1990. *Status Report on Dropouts and At-risk Students.* Austin, TX.

Vaughan, M. October 1990. "The Effects of Reform in Rural Schools." Paper presented at the NREA Rural Research Forum, Colorado Springs, CO.

William T. Grant Foundation Commission on Work, Family, and Citizenship. 1988. *The Forgotten Half: Non-College Youth in America.* Washington, DC.

8. Public School Finance Policies and Practices Affecting Rural Schools

"The problems of rural living . . .are nowhere more obvious than in the underfinanced local school systems that are found in every state in the nation. Rural schools in all states have less money and poorer educational programs than their more wealthy neighbors in urban areas.

Kern Alexander,
University Distinguished Professor
Virginia Polytechnic Institute, 1990

This chapter describes the major state school finance practices and their potential for benefiting pupils who attend rural schools. It also discusses litigation challenging the equity of school finance systems in several states—litigation that has been spearheaded or endorsed by many rural groups.

State Aid Strategies

General state aid. U.S. public schools are primarily supported by state and local funds.[1] States provide their basic aid funds—those allocated without specific expenditure restrictions—through one of just a few mechanisms. Flat Grants (five states) are fixed amounts that do not take need into account and thus compensate local school districts only partially for their incurred costs. States with full-funded programs (four states) provide more to those in greater need. Between the two are several strategies that offer some degree of fiscal equalization to offset local limitations in generating funds (41 states).[2] Table 8–1 displays these mechanisms along a fiscal equity continuum and identifies the states that use them as their primary form of revenue transfer to their school districts.

Figure 8–1 depicts a typical state system of public school finance and graphically displays the relative proportion each major grant type contributes, depending on whether the district has high or low fiscal capacity (i.e., is rich or poor).

Due to characteristics most rural school districts possess (figure 8–2), it is possible to determine which structural features of state school finance systems would benefit them more.

Since rural districts are generally poorer than ones located in nonrural areas, either the fiscal equalization or full state funding alternatives would bring them greater amounts of state aid from a given appropriated amount. Flat grants, by definition, do not take into consideration fiscal wealth and thus compensate local school districts only partially for their incurred costs; given a certain total appropriation, less afflu-

ent school districts would receive smaller amounts of state aid than they would through fiscal equalization grants. Eight states provide foundation grants based on instructional units (Verstegen 1990) that are more likely to help the low enrollment and poor schools and districts that exist throughout Rural America. Some fiscal equalization grant types (e.g., guaranteed tax yield programs) place the responsibility upon local citizens to establish funding levels toward which both would contribute. Given the current economic duress in many districts, taxpayers in some areas are unable or unwilling to generate sufficient funds to qualify for the state portion, leaving education needs unmet.

Locally generated funds. To augment the state contribution, most states

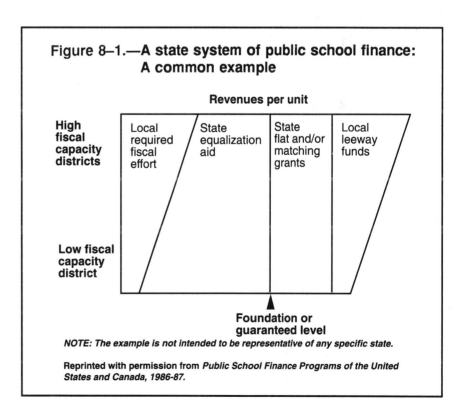

Figure 8–1.—A state system of public school finance: A common example

Revenues per unit

High fiscal capacity districts / **Low fiscal capacity district**

Local required fiscal effort | State equalization aid | State flat and/or matching grants | Local leeway funds

▲ **Foundation or guaranteed level**

NOTE: The example is not intended to be representative of any specific state.

Reprinted with permission from *Public School Finance Programs of the United States and Canada, 1986-87.*

Figure 8–2.— Characteristics of rural schools and rural school districts

- Rural schools and rural school districts usually enroll small numbers of pupils (i.e., fewer than 1,000 pupils per school district).

- Rural school districts commonly are experiencing significant enrollment decline.

- Rural residents report incomes significantly less than their urban and suburban peers.

- Rural school districts usually employ school buildings that house smaller numbers of pupils.

- Rural school districts typically are sparsely populated.

- Due primarily to small numbers of pupils generally located in large geographic areas, per-pupil transportation costs for rural schools are inordinately high.

- Due to the absence of significant trading centers, rural school districts often are nearly exclusively dependent on real property taxation for their local revenue.

permit school districts to raise their own revenues, which are called local leeway funds. Traditionally, these have been drawn from local property taxes. This practice has led to marked disparities in education funding levels across the country and even within states because tax yields are so uneven.

It is surprising then—given what is known about their low fiscal capacity—to find that on average, rural (nonmetropolitan) counties spend more per pupil in public elementary and secondary schools than do nonrural counties, $1,973 vs. $2,137 (Jansen 1991) (figure 8–3). This partly reflects the greater fixed costs for providing the basic elements of an education in smaller (often rural) districts (Walberg and Fowler 1987). To provide even a basic education, rural school district revenues often are obtained by imposing steeper tax rates than in nonrural areas where high property values yield more revenue at lower tax rates.

And averages mask the considerable range that exists, particularly in the more rural states, and that are a function of wide differences in wealth. Indeed, the range among rural counties is greater than that among metropolitan counties (Jansen 1991) (table 8–2). The variability within states as the driving issue for legal cases is discussed later in this chapter.

Categorical aid. States also provide some portion of their assistance to schools in the form of categorical aid (i.e., funds for certain clients like the handicapped, or programs like vocational education). Because they are usually small and less affluent, rural school districts often are inadequately compensated under these programs. This would be especially true if a flat grant allocation system were used. Here, a fixed amount of revenue multiplied by the number of identified clients may not yield enough to pay staff for the small numbers needing service. If either full-state assumption of costs or fiscal equalization grants are used

instead, small schools, including most rural schools, stand a better chance of getting sufficient funds for the purpose.

Small schools and districts are also penalized fiscally if the state uses a per pupil allocation system in a given categorical program (e.g., $1,000 per student). As in the example just given, there may not be enough pupils to draw enough money for the needed personnel. If a range (called brackets) of eligible pupils is instead used to calculate the allocation, say $10,000 for between 1 and 10 students, a school's ability to support the needed salary is enhanced.

State Aid Finance Structures and Their Impact Upon Rural Schools

In addition to the basic approaches governing the distribution of general and categorical aid, other state funding mechanisms exist that have a differential effect upon rural schools. These include: measures of fiscal wealth; transportation allocations; adjustments for enrollment changes; economies of scale provisions; sparsity and density provisions; consolidation and reorganization grants; and capital outlay and debt service assistance. Whether and how these are computed significantly affect the fiscal health of public schools in those states where they are employed.

Measures of fiscal wealth. Contained within the structure of all fiscal equalization grants is a method for determining school district capacity to raise funds. The traditional and near-universal source of local revenue, as noted above, is local property taxes, though a few states have allowed districts to use other measures (e.g., sales taxes and income measures).

Rural school districts receive more fiscal equalization aid to the extent they are unable to generate sufficient revenue. If a state allocates aid based upon assessed property values, rural school districts usually can demonstrate a need for more assistance. But there are circumstances when rural property values may be high relative to actual wealth. For this reason, some argue that income measures be used because these more accurately reflect the lower capacity of rural residents to fund education. Likewise, reliance on sales taxes will also necessitate greater state equalization aid because of the limited buying power of rural residents (Jansen 1990).

Pupil transportation. In 1991–92, 22.9 million public school students were transported on 391,000 buses, covering 3.7 billion miles at a cost of $8.7 billion in public funds (School Bus Fleet December/January 1993). While some places require student fees to partially cover transportation costs, most provide systems of free pupil transportation through a combination of state and local resources (Alexander, M.D. 1990). In urban communities, alternatives exist for transporting pupils, including private vehicles and public transit. But in most rural areas of the country, vehicles that are owned and maintained by the school district, are a virtual necessity. Consequently, pupil transportation costs, as a percentage of total current expenditures, are significantly higher for rural school districts (Alexander, M.D. 1990).

Less than one-third of the states (16) provide additional allotments for transportation where settlement is sparse (Bass 1988). As with general and categorical aid, state transportation assistance can take the form of flat, foundation, or equalization support, and so outcomes in terms of equity can be quite varied. Formulas can even vary within states. Reflecting this, aid formulas have long been the subject of considerable debate and continually undergo reevaluation and redesign. Still, the transportation of pupils to and from public schools, an expensive component for funding public schools in the rural communities of the nation, are often overlooked in larger policy discussions.

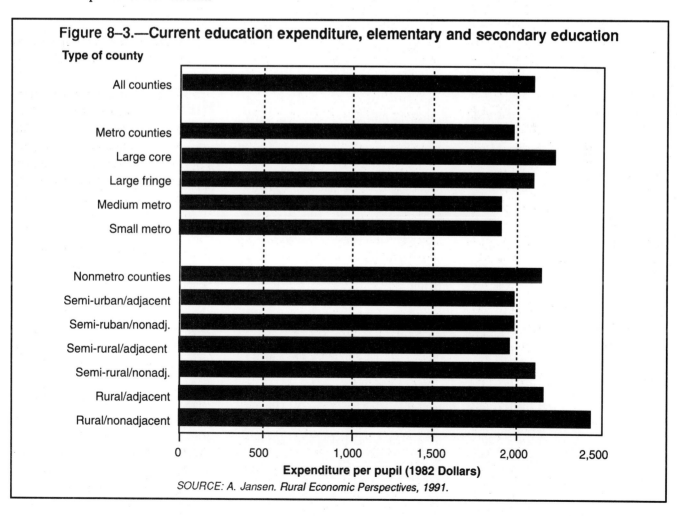

Figure 8–3.—Current education expenditure, elementary and secondary education

SOURCE: A. Jansen. Rural Economic Perspectives, 1991.

Enrollment adjustments. Emigration of pupils from rural schools places an additional fiscal burden upon the affected communities since the school district can experience corresponding losses in state aid based on per unit allocations. Nearly half the states (24) take this into account by delaying cuts in aid for a period of time through various formula adjustments (Salmon et al. 1988), thus reflecting a policy decision to educate the remaining children where they are (Bass 1988), at least for a time. Examples include limiting percentage aid reductions (Arizona, Delaware, and Idaho) and using the prior year count (Alabama, California, and Colorado) in calculating fund allocations.

Economies of scale provisions.

According to factory model production analysis, "diseconomies" occur when fewer units are produced or serviced (Swanson and King 1991). Some state formulas recognize that larger per pupil costs occur when small numbers of students are served, as in rural and small school districts. Ten states (table 8–3) provide extra funding based on small *size*—some at the district level and some at the school level (Verstegen 1990).

Sparsity weights. A similar approach is adding weights in state aid formulas to benefit geographically isolated schools, a practice in six states (table 8–3). It reflects an awareness of necessarily high per unit costs for instructional services and pupil transportation where the service area is sparsely populated. Note: Another 11 states (table 8–3) have provisions in the state funding formulas to add funds based on a combination of factors, including size and geographical isolation, while three other states use different factors (Verstegen 1990).

Consolidation and reorganization grants. Several states have established state aid provisions designed to encourage school districts to reorganize and consolidate with neighboring schools and school districts. Generally, such grants often provide transitional resources to the combining schools for a specified number of years after which they are obligated to function through the common funding system. Another approach is to discourage school districts from continuing to operate small schools by making unavailable certain state resources (e.g., capital outlays).

Capital outlay and debt service assistance. A major contributing factor to the poor fiscal health of rural schools is the absence of sufficient resources either to erect or to maintain school buildings. One study reported that the need for capital facilities by the nation's public schools is nearing crisis proportions (Education Writers Association 1989). This includes rural school facilities, many erected some decades ago and in dire need of replacement or renovation. A recent survey of capital needs for rural schools estimated that deferred maintenance costs now approach $2.6 billion, while costs required to replace existing rural school facilities were projected at $18 billion (Honeyman 1990).

Historically, many state legislatures have been reluctant to provide fiscal assistance to their local school districts for capital outlay and debt service.[3] Some state constitutions and statutes even prohibit small rural school districts from incurring debt sufficient to replace existing facilities. (Debt limitations prohibit a school district from incurring long-term debt in excess of a specified percentage of its assessed valuation of real property.) In addition, rural school districts in many states often lack sufficient property valuation to issue general obligation bonds or have low bond ratings and other related problems. The result for many rural school districts is the continued use of run-down, dilapidated, and outdated buildings.

Some states, to further encourage consolidation, have established capital outlay programs for those school districts that merge their schools or combine with other districts (e.g., the current West Virginia Public School Building Authority). And while most of the recent school finance fiscal equalization lawsuits focused primarily upon current operating costs, several courts also ordered their state legislatures to address capital facilities as well, seeing this issue as significant as current revenue in determining public education equity.

State and Federal Policies That Affect Rural Education

During the past decade, state legislatures have issued numerous mandates directed toward improving the quality of public education. Particularly hard-pressed to acquire the necessary additional resources have been the nation's small, rural school districts with low fiscal capacity. In some cases, through extraordinary local effort, full compliance with the state mandates has been met. In other cases, reform legislation has forced consolidation and reorganization of rural schools and school districts.

The federal government, through executive order, congressional action, or judicial intervention also has expanded requirements for public schools, thus increasing their operating costs. Occupational Safety and Health Administration rules governing safety standards for school buildings and employees; the Education for All Handicapped Children Act of 1975 mandating service; and the Vocational Rehabilitation Act (Section 504) requiring access by all students, have placed considerable demands upon local school systems. Most states require that the burden for compliance at least be shared, if not assumed, by their local school districts.

Again, rural and small school districts have found these requirements difficult to meet. Indeed, an array of legal issues continues to confront local school districts concerning such matters as special education services, liability and negligence, service for certain specified clients, and asbestos abatement programs. But the most far-reaching legal cases concern fiscal equity, an issue on which rural schools have been proactive.

School Finance Litigation

The complex system of school financing summarized in this chapter has largely failed to equalize funding of elementary and secondary education in this country. Since school finance litigation began in the late 1960s and early 1970s, over a quarter of the states have seen a challenge to the status quo whereby the extent of education support is largely determined by a student's residency (Franklin and Hickrod 1990).

The supreme courts in 12 states[4] now have ruled their state systems of school finance unconstitutional and have ordered the state legislatures to design and implement school finance systems that will withstand constitutional scrutiny. The impetus for judicial intervention and activism apparently has begun to accelerate; seven states—Kentucky,

Massachusetts, Montana, New Jersey (for the second time), Tennessee, Texas, and West Virginia have witnessed their highest courts rule their state school finance systems unconstitutional in just the last 5 years.

Almost without exception, state-guaranteed programs need to be substantially augmented by local funds. Rural school districts, with their modest fiscal bases, usually cannot generate sufficient local resources to supplement adequately the state programs the way more affluent localities can. Reflecting this situation, most lawsuits that challenged state school finance programs were filed by persons who resided in rural communities, for example, the pending 1991 Ohio suit by the *Coalition of Rural and Appalachian School Districts v. Walter*. In Kentucky, the successful *Rose* lawsuit was brought primarily by rural school districts and resulted in the largest state funding increase for public education in the state's history, with the poorer districts receiving increases of 25 percent.

Most of the litigation demonstrated the uneven results obtained by property poor and property wealthy districts on various fiscal input measures. Among them were average annual salaries paid classroom teachers, per pupil revenues or expenditures, breadth of the curriculum, quality of school facilities, number of library books per pupil, and funding for instructional supplies and equipment. The lawsuits were based primarily upon education clauses and articles of the states' respective constitutions. Phrases such as "thorough and efficient," "efficient system of common schools," and "uniform system of common schools," typify the constitutional foundations upon which the decisions were made.

Using instructional expenditures as the measure, recent research suggests a majority of states saw a lessening of funding disparities between 1980 and 1987. Exceptions included Montana, Kentucky, and New Jersey, whose systems were overturned, as well as several others where cases are pending. Significantly, those that had raised their school expenditures the most tended to be the ones that made the greatest progress toward equality, suggesting that attempts to improve quality were structured to address equity as well (Wyckoff 1992).

How much this lessening of disparities may have affected rural schools is not known, however. And progress toward funding equity may have been impeded as a result of the most recent recession. Revenue shortfalls at both state and local levels have been widely documented, with resulting cuts in education expenditures, including state compensation to property-poor districts (Fowler 1992).

Summary

Almost every state demonstrates resource disparities among local school districts, reflecting the relative wealth of the communities that support the districts. In most states, disparities primarily affect two classes of districts: those at the urban core and those in rural areas. For a variety of reasons, education in both settings is expensive as measured in per unit costs. The challenge of adequately funding rural schools has become more dramatic during recent years and is symptomatic of the generally unhealthy financial situation that currently confronts much of rural society throughout the United States.

While greater funding equity can be brought to rural schools through modifying various funding mechanisms described in this chapter, such as fiscal equalization formulas, capital outlay and debt service programs, or methods of assessing fiscal capacity and fiscal effort, change does not come easily. The present economic climate already seems to have slowed progress on these matters. Fiscal equity, even with the courts' intervention, may remain an elusive goal for many rural schools for some time to come.

Notes

1. The federal share has never exceeded 10 percent of the total; in 1992 the amount contributed to elementary and secondary education was estimated at 8.3 percent (Hoffman 1993).

2. Absolute fiscal equalization does not assure an efficient or adequately funded system of public elementary and secondary education. It suggests only that little, if any, fiscal disparity exists among a state's local school districts.

3. Capital outlay is defined as costs incurred for land or buildings, improvements of grounds, construction of buildings, additions to buildings, remodeling of buildings, or purchase and replacement of equipment. Debt service is defined as costs incurred for the repayment of loan or bond principal, interest, and service charges.

4. **Arkansas**, *Dupree v. Alma School District No.30*, 651 S.W.2d 90 (1983); **California**, *Serrano v. Priest*, 487 P.2d 1241 (1971); **Connecticut**, *Horton v. Meskill*, 376 A.2d 359 (1977); **Kentucky**, *Rose v. The Council for Better Education*, 790 S.W.2d 186 (1989); **Massachusetts**, *McDuffy v. Robertson*, 615 N.E.2d 516 (1993); **Montana**, *Helena Elementary School District No. 1 v. State*, 769 P.2d 684 (1989); **New Jersey**, *Robinson v. Cahill*, 303 A.2d 273 (1973) and *Abbott v. Burke*, 575 A.2d 359 (1990); **Tennessee**, *Small*

School Systems v. McWherter, 851 S.W.2d 139 (1993); **Texas**, *Edgewood Independent School District v. Kirby*, 777 S.W. 2d 391 (1989); **Washington**, *Seattle School District No. 1 of King County v. State*, 585 P.2d 71 (1978); **West Virginia**, *State Ex Rel. Board of Education for Grant County v. Manchin*, 366 S.E.2d 743 (1988); **Wyoming**, *Washakie County School District No. 1 v. Herschler*, 606 P.2d 310 (1980). At the same time, supreme courts in approximately the same number of states have upheld existing school finance systems. In other states, most recently Alabama and Missouri, challenges were successful in lower courts (Fulton and Long 1993).

References

Alexander, K. Fall 1990. "Rural Education: Institutionalization of Disadvantage." *Journal of Education Finance* 16:2.

Alexander, M.D. Fall 1990. "Public School Pupil Transportation: Rural Schools." Journal of Education Finance 16:2.

Bass, G. 1988. "Financing for Small Schools." The Rural Educator 9:2.

Education Writers Association. 1989. *Wolves at the Schoolhouse Door.* Washington, DC.

Fowler, W.J. 1992. *What Should We Know about School Finance?* Paper presented at the American Education Finance Association Annual Meeting, New Orleans, LA.

Franklin, D.L., and G.A. Hickrod. 1990. "School Finance Equity: the Courts Intervene." *Policy Briefs.* Elmhurst, IL: North Central Regional Educational Laboratory.

Fulton, M., and D. Long. 1993. *School Finance Litigation: A Historical Summary.* Denver, CO: Education Commission of the States.

Hoffman, C.M. 1993. *Federal Support for Education: Fiscal Years 1980 to 1992.* Washington, DC: U.S. Department of

Education, National Center for Education Statistics.

Honeyman, D.S. Fall 1990. "School Facilities and State Mechanisms That Support School Construction: A Report From the Fifty States." *Journal of Education Finance* 16:2.

Jansen, A.C. 1990. "Can Sales Tax Revenue Equitably Finance Education?" Paper presented at the Association of Collegiate Schools of Planning Annual Conference, Austin TX.

Jansen, A.C. October–January 1991. "Rural Counties Lead Urban in Education Spending, But is That Enough?" Rural Economic Perspectives. Washington, DC: U.S. Department of Agriculture, Economic Research Service.

Salmon, R.G., et al. 1988. *Public School Finance Programs of the United States and Canada, 1986–87.* Blacksburg, VA: Virginia Polytechnic and State University.

School Bus Fleet Fact Book 1993. December/January 1993. Redondo Beach, CA: Bobit Publishing Company 37:1.

Swanson, A.D., and R.A. King. 1991. *School Finance: Its Economics and Politics.* New York: Longman.

Verstegan, D. Fall 1990. "Efficiency and Economies-of-Scale Revisited: Implications for Financing Rural School Districts." *Journal of Education Finance* 16:2.

Walberg, H. J., and W.J. Fowler. 1987. "Expenditure and Size Efficiencies of Public School Districts." *Educational Researcher* 16:7.

Wyckoff, J.H. 1992. "The Intrastate Equality of Public Primary and Secondary Education Resources in the U.S., 1980–1987." Economics of Education Review 11:1.

9. Assessment of Student Performance in Rural Schools

With rural communities facing many challenges today, gauging their schools' educational quality is more important than ever. It is a time of increased expectations, rising accountability demands, and growing competition for scarce budget dollars. National data reported below compare the academic performance of rural students with that of nonrural students. In this context, emerging research information on the relative merits of small-scale schooling, including the availability of high school courses, is also presented.

Academic Performance by Rural Students

Rural education often has been discussed as a deficit model of instruction from which relatively low outcomes can be expected (Edington and Koehler 1987). While this perspective was reinforced by some local studies, most data, as presented below, do not support this view.

National Assessment of Educational Progress. The most comprehensive data on student achievement in this country is gathered by the National Assessment of Educational Progress (NAEP), administered by the National Center for Education Statistics (NCES). Established in 1969, NAEP periodically reports information on the educational progress of American students in reading, writing, mathematics, science, and social studies, as well as other subjects. Performance is measured along a proficiency scale that ranges from 100 to 500, allowing comparisons across groups, age levels, and years of assessment. For example, a proficiency level of 250 in mathematics skills indicates students can use multiplication and solve simple problems.

Comparing rural performance to the national average. NAEP uses a definition of rural, called *Extreme Rural*, that encompasses students in nonmetropolitan areas with a population below 10,000 and where many parents are farmers or farm workers. In the earliest NAEP assessments, these students consistently scored below the national average on nearly every subject (Martin 1983). However, by the 1980s, at the same time state education reforms got underway, the scores of rural students were equivalent to the national average in virtually all subjects tested (NCES 1991a).

For example, rural reading scores were below the national mean in 1971 for all three ages groups (9, 13, and 17) and in 1975 for 9- and 13-year-olds. However, from 1980 to 1990, of the 12 total scores (4 assessments times 3 ages), rural students were below the national mean proficiency level only once (age 9 in 1984) (table 9–1). Nor were rural writing scores significantly below the national mean at any time during the decade: 1984, 1988, and 1990 (table 9–2). In this subject, scores of rural 8th and 11th graders did not change significantly over time, but those of rural 4th graders improved dramatically in 1988 and that gain was essentially sustained in 1990.

On the NAEP mathematics assessments in 1978 and 1982, the mean proficiency scores for rural students were below the national average for all three age groups tested except for one (age 9 in 1978). But by 1986 and again in 1990, rural mean scores essentially matched the national average (table 9–3). The story is similar for science. In the 1970 and 1973 assessments, rural students were below national means on the proficiency scale, but in 1977 (Welch and Wagner 1989) and thereafter, rural students were at the mean proficiency level at each age tested: 9, 13, and 17 (table 9–4).

The academic standing of rural students may be illustrated further by examining their scores on recent assessments for history and civics (NCES 1990a and NCES 1990b). Rural scores were equivalent to the national mean in every instance and in eighth-grade civics were significantly above the national mean (table 9–5).

Note should be taken of the general disappointment with the overall quality of student performance as revealed by NAEP. Although students are able to perform basic skills, they have demonstrated limited success on measures of higher order thinking skills. While rural NAEP mean scores now approximate national averages, much remains to be done to enhance rural student achievement as well as that of all students in this country. However, focusing on the issue of rural student performance, the fundamental finding is that

- NAEP assessment levels of students living in *Extreme Rural* areas are now consistently comparable to the national mean proficiency levels and have been for a decade.

Comparing rural and nonrural students. It is also possible to compare rural student performance with that of students attending schools in other types of communities. As defined by NAEP, the *Advantaged Urban* setting covers schools in or around large cities where a high proportion of the residents are in professional or managerial positions, while the *Disadvantaged Urban* setting encompasses schools in or around large cities with a high proportion of residents on welfare or not regularly employed. The rank of rural students relative to these two metropolitan groups has been fairly consistent across subjects.

- NAEP scores of *Extreme Rural* students were generally higher than those of the *Disadvantaged Urban* group and lower than those of the *Advantaged Urban* group.

However, rural contrasts with these two groups were not uniform. For example, on the six subjects noted above across the three grade (or age) levels, *Extreme Rural* students scored an average of 21 points higher than *Disadvantaged Urban* students. The range of differences on the 18 comparisons was +10 to +40, most of which were statistically significant (table 9–6). But rural students averaged only 13 points lower than *Advantaged Urban* students. And the range of differences was -1 to -19, with two out of three score differences statistically significant (table 9–7). This means the performance edge *Extreme Rural* students had compared to *Disadvantaged Urban* students was more marked and consistent than their shortfall relative to *Advantaged Urban* students.

(Note: When the 1988 12th-grade data were examined by county type, metropolitan and nonmetropolitan score differences were found to be negligible. At the same time, an in-depth analysis pinpointed the source of any lower nonmetropolitan scores as coming from the most rural counties as defined by low population density and distance from metropolitan centers (Greenberg, et al. 1992), a finding that suggests an important area for further research.)

National Education Longitudinal Study of 1988.

Rural student performance has been documented as well on the National Education Longitudinal Study of 1988 (NELS:88), also administered by NCES. The survey of nearly 25,000 randomly selected eighth graders covered three community types: *urban*, meaning central city; *suburban*, the area surrounding a central city within counties constituting the Metropolitan Statistical Area (MSA); and *rural* (i.e., outside an MSA). This definition of rural is thus far broader than that used by NAEP; essentially, rural means nonmetropolitan in NELS. In this study,

- Rural eighth graders scored at or about the national average on measures of science, mathematics, reading, and history-government. However, they scored significantly lower than their suburban counterparts on all four achievement tests, but significantly higher than urban students (table 9–8) (NCES 1991b).

In summary, the results from two high quality national surveys are consistent. Whether rural students are defined narrowly as with NAEP or broadly as with NELS, their scores approximated the national average. Marked contrasts appear, however, when comparing their scores to students in other locations. Rural students scored significantly higher than urban students and lower than their suburban counterparts on all four NELS:88 tests and placed between *Advantaged* and *Disadvantaged Urban* students on most NAEP assessments.

These score differences suggest the need to examine the situation of rural students more closely. Research has associated weak scores and other poor educational outcomes with students having to cope with multiple risk factors. Several of these factors were identified in the NELS report (NCES 1991b)—single-parent family; parents have no high school diploma; limited English speaking proficiency; family income less than $15,000; having a sibling who dropped out; and student home alone more than 3 hours per day.

Essentially one of four eighth graders had one risk factor regardless of setting (table 9–9). The percentage of rural eighth graders that had each risk appears in figure 9–1.

Compared to suburban students, the rural rate was significantly greater in three factors: low-parental education, low-family income, and a sibling who dropped out. Rural students appeared in each risk category at rates comparable to urban students, except for the single-parent family category where the urban rate was considerably higher (table 9–10). Somewhat more than half (52 percent) of rural eighth-grade students were estimated to have no listed risk factors (table 9–9). This was true for 47 percent of urban students but 60 percent of suburban students.

In the NELS survey, lower test scores, lower grades, more school absences, and lowered expectations for graduation were documented for students as the number of risk factors increased (NCES 1991b). Using two or more factors as the threshold,

- About one out of five rural eighth graders were at risk of having serious educational problems.

As with performance scores, the rate for rural students (22 percent) on this indicator fell between that of urban students (26 percent) and that of suburban students (15 percent) (table 9–9).

Research on Small-Scale Schooling

Whether rural and urban differences exist in student outcomes has drawn little research attention until very recently. Somewhat more focus has been given to contrasting small and large schools. This research relates to the condition of rural schools for two reasons. First, the preponderance of rural schools remains small. Second, the movement to consolidate or reorganize small schools and districts into larger units, a strategy that dominated educa-

tion policy in the 20th century, has been revived in a number of states faced with dwindling populations and budgetary pressures (e.g., Georgia, Iowa, Massachusetts, New York, North Carolina, Rhode Island, Utah, West Virginia, and Vermont).

Consolidation. Nearly 30 years ago, a study was released that compared certain non-academic outcomes in small and large high schools in Kansas (Barker and Gump 1964). The researchers found clear evidence of affective advantages for students in smaller schools, for example, greater participation in sports and extracurricular activities (e.g., chorus, band, plays, student newspaper) and greater

personal satisfaction (Fowler 1992). The 1964 study received little attention at the time; rather, the country soon after experienced widespread efforts to enlarge schools and districts (Fowler 1992). These state policies stemmed from recommendations made by James Conant, president of Harvard University, who argued in 1967 that high school classes of at least 100 were needed for curriculum comprehensiveness, particularly in foreign languages and advanced subjects.

School and district consolidation was hardly an innovative strategy by the 1960s. On the contrary, since the turn of the century, states have consistently viewed the merger of small, usually rural, entities into larger units as a major solution to the twin challenges of achieving quality and reducing the cost of education in sparsely settled areas (Monk 1988). Successive waves of consolidation, including that following the Conant recommendations, reduced the number of districts from a high of 128,000 in 1932 to 22,000 by the end of the 1960s. There are currently about 15,000 school districts (NCES 1992).

Earlier consolidations succeeded in broadening the tax base and increasing enrollment size, likely bringing curricular and school finance advantages to many rural areas. But with district reorganizations encompassing larger geographic areas and with associated problems emerging, consolidation is not proceeding without challenge to its underlying assumptions.

Research Findings on School Size

No comprehensive analysis has been undertaken yet to determine the extent to which consolidation has addressed the problems for which it has been advocated—school quality and cost-sav-

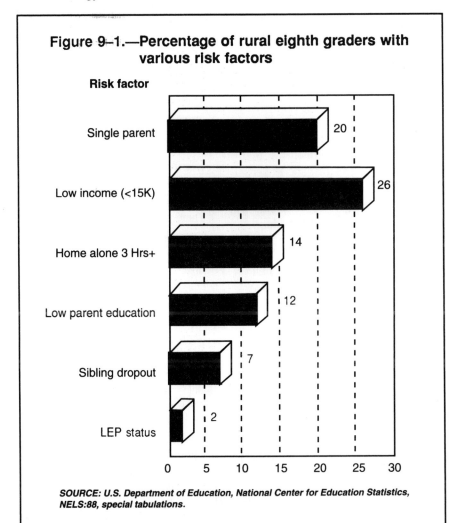

Figure 9–1.—Percentage of rural eighth graders with various risk factors

Risk factor

SOURCE: U.S. Department of Education, National Center for Education Statistics, NELS:88, special tabulations.

ings (Rincones 1988). In fact, the strong push to create large schools and districts frequently has been based on anecdotal evidence of the advantages. The limited research carried out in recent years has revealed larger size does not necessarily yield the anticipated benefits.

Costs. One key analysis determined that costs in very small and very large schools were higher than for mid-size schools, suggesting an upper limit to optimal school size (Fox 1981). Transportation costs in rural areas have become significant, substantially cutting into cost savings expected from consolidation. Moreover, student time on buses can be considerable (Carlsen and Dunne 1981) and has been shown to undermine student performance (Lu and Tweeten 1973).

Attitudes and behavior. Many feel the material limitations rural schools often experience are somehow compensated for by the supportive ethos found in smaller communities and their generally smaller schools. There is a basis in research for this view. A recent examination of school size studies found small size had "an independent, positive effect on student achievement, extracurricular participation, student satisfaction, and attendance" (Fowler and Walberg 1991). For example, major studies found a correlation between low dropout rates and small school size; increasing size negatively influenced school climate that in turn contributed to the dropout rate (Pittman and Haughwort 1987; Bryck and Thum 1989).

Moreover, studies replicating elements of the 1964 size-effects research at the state and national levels were consistent in finding that students in small schools fared better than their peers in large schools regardless of measure. Among the results documented were that students from smaller schools had greater voluntary participation in extracurricular activities; a greater sense of obligation; more feelings of satisfaction and sense of belonging; less loneliness; and less use of drugs and alcohol (Fowler 1992).

Course availability. The longstanding presumption has been that school size is strongly and uniformly related positively to the breadth and depth of curricular offerings, meaning larger schools unambiguously are able to offer superior educational opportunities to their students. For example, one national sample survey of public high school principals in school year 1983–84 documented that the variety of courses offered in small schools was less than in large schools, with differences particularly sharp in the areas of foreign languages and advanced placement courses (Barker 1985).

Research conducted since the late 1980s has prompted a refinement of the prevailing view (Monk and Haller 1986; Monk 1987; Monk 1988; Haller et al. 1990; Monk 1991; Monk and Haller 1993). The cumulative findings follow:

- The effects of school size on high school curricular offerings vary depending on the subject area. For example, school size is much less likely to impact course offerings in social studies and science than in foreign languages and the performing and visual arts.

- The strength of the relationship between school size and curricular offerings diminishes as schools become larger. Increases in the size of very small schools are associated with greater curricular gains than increases in the size of larger schools.

- School size is related to the types of courses added within subject areas. In particular, school size is positively related to the share of the academic curriculum devoted to advanced and remedial courses. In most subjects, though, advanced courses grow more rapidly with school size than do remedial courses. (See tables 9–11a through 9–11d with national data supporting these conclusions.)

A recent analysis of NAEP data revealed extremely low rates in the availability of advanced courses for 12th graders in schools located in nonmetropolitan counties compared to metropolitan counties (Greenberg, et al. 1992). Nevertheless, the impact of a rural location per se on curricular offerings is generally considered smaller than the impact of school size.

- Substantial variation in curricular offerings among high schools remains after the effects of school size and rural location are removed. There are small schools with rich curricular offerings just as there are large schools with modest offerings. School size alone explains roughly half of the variation in course offerings among high schools.

- The mere presence of a course in a curriculum is no guarantee of widespread student participation. Remarkably small percentages of students within a school take advantage of those courses found only within large school curricula.

Academic performance. With a better understanding of the relationship between school size and both stu-

56

dent behaviors and course availability, one may now examine available findings on academic outcomes. In most studies, some dating back to the 1920s, little if any difference has been found in student achievement in small vs. large schools (Howley 1989). The recent summary of school size effects noted above (Fowler 1992) also identified studies (e.g., Marion et al. 1991) that revealed a positive relationship between small size and achievement.

Data from NELS analyzed for this report are consistent with such findings about the advantages of small-scale schooling. Student scores from smaller schools (less than 500 enrollment) were higher than those from medium (500 to 999 enrollment) or larger schools (greater than 1,000) (table 9–12).[1] In fact,

- Students in the smallest schools scored higher than the national average, and students in the larger schools scored significantly lower on all four NELS:88 tests.

Discussion of student performance. As noted above, while rural school outcomes have improved in recent years, there are deficiencies relative to suburban settings as well as advantages over urban settings. At issue is the cause of both the improvements and the differences. Regarding the latter, what may be the stronger influence depressing rural performance is the poverty of many students rather than any limitations imposed by type of location (Edington and Koehler 1987).

The validity of this hypothesis has been largely borne out in studies that control for socioeconomic status (SES). Results are consistent whether the studies have been of students in rural vs. urban settings (e.g., Edington and Martellaro 1984) or in small vs. large schools (e.g.,

Walberg and Fowler 1987). Indeed, recent studies demonstrated small-scale schooling has a positive effect on student achievement, while large-scale schooling has a decidedly negative effect, particularly where low SES students were concerned (Friedkin and Necochea 1988, per Howley 1989).

If poverty retards student performance, what then accounts for overall rural improvement? And why do students from small schools, with relatively limited curricula, match or sometimes even surpass students from larger schools? And similarly, how can nonmetropolitan students with fewer advanced courses to take perform nearly as well as metropolitan students? Generally, researchers have expected inequities in what is called "opportunity to learn"(NCES 1988) to hold back rural and small school students on achievement measures (Barker 1985).

An illustration of this issue may be found in students' exposure to science. While significantly less involvement in science learning activities and science course taking among rural 13- and 17-year-old students was documented in 1983, their NAEP scores even at that time were comparable to the national averages. Perhaps intervening to offset input limitations was the supportive ethos of small schools. That rural students are outdistanced by more advantaged students suggests that with greater curricular opportunities, rural performance could improve still more (Welch and Wagner 1989).

The perennial challenge faced by rural schools to provide cost-effective, quality schooling persists and will surely increase as standards and expectations are raised for all students. These research findings suggest there is value in small size just as proponents of rural schools have traditionally claimed

(Barker 1985; Swanson 1988). Any agenda for improving the outcomes of rural education could consider how to capitalize on the advantages of small scale while at the same time finding ways to improve or expand opportunities to learn in smaller schools, particularly for those students seeking advanced courses.

And given that many rural students are poor and live in communities whose fiscal resources are limited, the level of their performance is encouraging. Indeed, it suggests that rather than a deficit model, rural schools, having achieved so much with so little, can provide instead a model of strength (Edington and Koehler 1987) worth studying and emulating.

Summary

NAEP assessment scores for rural students in Extreme Rural settings have risen in the last 10 years and now approximate the mean, a finding that was maintained when "rural" was defined to include a much wider population in the NELS:88 survey. At the same time, research on small schools, which includes the large majority of rural schools, revealed definitive advantages as measured by student attitudes and behavior. But other research documented inequities in the availability of courses at the secondary level, though most small schools offered a basic curriculum and not all large schools offered an enriched one. Nevertheless, student achievement in small schools equaled or exceeded that of students in large schools, suggesting that the climate in small schools may propel students to excel in spite of certain material disadvantages. These findings have policy implications not only for rural schools, but for schools in any setting.

Notes

1. Given that rural schools are generally small, it is unclear why eighth-grade students in smaller schools exceed the mean while those in rural schools approximate the mean. What may be occurring is the less-than-500 category draws in some higher scoring small nonrural schools thus raising the group mean. However, little is known about the mix and variety of schools that comprise the "small" category in the NELS sample, and results are not reported for rural schools by enrollment size. (NAEP does not report results by school enrollment so confirmation checks are not possible in that data set regarding school size effects.)

References

Barker, B. 1985. "Curricular Offerings in Small and Large High Schools: How Broad is the Disparity?" *Research in Rural Education* 3:1.

Barker, R.G., and P.V. Gump. 1964. Big School, Small School: High School Size and Student Behavior. Stanford, CA: Stanford University Press.

Bryck, A.S., and Y.M. Thum. 1989. "The Effects of High School Organization on Dropping Out: An Exploratory Investigation" (Report No. RR–012). Center for Policy Research in Education.

Carlsen, W.S., and F. Dunn. 1981. "Small Rural Schools: A Portrait." *High School Journal* 64:7.

Edington, E.D., and H.C. Martellaro. 1984. "Variables Affecting Academic Achievement in New Mexico Schools." Paper presented at the American Educational Research Association Conference, New Orleans, LA.

Edington, E.D., and L. Koehler. 1987. "Rural Student Achievement: Elements for Consideration." *ERIC Digest.* Las Cruces, NM: ERIC Clearinghouse on Rural Education and Small Schools.

Fowler, W.J. April 1992. "What Do We Know About School Size? What Should We Know?" Paper presented at the American Educational Research Association Conference, San Francisco, CA.

Fowler, W.J., and H.J. Walberg. 1991. "School Size, Characteristics, and Outcomes." *Educational Evaluation and Policy Analysis* 13:2.

Fox, W.F. 1981. "Reviewing Economies of Size in Education." *Journal of Education Finance* 6:3.

Friedkin, N., and J. Necochea. 1988. "School System Size and Performance: A Contingency Perspective." Educational Evaluation and Policy Analysis 10:3.

Greenberg, E.J., P.L. Swaim, and R.A. Teixiera. December, 1992. "Can Rural Workers Compete for the Jobs of the Future?" Paper prepared for the Agricultural Outlook Conference, Washington, DC.

Haller, E.J., D.H. Monk, A. Spotted Bear, J. Griffith, and P. Moss. 1990. "School Size and Program Comprehensiveness: Evidence From High School and Beyond." *Educational Evaluation and Policy Analysis* 12:2.

Howley, C. 1989. "Synthesis of the Effects of School and District Size: What Research Says about Achievement in Small Schools and School Districts." Journal of Rural and Small Schools 4:1.

Lu, Y., and L. Tweeten. 1973. "The Impact of Busing on Student Achievement." *Growth and Change.*

Marion, S.F., W.G. McIntire, and H.G. Walberg. April 1991. "The Effects of Per-pupil Expenditures, School Size, and Student Characteristics on Student Achievement and Educational Attainment in Rural Schools." Paper presented at the American Educational Research Association Conference, Chicago, IL.

Martin, W.H. 1983. "Student Achievement in Rural Schools: A View from the National Assessment Data." In J. Fletcher (Ed.). *Rural Education: A National Perspective.* International Dialogue Press.

Monk, D.H., and E.J. Haller. 1986. *Organizational Alternatives for Small, Rural Schools.* Ithaca, NY: Department of Education, Cornell University.

Monk, D.H. 1987. "Secondary School Size and Curriculum Comprehensiveness." *Economics of Education Review* 6:2.

Monk, D.H. 1988. "Disparities in Curricular Offerings: Issues and Policy Alternatives for Small, Rural Schools. Policy Issues. Policy and Planning Center, Appalachia Educational Laboratory, Charleston, WV.

Monk, D.H. 1991. "The Organization and Reorganization of Small, Rural Schools." *Rural Education: Issues and Practice.* A.J. De Young (Ed.). New York: Garland Publishing, Inc.

Monk, D. H., and E.J. Haller. Spring 1993. "Predictors of High School Academic Course Offerings: The Role of School Size." *American Educational Research Journal* 30:1.

National Center for Education Statistics. 1988. *1988 Education Indicators.* J. Stern (Ed.). Washington, DC: U.S. Department of Education.

National Center for Education Statistics. 1990a. *The U.S. History Report Card.* Washington, DC: U.S. Department of Education.

National Center for Education Statistics. 1990b. *The Civics Report Card.* Washington, DC: U.S. Department of Education.

National Center for Education Statistics. 1991a. *Trends in Academic Progress.* Washington, DC: U.S. Department of Education.

National Center for Education Statistics. 1991b. *The Tested Achievement of the National Education Longitudinal Study of 1988 Eighth Grade Class.* Washington, DC: U.S. Department of Education.

National Center for Education Statistics. 1992. *Digest of Education Statistics.* NCES 92–097. Washington, DC.

Pittman, R.B., and P. Haughwort. 1987. "Influence of High School Size on Dropout Rate." *Educational Evaluation and Policy Analysis* 9:4.

Rincones, R. 1988. "Rural Education: Exploring Alternatives to Consolidation." ERIC Clearinghouse on Rural Education and Small Schools. (ERIC Document Reproduction Service No. ED 296 817/EDO–RC–88–05). Las Cruces, NM.

Swanson, A.D. 1988. "The Matter of Size: A Review of the Research on Relationships Between School and District Size, Pupil Achievement, and Cost." *Research in Rural Education* 5:2.

Walberg, H.J., and W.J. Fowler. 1987. "Expenditure and Size Efficiencies of Public School Districts." *Educational Researcher* 16:7.

Welch, W.W., and T.G. Wagner. 1989. *Science Education in Rural America*. Elmhurst, IL: North Central Regional Educational Laboratory.

Computer training at the Miami Valley Career Technology Center (enrollment: 1,772 students, grades 11–12), Clayton, Ohio (pop. 600). In a pattern typical of many rural areas, Miami Valley draws students from high schools in several neighboring counties for its programs in vocational and technological education. **Photo from the National FFA Center, Alexandria, Virginia**.

Biology class, Anderson Valley Junior-Senior High School (enrollment: 217 students), Anderson Valley, California. **Photo from the National FFA Center, Alexandria, Virginia.**

10. Education and Work Experiences of Rural Youth

To understand the potential for America's rural youth to participate in today's competitive global economy, this chapter examines rural students' aspirations, preparation, academic achievements and vocational careers. Contrasts are made not only with their nonrural counterparts, but between rural youth who remained in their home communities and those who left. Some regional differences are also touched upon.

Rural Youth in the 1980s

Employment opportunities in agriculture, mining, construction, and manufacturing industries—principal sources of rural jobs—are projected to continue declining, while information-based industries are predicted to grow (Hamrick 1991–92). An estimated six million jobs will open up nationally in highly skilled occupations during the decade of the 1990s (World Future Society 1988).

To gauge the readiness of rural youth for the rapidly changing economy, this chapter examines the Class of 1980 and, to some extent, the Class of 1982, from the longitudinal survey, High School and Beyond, administered by the National Center for Education Statistics (NCES). Youth were considered rural if they went to high schools in nonmetropolitan counties as defined by the Census Bureau. Nonrural students were those who went to a high school within a metropolitan area—urban or suburban. (Appendix B provides more information on the survey.)

Aspirations. Rural students share certain attitudes and values that are less common among nonrural students. For

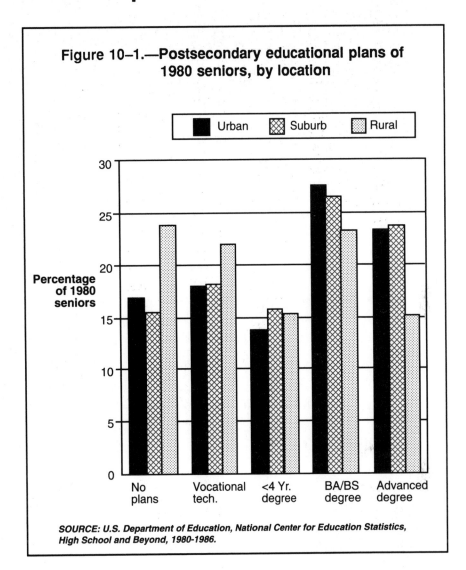

Figure 10–1.—Postsecondary educational plans of 1980 seniors, by location

SOURCE: U.S. Department of Education, National Center for Education Statistics, High School and Beyond, 1980-1986.

example, compared to nonrural students, seniors in rural high schools in 1980 said they valued their jobs more and academics less (Cobb, McIntire, and Pratt 1989). This perception contributed to differences between the ambitions of rural youth and their nonrural counterparts.

For example, rural students envisioned themselves more often in lower level, less skilled positions than did nonrural youth (table 10–1). Thus rural youth expected to complete their full-time

education at lower levels of attainment than did either urban or suburban students (tables 10–2 and 10–3). These aspirations translated into clear differences in postsecondary education plans as presented in figure 10–1 (table 10–4).

Proportionately fewer rural than nonrural seniors intended to pursue college and advanced degrees. And more rural seniors than nonrural seniors had no plans at all (table 10–4).

Preparation. Reflecting these long-range perceptions about the future, seniors in rural high schools were less likely to have enrolled in academic programs that would prepare them for further academic study and more likely to be enrolled in general studies programs (figure 10–2) (table 10–5).

As a result, rural seniors in the high school Class of 1980 completed somewhat less course work in the subjects students need for college (Algebra I and II, Trigonometry, Calculus, Chemistry, and Physics). Rather, they took more vocational and business courses (Pollard and O'Hare 1990).

Postsecondary education. Lower academic aspirations and less preparation translated into lower college-going rates for rural youth. During the 4 years following high school graduation (1980–1984), significantly fewer rural (62 percent) than urban (70 percent) or suburban (73.5 percent) youth attended at least one term of college, either part-time or full-time (Marion, McIntire, and Walberg 1991).

At the end of 6 years, 18 percent of rural members of the Class of 1980 had earned at least a bachelor's degree compared to 21 percent for nonrural youth (Pollard and O'Hare 1990).[1]

Given that educational attainment is a strong predictor of future income,

- The lower college-going and completion rates among rural students are important indicators that rural youth will have comparatively lower future earnings and job status.

Reasons for Rural-Nonrural Differences in Educational Attainment

An important issue in examining the educational orientation of rural and nonrural youth is how much the distinctions between them may somehow be a function of setting. A small but growing body of literature argues for considering factors other than place of residence to account for rural-nonrural differences.

For example, one factor depressing the education ambitions of rural youth may be the lower prevalence in their communities of professional and technical jobs that could serve as vocational goals (Haller and Virkler 1992). In fact, a smaller proportion (-9.2 percent) of rural youth from the Class of 1980 (Haller and Virkler 1992) aspired to those categories of employment requiring college degrees and for which few rural opportunities exist.

Another major factor is socioeconomic status (SES). The relationship between SES and educational outcomes has been documented in the educational and psychological literature (e.g., Anderson et al. 1992; White 1982). As a group, rural students ranked lower on the High School and Beyond socioeconomic scale compared with suburban students, though they had about the

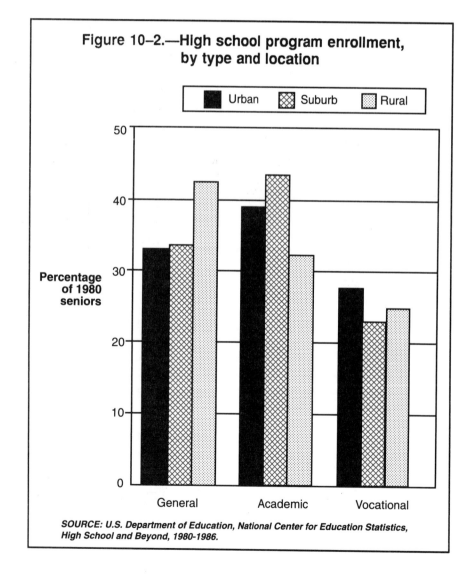

Figure 10–2.—High school program enrollment, by type and location

SOURCE: U.S. Department of Education, National Center for Education Statistics, High School and Beyond, 1980-1986.

same ranking as urban students (Marion, McIntire, and Walberg 1991). Thus the generally lower aspirations of 1980 rural seniors reflected that a large proportion came from families ranking lower in socioeconomic status (Coladarci and McIntire 1988; McIntire and Marion 1989).

One element of this status is parental education levels. For half of the rural students, parents had at most a high school education, whereas this circumstance applied to just one-third of the nonrural students; at the same time, 12 percent of rural seniors had parents with at least a bachelor's degree, compared to 19 percent of nonrural seniors (Pollard and O'Hare 1990). To the extent well-educated parents encourage their children to pursue more schooling, nonrural seniors had an advantage many rural seniors did not (Pollard and O'Hare 1990), and this background may help to account for the differences in their ambitions and choice of course study.

For example, compared to their counterparts elsewhere, proportionately more rural than nonrural seniors reported their fathers were inclined to encourage them to obtain full-time jobs (14 vs. 9 percent) or to attend trade school (10 vs. 6 percent) (table 10–6). Proportionately fewer rural students reported they thought their mothers were supportive of full-time college attendance (60 vs. 72 percent) (table 10–6). In addition, while half of the rural seniors said their guidance counselors and teachers thought they should go to college, the proportion was less than for nonrural seniors (56 percent) (Cobb, McIntire, and Pratt 1989). In sum,

- Youth in Rural America often perceive themselves as lacking guidance and support for pursuing advanced educational studies.

Nevertheless, one must keep the locational differences in perspective. Though below nonrural rates, a large proportion of rural students had professional ambitions. For example, nearly one-fourth of 1980 rural seniors (vs. 29 percent nonrural) said they expected to have low-level professional jobs by the age of 30, and about 9 percent (vs. 15 percent nonrural) saw themselves as high-level professionals—the same proportion as expected to become craftsmen. These aspirations translated into significant levels of educational attainment for many rural students, many of whom migrated out of rural areas to realize them. Specifically, for those rural youth from the Class of 1980 who did go to college, well over one-third (36 percent) remained for 4 years of education (table 10–7).

This rate of persistence in college, while below that of suburban college-going youth (40 percent), was about the same as urban students (37 percent). Moreover, when groups of rural and nonrural students from the high school Class of 1980 were matched by SES, there was little difference between them in terms of higher educational outcomes. In the top half of the SES distribution, in fact, proportionately more rural than nonrural students completed a 4–year degree or advanced degree (Marion, McIntire, and Walberg 1991). Together these data suggest

- Rural students who enter college have the capacity to succeed; coming from a rural area need not be an impediment to completing college.[2]

Leavers and stayers. Rural communities have a long history of losing large proportions of their academically accomplished youth to urban and suburban communities, a phenomenon caused by limited educational opportunities locally and better employment

prospects elsewhere. By 1984, approximately one-third of rural students of the Class of 1980 had left for nonrural areas, with males and females equally represented among them (Cobb, McIntire, and Pratt 1989). Contrasting "leavers" (rural youth who left) with "stayers" (those who stayed in Rural America) provides yet another perspective on rural diversity.

Those who left scored significantly higher on the survey's aptitude tests and came from higher socioeconomic status families than did those who stayed. In fact, "leavers" most resembled suburban youth in their postsecondary aspirations, educational attainment, and quality of life aspirations. For example, of the rural "stayers," less than half (46 percent) aspired to a college degree while 61 percent of rural "leavers" did—nearly the same as graduates from cities and suburbs (table 10–8). Rural "leavers" actually attained some college or a college degree more often than all other groups (Cobb, McIntire, and Pratt 1989).[3]

High School Dropout Rates

Comparing dropout rates. Looking at the Class of 1982 permits an examination of dropping out between the sophomore and senior years of high school. Between 1980 and 1982, rural sophomores had a dropout rate of 16 percent, which was below the national average and comparable to the suburban rate. The urban rate was considerably higher at 24.5 percent (Alsalam et al. 1992). What is not known is the degree to which rural students for this cohort had dropped out before the sophomore year.

Light is shed on this question by recent data on younger students showing 7 percent of rural students dropped out between the 8th and 10th grades (1988–90) compared to 5 percent of suburban students and 9 percent of urban students (Kaufman and McMillan 1991). This two percentage points disadvantage relative to suburban rates suggests the 1980 to 1982 rural dropout rate may understate the longer term rate.

As with plans for college attendance, however, an analysis of the High School and Beyond data set revealed that dropping out could not be attributed primarily to urban, suburban, or rural location but to differences in the demographics and social characteristics of students who lived in those places (Barro and Kolstad 1987). Dropouts gave the same primary reasons for leaving school regardless of high school location, namely low grades and "school wasn't for me" though rural dropouts had the lowest educational aspirations and lowest self esteem of any group (McCaul 1989).

Late completion. An understanding of the phenomenon of dropping out must include an awareness that a significant proportion of students who do not graduate with their class either take longer to complete high school or pass a high school equivalency examination. Of the Class of 1982, 84 percent of rural students completed high school on time, a rate comparable to that of suburban students (85 percent). (Of the urban students, 76 percent completed on time, i.e., by June 1982.) But these completion rates changed significantly over the next 6 years. In urban and suburban areas, completion rates rose 11 and 8 percentage points respectively. They rose least in rural areas—6 points—reflecting the lower availability of programs to prepare youth for equivalency tests (Sherman 1992). As a result, the rural high school completion rate fell behind the suburban rate—90 vs. 93 percent, and urban-rural

differences lessened (Alsalam et al. 1992).

Minority dropout rates. Black and Hispanic students in rural areas were far more likely to drop out than were metropolitan members of these minorities. In comparing groups 25 years of age and older, for example, rural black and Hispanic residents in 1991 were far less likely to have had schooling comparable to 4 years of high school or more than their nonrural counterparts (table 10–9). Rural rates for both groups were low, but the contrast was particularly great between blacks in the two sectors: 49 vs. 70 percent for blacks and 47 percent vs. 52 percent for Hispanics. (School completion rates for whites in rural areas were also far lower than for their metropolitan counterparts—74 vs. 82 percent.)

Minority groups in rural areas also had higher rates of functional illiteracy (defined as having completed less than 5 years of elementary school)—compared to rural whites and to minority groups in nonrural areas (table 10–10). Rural blacks 25 years of age and older were twice as likely as metropolitan blacks to be illiterate (8 vs. 4 percent). Rates for Hispanic residents were highest, though the rural-nonrural distinction was less extreme (15 vs. 12 percent). (Two percent of whites matched the criterion, and there was no difference by place of residence). But though illiteracy rates remain high, it is important to note the progress made in the last two decades. The illiteracy rates of black and white Americans have been cut by more than half, and Hispanic adults have seen dramatic improvements in this measure as well.

Factors influencing dropping out. Given that educational differences are not purely a function of location but of other circumstances, it is

useful to explore further some of those other influences. For example, in local communities where obtaining a high school degree offers no apparent advantage because of limited economic opportunities, students may tend to drop out more (Bickel and Papagiannis 1988). Additional light has been shed by recent studies using the High School and Beyond data set to track 10th graders in the South between 1980 and 1982 (Smith et al. 1992; Beaulieu et al. 1990). These studies highlighted two influences on high school dropout behavior: family and society.[3]

Taken separately, family and community elements showed varying but significant influences on dropout behaviors. In combination, however, they exerted a powerful force. When family and community influences were weak, the dropout rate exceeded 50 percent; when both were strong, students were virtually assured of completing their high school studies (Beaulieu et al. 1990). The rise in single parent households in Rural America, as elsewhere, and the extensive population migration in the last decade reflect unsettled economic and social conditions that could negatively affect not only persistence in school, but also a host of other behaviors associated with preparation for independent adulthood and responsible citizenship.

Educational Attainment of the Rural Workforce

In examining the personal and employment potential of rural students, it is useful to consider levels of schooling from a broader group of working-age rural residents. But first, it is important to note the tremendous strides Rural America has made in better educating its students in the last several decades. Just 30 years ago the average rural resident had a ninth-grade education, whereas today the norm is to have a high school diploma (McGranahan et al. 1986). And in spite of the employment problems of the last decade, a smaller proportion of rural youth age 16–24 had dropped out of high school in 1990 (12 percent) than did in 1975 (16.8 percent), reducing the gap between rural and national totals during that period (Kaufman and McMillan 1991) (table 10–11).

Those of working age (25–44) also narrowed the rural-nonrural gap in high school graduation rates (Swaim and Teixeira 1991) (table 10–12). Examining this age group's further educational attainment tells a more complex story, however. Not only were rural residents far less likely to have attained 4 or more years of college (16 vs. 27 percent), but after 1979, the difference in rural-nonrural rates for college attendance and for college completion widened considerably (Swaim and Teixeira 1991). The proportion of rural people completing 1 to 4 years of college did not decline; in fact, it increased, at least through 1983. The primary cause of the disparity is the even greater increase in the proportion of nonrural workers who obtained higher education. Several factors contributed to this phenomenon.

First, as noted, rural students had lower aspirations for higher education. In addition, rural residents have limited access to institutions of higher education (Swaim and Teixeira 1991), an element that could also have helped restrain their aspirations. For example, nonrural counties were three times more likely than rural counties to have some kind of public college (table 10–13). Even in the case of 2-year colleges, half the metropolitan counties had one,

while only 15 percent of the rural counties did.[4]

The third factor was that in the 1980s, the more educated rural residents left for nonrural areas, constituting a return to the historical pattern. (The influx of metropolitan residents to the countryside during the 1970s turned out to have been a temporary phenomenon.) In these data, such workers, though born in rural areas, are now nonrural residents and are counted among them.

Employment

According to the U.S. Department of Agriculture's Economic Research Service (ERS), the source of the rural employment crisis is that the new economy is an urban economy (McGranahan and Ghelfi 1991). This means jobs that support this economy, which demands a highly educated workforce, became concentrated in metropolitan areas. The result has been an increase in the rural-urban division of labor (McGranahan and Ghelfi 1991) whereby low-education, low-skill jobs stay in the countryside, while high-education, high-skill jobs are in the cities and suburbs.

As these work distinctions sharpened in the last decade, earnings disparities widened correspondingly. In 1979, the difference between the two sectors was probably close to the difference in cost of living; but by 1987, the pay difference for rural and nonrural high school graduates had grown to 15 percent and for college graduates to twice that percentage (McGranahan and Ghelfi 1991).

These economic facts of life—jobs and pay—governed migration patterns in the last decade. As one analyst summarized it, "Rural areas were net exporters of educated workers" (McGranahan

1988). Rarely noted, but relevant to the issues of jobs and pay, is that at the same time, those with the lowest levels of skills and education increasingly tended to leave metropolitan areas to settle in rural counties (Lichter et al. 1991).

As for the members of the Class of 1980, these economic circumstances naturally impacted them, as it did others. Six years after high school, not only were rural members of the class generally less likely to be in white collar jobs (50 vs. 61 percent), but this was true even for college graduates (77 vs. 84 percent) (Pollard and O'Hare 1990). Factors included differences in aspirations, preparation, and educational attainment. The outcome also reflects the limited availability of such jobs in the countryside, as mentioned above.

Members of the Class of 1980 who did not obtain a college degree (i.e., those with a high school diploma or less, a license or certificate, or a 2–3–year vocational degree) also had difficulties that reflected the broader analysis. Persons from rural schools were earning less and had significantly more unemployment than did those from urban and suburban schools (Pollard and O'Hare 1990).

Regional Differences

All the findings regarding the Class of 1980 were not uniform among the nine regional divisions. One of the most striking differences concerned SES. Rural students from New England had the highest average SES, while rural students from the East-South Central and West-South Central divisions had the lowest. Consistent with the national correlations of SES and outcomes discussed above, New England stood out as the only census division with a majority of its rural students in academic programs. This region had the highest proportion of its students entering college and the highest proportion with at least a bachelor's degree (30 percent) by 1986 (table 10–14). In the Mountain states, only 7 percent of the rural students had attained a college degree.

Regional differences also occurred for dropout rates according to the Current Population Survey. Most regions saw a decline in dropout rates for 16- to 24-year-olds, but again, variations by region were considerable (table 10–11). For example, rates in the South, though declining, remained high during the 15-year period, while rates in the West actually rose. Clearly, policies designed to aid rural schools must take into account circumstances peculiar to the region.

In the South and the Pacific regions, the persistence of low average incomes, high rates of poverty, and low educational achievement point to the need for a regional emphasis on creating higher value economic activity and a workforce qualified for better jobs and improved incomes. In the rural Midwest, where education and incomes are high relative to other regions, creating jobs in new industries that can stem population losses is more of a concern. The greatest challenges for amenity-rich areas on both coasts are to manage the impacts of growth and assure the benefits are shared with all their residents (Reid and Frederick 1990).

In light of the education and job disparities in Rural America, increasing attention is being paid to finding ways to conserve human resources. To raise the standard of living in rural communities, rural youth clearly must qualify for better jobs through education and training. But this strategy depends on the availability of such jobs. The President's Rural Development Initiative has recognized this two-way relationship, and has made rural community and economic development a primary focus. It is important that schools and students not be left out of the process but participate fully in rural development efforts. The application of school resources, such as faculty release time, adult education, and class projects that directly involve students in community projects have the potential to strengthen the educational institutions and the communities.

Summary

Proportionately more rural than nonrural students have been shown to come from families with lower SES, a factor that contributes significantly to their somewhat lower career aspirations and lower tendency to prepare for and enroll in postsecondary education programs. Other factors include the presence in rural areas of fewer jobs requiring a college education and the dearth of institutions of higher education in rural counties. Yet diminished aspirations and lack of continuing education opportunities come at a time when every indication is that more knowledge and skills are necessary for well-paying jobs, typically located in nonrural areas. Many of those who do prepare, therefore, leave for jobs in metropolitan locations. The new economy has thus contributed to the emigration of Rural America's better educated workers, a phenomenon that will continue to challenge educators and communities in the years ahead.

Notes

1. This actually understates the rural shortfall because it compares those who had reached their senior year and does not reflect the higher dropout rates for rural students *prior* to that year. According to the Census Bureau, in the late 1970s, when 1980 seniors would have been in their sophomore and junior years, 9.7 percent of rural youth age 16–17 had dropped out, that is were neither in school nor had a high school diploma, compared to 8.3 percent for nonrural youth (Reid and Frederick 1990).

2. One of the most dramatic illustrations of the potential of rural schooling comes from a recent study that examined the high school Class of 1983 in 11 school districts in Iowa. A striking 75 percent of those students who entered either 2– or 4–year colleges received their degrees within 5 years of high school graduation. Almost all of these students grew up in families that valued perseverance and education. These students, in contrast to the general HSB finding, credited their parents with encouraging their post-high school plans. Also credited was the "ethos" in their rural schools that fostered a positive school climate and sense of belonging that influenced college performance (Schonert et al.).

3. Cobb, McIntire, and Pratt contrasted rural students who had attended a rural high school in 1980 and who, 4 years later, were living in a rural area or small town of less than 50,000 ("stayers") with those now residing in more urbanized areas ("leavers"). Other researchers use different reference points to determine migration, including simply leaving the hometown (Pollard and O'Hare 1990) or migrating 50 miles from home (Pollard et al. 1990). However defined, rural "leavers" ("migrants" in Pollard's work) have more advantaged backgrounds and progress further academically than "stayers" ("nonmigrants"). — Ed.

4. Family variables included socioeconomic status and family configuration (e.g., number of siblings, whether the mother worked) while "community social capital" included positive action on school bond issues and how well the student was integrated into the community as measured by long-term residence and church participation.

5. Interestingly, the difference in the availability of colleges and universities located in rural counties adjacent and nonadjacent to metropolitan counties was not particularly great.

References

Alsalam, N., L.T. Ogle, G.T. Rogers, and T.M. Smith. 1992. *The Condition of Education 1992*. Washington, DC: U.S. Department of Education, National Center for Education Statistics.

Anderson, J., D. Hollinger, and J. Conaty. 1992. *Poverty and Achievement: Re-examining the Relationship Between School Poverty and Student Achievement*. Washington, DC: U. S. Department of Education, Office of Research.

Barro, S.M., and A. Kolstad. 1987. *Who Drops Out of School? Findings from High School and Beyond*. Washington, DC: U.S. Department of Education, National Center for Education Statistics.

Beaulieu, L.J., G.D. Israel, M.H. Smith. 1990. "Community as Social Capital: The Case of Public High School Dropouts." Paper presented at the Annual Meeting of the Rural Sociological Society. Norfolk, VA.

Bickel, R., and G. Papagiannis. 1988. "Post-high School Prospects and District-level Dropout Rates." *Youth and Society* 20:2.

Cobb, R.A., W.G. McIntire, and P.A. Pratt. 1989. "Vocational and Educational Aspirations of High School Students: A Problem for Rural America." *Research in Rural Education* 6:2.

Coladarci, T., and W.G. McIntire. 1988. "Gender, Urbanicity, and Ability." *Research in Rural Education* 5:1.

Haller, E.J., and S.J. Virkler. October 1992. "Another Look at Rural-Urban Differences in Students' Educational Aspirations." Paper presented at the Rural Research Forum of the National Rural Education Association meeting in Traverse City, MI.

Hamrick, K.S. Winter 1991–1992. *Rural Conditions and Trends*. U.S. Department of Agriculture, Economic Research Service.

Kaufman, P., and M.M. McMillan. 1991. *Dropout Rates in the United States: 1990*. Washington, DC: U.S. Department of Education, National Center for Education Statistics.

Lichter, D.T., D.K. McLaughlin, and G.T. Cornwell. 1991. "Migration and the Loss of Human Resources in Rural America." Paper prepared for the Population Issues Research Center, Institute for Policy Research and Evaluation. Pennsylvania State University.

Marion, S.F., W.G. McIntire, and H.G. Walberg. April 1991. "The Effects of Per-pupil Expenditures, School Size, and Student Characteristics on Student Achievement and Educational Attainment in Rural Schools." Paper presented at the American Educational Research Association Conference, Chicago, IL.

McCaul, E.J. 1989. "Rural Public School Dropouts: Findings from High School and Beyond." *Research in Rural Education* 6:1.

McGranahan, D.A. 1988. "Rural Workers in the National Economy." *Rural Economic Development in the 1980s*. Rural Development Research Report No. 69. Washington, DC: U.S. Department of Agriculture, Economic Research Service.

McGranahan, D.A., J.C. Hession, F.K. Hines, and M.F. Jordan. 1986. *Social and Economic Characteristics of the Population in Metro and Nonmetro Counties, 1970–1980*. Washington, DC: U.S. Department of Agriculture, Economic Research Service.

McGranahan, D.A., and L.M. Ghelfi. 1991. "The Education Crisis and Rural Stagnation in the 1980s." *Education and Rural Economic Development: Strategies for the 1990s*. Washington, DC: U.S. Department of Agriculture, Economic Research Service.

McIntire, W.G., and S.F. Marion. March 1989. "Academic Achievement in America's Small Schools: Data from High School and Beyond." Paper presented at the National Rural and Small School Consortium Conference, Fort Lauderdale, FL.

Pollard, K. M., and W.P. O'Hare. March 1990. "Beyond High School: The Experience of Rural and Urban Youth in the 1980s." Staff Working Paper prepared for the Population Reference Bureau, Washington, DC.

Pollard, K. M., W.P. O'Hare, and R. Berg. "Selective Migration of Rural High School Seniors in the 1980s." Staff Working Paper prepared for the Population Reference Bureau, Washington, DC.

Reid, J.N., and M. Frederick. August 1990. *Rural America: Economic Performance, 1989*. AIB–609. Washington, DC: U. S. Department of Agriculture, Economic Research Service.

Schonert, K.A., J.P. Elliott, and D. Bills. 1991. "Rural Iowa Youth: A Descriptive Summary of Postsecondary Persistence Five Years After High School." *Research in Higher Education* 32.

Sherman, Arloc. 1992. *Falling by the Wayside: Children in Rural America*. Washington, DC: The Children's Defense Fund.

Smith, M. H., L.J. Beaulieu, and G.D. Israel. Winter, 1992. "Effects of Human Capital and Social Capital on Dropping Out of High School in the South" *Journal of Research in Rural Education* 8:1.

Swaim, P., and R. Teixeira. 1991. "Education and Training Policy: Skill Upgrading Options for the Rural Workforce." *Education and Rural Economic Development: Strategies for the 1990s.* Washington, DC: U.S. Department of Agriculture. Economic Research Service.

White, K.R. 1982. "The Relation Between Socioeconomic Status and Academic Achievement." *Psychological Bulletin* 91:3.

World Future Society. 1988. *Into the 21st Century: Long Term Trends Affecting the United States.* Bethesda, MD.

First grade graduates: Tornillo Independent School District, Tornillo, Texas (pop. 600). **Photo by Roz Alexander-Kasparik, Southwest Educational Development Laboratory (SEDL), Austin, Texas.**

11. Looking Ahead

Reporting the Condition of Education in Rural Schools

By the most conservative definition of rural, some 6.6 million students are enrolled in some 22,000 public elementary and secondary schools located in rural communities. Size alone—nearly 17 percent of America's students attending 28 percent of its schools—warrants considerable attention by policymakers to rural issues. Summarized below are the problems and the achievements of rural schools, as well as samples of missing information, implications for resolving the perennial problem of defining rural, and a vision for the future.

Identified problems. Along with traditional challenges to education imposed by location and demography, Rural America faced additional stresses during the last decade, difficulties that have continued into the 1990s.

- The stability of rural communities was severely undermined because economic problems in all traditional sources of rural employment occurred simultaneously. The resulting unemployment and underemployment led to increased poverty, emigration, and a dramatic surge in single-parent families.

- This decline in resource capacity and increase in service need occurred at a time of greater educational demands imposed not only by state reforms but also by the emergence of a new economy that called for different employment skills.

Many rural schools are ill-equipped to meet these challenges.

- Yet the system of school finance in the states leaves property-poor school districts at a disadvantage in providing adequate support for schools. High per pupil expenditures are a consequence of sparse population concentrations and the high cost of transporting pupils. State measures to achieve fiscal equity have, by and large, not been successful. One result is many rural districts have initiated or joined legal challenges to state systems of education financing.

- Teachers in rural schools have more preparations, and rural principals often have multiple responsibilities. Yet both receive considerably less compensation by way of salaries and benefits. This is due in part to their relative youth, their somewhat lower frequency of advanced degrees, and the small size of their schools. Turnover in *small* schools is particularly high, and it is especially difficult to recruit science and special education teachers to rural areas.

- Facilities are in great need of repair or replacement, but many districts are hampered in their ability to raise the necessary funds.

- The depth and breadth of curricula in small secondary schools are generally less than in larger schools, that is, there are relatively limited opportunities for alternative and advanced courses.

- While rural students in general do as well as the national average and

better than urban students on certain measures of achievement, they do less well than suburban students. Aspirations are lower, and they do not continue in higher education at the same rate as their nonrural counterparts.

- Perhaps most alarming for the future of Rural America is the extent to which its more educated residents continue to leave their communities.

Identified successes. Rural communities over the years have shown a remarkable resilience in the face of difficulties. Now is no exception.

- The link between the community and the school is a defining feature of most rural settlements and can be a major source of strength to its citizens and to the quality of education offered there. Many communities are exploring new avenues for this relationship to the mutual benefit of the school and the community.

- Rural America has made considerable progress in the last several decades in increasing the education levels of its people and improving the test scores of the students. Rural students who do go on to college stay the course as often as nonrural students.

- In the face of the misconception by some that rural education is somehow inferior, learning outcomes have been shown to be related to economic and social circumstances (e.g., parents' education rather than to community type. Moreover, research has documented certain strengths of small-scale schooling.

- The existence of a basic curriculum is not necessarily constrained by size or location, and many small schools have curricula as diverse as those of larger schools. Many schools address the needs of students desiring advanced courses in innovative ways, including cooperation with other districts, the state, or regional service centers. Telecommunications technology applications have mushroomed this last decade to provide courses to both students and teachers in rural areas.

- Interest in the needs of rural students and in the problems faced by rural communities has grown in recent years. At the federal and state levels and in the private sector, a variety of programs were established, organizations formed, and policies fashioned to address their unique needs.

The definitional Issue. At one time, when the United States was largely an agrarian society, "rural" simply meant a farming community, and those who had attended rural schools were the vast majority of the population. Indeed, not until 1918 did the urban population exceed that of rural communities. But with the urbanization that took place in this century, a variety of rural communities has emerged. That is the crux of the problem: there is no longer a single way to describe "rural." Though definitions abound, an adequate definition does not exist. What is known with certainty is that Rural America is diverse. What constitutes rural in terms of geography, economy, and culture in a Maine coastal island has little in common with the Mississippi Delta, the high plains of Kansas, or the mountains of Montana. And as the communities differ, so do the schools.

Given this diversity, one must approach national data on rural education realistically. Conditions in a given rural area may be better or worse than national averages suggest—whether the measure is dropout rates, school building quality, or test scores. For optimum practical utility, data need to be disaggregated to reflect each rural reality—a task beyond the scope of this report.

Gaps in information. The breadth of this report was possible because of the timing of a number of surveys by the National Center for Education Statistics (NCES) that tapped information on rural schools, educators, and student performance. Yet there remains much undocumented for lack of data. Examples follow.

- The impact of programs that assist rural students—either by design or because they are included among eligible recipients—is largely unavailable. Need for this information on the large entitlement programs is especially great.

- What limited material is available suggests the ongoing reform movement has had a strong effect on rural schools. But no national data exists on how states have targeted rural areas or designed strategies to address particular circumstances. Nor has there been adequate research on how different rural districts have responded or lacked the capacity to respond to reform mandates.

- There is a paucity of information on how rural youth who do not go to college cope with the ongoing change to the rural economy.

Research on rural education has not attracted a great deal of interest in most academic circles. The research base is small, with comparatively few profes-

sionals devoting time and energy to it. These omissions reflect the relatively low priority given to rural education information at top policy levels. To spur more interest, the U. S. Department of Education's Office of Educational Research and Improvement (OERI) published a research agenda in 1990 and has conducted seminars for rural researchers in 1993 to acquaint them with new NCES data bases. But more needs to be done at all levels to expand an understanding of the complexities of rural education that will in turn yield suitable policies.

Next Steps

These issues—resolution of the definitional problem and research-based school improvement strategies—demand a variety of responses from policymakers and decisionmakers. Some activities are underway; for others, options still need to be formulated.

Toward a typology of rural communities and schools. A necessary next step in better understanding the condition of the nation's rural schools is to move ahead in the creation of a typology of rural communities. This does not have to start from scratch because important progress has already been made.

In 1985, to portray better the new reality of a diverse Rural America, the U.S. Department of Agriculture (USDA) began developing county classification systems. One grouped the 2,443 rural counties according to their principal sources of income, employment, or both (Bender et al. 1985) (e.g., farming, retirement, manufacturing, mining, and federal lands) while another (Butler 1990) documented ranges of population density. Chapter 3 of this report includes the first attempt by a researcher to combine those typologies with data on schools. The approach holds considerable potential for further refinement and application for policy purposes.

Concurrently, NCES has linked its basic school district data file to 1990 Census data. This will allow access to a vast resource of demographic information that can be analyzed by school district. In 1992, NCES invited suggestions from rural education experts in the 10 regional educational laboratories for identifying benchmarks to better reflect rural districts in this system. In addition to gradations of low population density, dimensions built into this new rural school district typology include adjacency to metropolitan areas and isolation of settlement. Significantly, the resulting classification system encompasses rural districts in metropolitan counties as well as in nonmetropolitan ones.

Rather than comparing broad community types, a typology—whether at the county level (USDA) or the district level (NCES)—is important for differentiating among the multiple rural realities. For example, with a classification system, high school dropout rates, college-going rates, or test scores could be compared within or across a range of rural community types. By more precisely identifying the locations of specified problems, more focused public policy can be crafted at national, state, and local levels. The most isolated schools might well be targeted for special electronic distance-learning initiatives. Rural communities experiencing declining populations could be helped with programs that better involve schools in economic development efforts to retard emigration.

Moreover, the technology for such analyses will be user friendly under the NCES system. Information will be on CD-ROM and will be accessible through software that will guide the user; one need not be a statistician to locate and analyze the data. Thus, at the local, state, regional, or national level, those who need information on rural school districts will be able to obtain more of it than ever before, and with unprecedented ease.

Redesigning Rural Education

Rural America is being challenged to devise new approaches to educating and preparing its youth for the future. A number of elements need to be considered.

Dilemmas. Rural communities must decide whether, and to what extent, they should expand their educational programs. Without better education, their children's economic futures may be limited; education makes an acknowledged critical contribution to individual economic and social advancement. But from a rural development perspective, rural schools have been one of the largest economic drains locally as communities tend to tax themselves more heavily to support their schools.

For Rural America to be revitalized, attracting and keeping enough of the more educated and talented individuals who have high aspirations for themselves and their communities is essential. In the present structure, realizing high personal aspirations usually can only be achieved by moving to larger urban areas. At the same time, although skilled workers are needed for the jobs being created in new industries, some rural workers may have little incentive to learn those skills before the jobs actually exist. In that important sense, economic development is actually needed as a precursor to educational improvements in important parts of the rural population (Reid and Frederick 1990). Communities thus often have painful choices about where to invest resources—development or education.

And there remains a fundamental issue about the fairness of an educational finance system that puts so much burden on those citizens who can afford it the least and whose share in the benefits is so low. It is, after all, urban and suburban areas that are the recipients of Rural America's more educated youth, and thus the net beneficiaries from rural school spending.

Creating opportunities. Many analysts argue rural communities have not been well served by the mass-production model of schooling that has for so long characterized public education. Just as education everywhere must change in the information age, schools in modern rural societies must become quite different from those that currently exist. Pilot programs that have used the community as the focus of study and involved schools in community development suggest that as students are integrated in a significant way in the life of their community, their attitudes change. They begin to see the community as a possible place to stay in or return to, rather than as a place to depart from as soon as possible. This report notes examples of curricula that offer training in entrepreneurial skills in a context that allows students to create their own employment rather than depend on finding an existing job—often somewhere else.

Certain changes promoted for rural school redesign are the same suggested in the research literature for education generally. They are embedded in the recommendations of national curriculum studies such as those of the American Association for the Advancement of Science's "Project 2061," *Becoming a Nation of Readers* published by the U.S. Department of Education, and the national standards proposed in 1992 by the National Council on Education Standards and Testing. But because of the small scale of rural schools and the attendant lack of bureaucracy, because members of rural communities are more likely to share common values, and because rural schools have ready access to the surrounding environment for learning, education in a rural setting holds the potential to be at the forefront of the drive to redesign America's schools.

But barriers exist. For example, in terms of programmatic policy, rural schools have been disadvantaged on at least two major counts. First, few funded programs in either the public or private sector have specifically targeted small, rural schools. Second, even where resources have been available, access has been limited because the expertise and the luxury of time to pursue development funds do not exist within the small staffs of rural schools. Decisionmakers could help remove these barriers with legislation or administrative adjustments. Involving rural schools in opportunities for school redesign and in the establishment of partnerships with neighboring institutions of higher education and technical assistance providers represents yet another way rural schools could build on their strengths to help transform American education. Such cooperation and pooling of resources could help those affected respond better to changing educational and social conditions in the countryside.

Reversing the decline of much of Rural America and building sustainable rural communities will take some rethinking and certain changes in public policy. For instance, the policy concerning school district organization, which is based on the industrial notion that efficiency and effectiveness are directly tied to school size and therefore the solution to the rural school problem is school consolidation, should be reconsidered. Because it is the cornerstone of the rural community and a critical component of rural development, many believe the rural school needs to be nurtured as long as there is a rural community to serve.

Concluding Observations

This report documents how rural conditions are sufficiently different from urban ones to warrant being examined independently. It endorses the hypothesis that a single set of public policies may not be the best way to address adequately the various issues involving education in rural vs. urban settings.

While many might be discouraged by some data reported here and by projections for future change that do not bode well for Rural America, some see hope for the future in the characteristics of rural society itself. As the industrial society gives way to an information society, the norms and practices that are valued are changing. For instance, centralization is giving way to decentralization; the integration of service delivery is being seen as more effective than disconnected, specialized service delivery; and uniformity as a value is being replaced by an increased recognition of the strengths inherent in diversity.

These emerging norms and practices are reflective of rural reality and as they increase, could enhance the chances for many communities to survive. Moreover, in an information society, what one does for a living and where one lives are no longer as tightly connected. With access to the information infrastructure, there is potential for an array of job opportunities to develop for those wishing to live in rural communities. Finally, some observers hold that concerns for the environment, accompanied by the search for more sustainable agriculture, could increase the opportunities to live and work in the nation's countryside.

The rural school once produced most of America's workforce. Today, a smaller but a still significant portion of the school-age population is enrolled in rural schools. Though the data demonstrate overall strength by rural schools in terms of academic outcomes, many of these schools are suffering the effects of major economic upheavals and social dislocation. In the face of these larger forces, the challenge becomes how best to safeguard the human resources in rural communities. Strategies are needed to improve the potential of local schools to better educate their students for the future. Potentially productive avenues discussed in this report involve strengthening the school's connection with the community, using advanced technologies, and collaborating among a host of service agencies.

In sum, despite the severe problems this report has documented, the potential for rural schools to thrive does exist. With an improved research capacity to better target rural needs, and with the lead of model rural schools that are successfully serving their students, strategies can be designed to extend educational opportunities to students everywhere. This report has not offered a blueprint for success. Given the diversity of Rural America and the primacy of local control, that would not be appropriate. But in presenting a current profile of rural education, highlighting successes, and suggesting directions for improvement, this volume may spark greater interest in Rural America and serve as a resource to those who would design programs and strategies to help rural students successfully enter the 21st century.

References

Bender, L.D. (Ed.), B.L. Green, T.F. Hady, J.A. Kuehn, M.K. Nelson, L.B. Perkinson, and P.J. Ross. 1985. *The Diverse Social and Economic Structure of Nonmetropolitan America*. Rural Development Research Report No. 49. Washington DC: U.S. Department of Agriculture, Economic Research Service.

Butler, M.A. 1990. *Rural-urban Continuum Codes for Metro and Nonmetro Counties*. Washington DC: U.S. Department of Agriculture, Economic Research Service.

Reid, J.N., and M. Frederick. August 1990. *Rural America: Economic Performance, 1989*. AIB–609. Washington, DC: U.S. Department of Agriculture, Economic Research Service.

Two-room school house built in 1813 and in continuous operation through 1993; Washington Center School (enrollment: 37 students, grades 1–5), Washington, New Hampshire. **Photo by Joyce Stern, Washington, D.C.**

Elementary grade class at the Hanna School (enrollment: 91 students, grades PK–12), Hanna, Oklahoma. **Photo by Edward W. Chance, Center for the Study of Small/Rural Schools, University of Oklahoma, Norman.**

Appendices

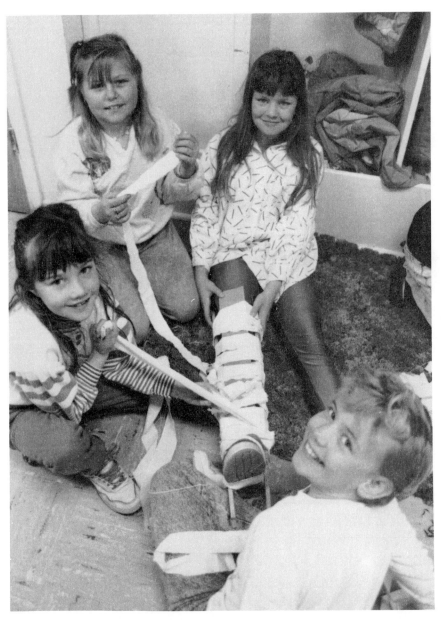

First-aid instruction at Seeley Lake Elementary School (enrollment: 186 students, grades K–6), Seeley Lake, Montana. **Photo by Tony Kneidek, Northwest Regional Educational Laboratory (NWREL), Portland, Oregon**.

Dot Lake School (enrollment: 16 students, grades 1–10), Dot Lake, Alaska Gateway School District, Alaska. **Photo by Tony Kneidek, Northwest Regional Educational Laboratory, (NWREL), Portland, Oregon.**

A. Supporting Tables

Table 3–1.—Number and percentage of regular public schools, students, and average school enrollment, by NCES locale code: 1991–92

Selected indicators	Total	Locale code			
		City	Urban fringe	Town	Rural
Regular public schools					
Number	79,876	18,420	19,073	20,013	22,370
Percentage	100	23.1	23.9	25.1	28.0
Students (in millions)					
Number	41.3	12.5	12.0	9.9	6.9
Percentage	100	30.3	29.1	23.9	16.7
Average school enrollment	521	683	637	498	310

SOURCE: U.S. Department of Education, National Center for Education Statistics, Common Core of Data Public School Universe, 1991–92.

Table 3-2.—Percentage distribution of regular public schools and students by school enrollment size and type of school, by rural and urban locale: 1991–92

School size	Primary		Secondary		Combined	
	Urban	Rural	Urban	Rural	Urban	Rural
Percentage of schools						
Under 100	1.9	14.6	1.9	21.1	3.6	20.3
100 to 199	5.7	23.5	2.7	24.7	4.2	20.2
200 to 399	30.4	34.1	12.0	27.5	17.6	30.3
400 to 799	53.2	24.9	34.0	19.9	49.3	24.4
800 to 1,199	7.9	2.7	23.4	4.5	20.2	4.2
1,200 or more	0.9	0.1	26.0	2.4	5.0	0.7
Percentage of students						
Under 100	0.2	2.6	0.1	4.0	0.3	3.0
100 to 199	1.9	11.5	0.5	11.3	1.1	9.7
200 to 399	19.6	32.8	4.0	24.6	8.7	28.5
400 to 799	60.7	44.2	21.9	34.6	46.9	42.9
800 to 1,199	14.9	8.2	24.8	13.4	31.1	12.7
1,200 or more	2.7	0.6	48.8	12.1	11.9	3.2

SOURCE: U.S. Department of Education, National Center for Education Statistics, Common Core of Data Public School Universe, 1991–92.

Table 3-3.—Student teacher ratios by school, type, size, and locale: 1991–92

Locale	Primary		Secondary	
	Fewer than 400 students	More than 400 students	Fewer than 400 students	More than 400 students
Rural	17.0	19.2	13.4	17.3
Urban	18.7	19.9	14.4	18.0

SOURCE: U.S. Department of Education, National Center for Education Statistics, Common Core of Data Public School Universe, 1991–92.

Table 3-4.—Number and percentage distribution of rural schools and students, by division and state: 1991–92

Census division	State	Number of schools	Number of students	Number of rural schools	Percent rural schools	Number of rural students	Percent rural students	Schools per 100 sq. miles	Students per sq. mile
	United States	79,876	41,282,415	22,370	28.01	6,890,334	16.69	2.26	11.67
New England		4,435	1,904,516	864	19.48	232,143	12.19	7.06	30.32
	Connecticut	933	464,319	48	5.14	16,061	3.46	19.26	95.83
	Maine	712	211,479	299	41.99	60,135	28.44	2.31	6.85
	Massachusetts	1,701	815,119	176	10.35	86,255	10.58	21.70	104.00
	New Hampshire	449	177,138	158	35.19	33,538	18.93	5.01	19.75
	Rhode Island	306	140,592	14	4.58	6,919	4.92	29.28	134.54
	Vermont	334	95,869	169	50.60	29,235	30.49	3.61	10.37
Middle Atlantic		10,617	6,226,393	1,518	14.30	699,509	11.23	9.54	55.97
	Delaware	146	95,534	49	33.56	30,548	31.98	7.47	48.87
	District of Columbia	162	77,640	0	0.00	0	0.00	265.57	1,272.79
	Maryland	1,149	719,976	193	16.80	101,736	14.13	11.75	73.65
	New Jersey	2,160	1,086,792	150	6.94	68,209	6.28	29.11	146.49
	New York	3,898	2,588,911	524	13.44	244,079	9.43	8.25	54.82
	Pennsylvania	3,102	1,657,540	602	19.41	254,937	15.38	6.92	36.98
Midwest		16,196	7,582,309	4,508	27.83	1,418,129	18.70	5.01	23.46
	Illinois	3,929	1,814,760	962	24.48	209,203	11.53	7.07	32.64
	Indiana	1,815	950,485	461	25.40	187,864	19.77	5.06	26.50
	Michigan	3,257	1,576,495	651	19.99	236,212	14.98	5.73	27.75
	Minnesota	1,516	670,773	698	46.04	205,657	30.66	1.90	8.42
	Ohio	3,684	1,761,353	982	26.66	379,764	21.56	9.00	43.01
	Wisconsin	1,995	808,443	754	37.79	199,429	24.67	3.67	14.88
West North Central		7,784	2,278,149	4,369	56.13	802,703	35.23	1.82	5.32
	Iowa	1,550	486,752	758	48.90	152,101	31.25	2.77	8.71
	Kansas	1,466	441,435	964	65.76	228,254	51.71	1.79	5.39
	Missouri	2,067	821,807	836	40.45	215,743	26.25	3.00	11.93
	Nebraska	1,432	278,339	861	60.13	93,579	33.62	1.86	3.62
	North Dakota	613	120,098	447	72.92	51,932	43.24	0.89	1.74
	South Dakota	656	129,718	503	76.68	61,094	47.10	0.86	1.71
South Atlantic		9,407	6,114,218	2,631	27.97	1,248,126	20.41	3.70	24.03
	Florida	2,179	1,893,803	312	14.32	217,269	11.47	4.04	35.07
	Georgia	1,709	1,170,703	348	20.36	201,628	17.22	2.95	20.21
	North Carolina	1,887	1,091,182	647	34.29	310,428	28.45	3.87	22.40
	South Carolina	1,022	624,986	295	28.86	131,831	21.09	3.39	20.76
	Virginia	1,683	1,014,143	561	33.33	251,660	24.82	4.25	25.61
	West Virginia	927	319,401	468	50.49	135,310	42.36	3.85	13.26
East South Central		4,946	2,697,691	1,649	33.34	728,121	26.99	2.77	15.10
	Alabama	1,285	723,356	374	29.11	181,170	25.05	2.53	14.25
	Kentucky	1,330	644,009	527	39.62	194,318	30.17	3.35	16.21
	Mississippi	865	501,029	370	42.77	192,882	38.50	1.84	10.68
	Tennessee	1,466	829,297	378	25.78	159,751	19.26	3.56	20.12
West South Central		10,054	5,225,598	2,986	29.70	854,590	16.35	2.36	12.26
	Arkansas	1,096	437,815	481	43.89	128,455	29.34	2.10	8.41
	Louisiana	1,357	768,917	329	24.24	139,951	18.20	3.11	17.65
	Oklahoma	1,799	584,496	800	44.47	143,223	24.50	2.62	8.51
	Texas	5,802	3,434,370	1,376	23.72	442,961	12.90	2.22	13.11
Mountain		5,859	2,675,224	2,147	36.64	420,982	15.74	0.68	3.12
	Arizona	1,026	647,629	157	15.30	41,211	6.36	0.90	5.70
	Colorado	1,331	587,308	390	29.30	82,687	14.08	1.28	5.66
	Idaho	547	222,688	246	44.97	57,662	25.89	0.66	2.69
	Montana	897	155,315	645	71.91	54,230	34.92	0.62	1.07
	Nevada	349	207,687	128	36.68	46,365	22.32	0.32	1.89
	New Mexico	652	306,880	223	34.20	46,628	15.19	0.54	2.53
	Utah	651	448,473	173	26.57	72,911	16.26	0.79	5.46
	Wyoming	406	99,244	185	45.57	19,288	19.43	0.42	1.02
Pacific		10,578	6,578,317	1,698	16.05	486,031	7.39	1.18	7.35
	Alaska	453	113,432	294	64.90	30,294	26.71	0.08	0.20
	California	7,077	4,947,223	715	10.10	249,267	5.04	4.54	31.72
	Hawaii	233	174,581	43	18.45	27,752	15.90	3.63	27.18
	Oregon	1,157	493,764	200	17.29	38,589	7.82	1.21	5.14
	Washington	1,658	849,317	446	26.90	140,129	16.50	2.49	12.76

SOURCE: U.S. Department of Education, National Center for Education Statistics, Common Core of Data Public School Universe, 1991–92.

79

Table 3-5.—Number of rural schools and percentage, by enrollment size, by division and state: 1991–92

Census division	State	Number of rural schools	1-99	100-199	200-399	400-799	800-1,199	1,200+
	United States	22,370	17.94	23.00	31.18	23.33	3.60	0.94
New England		864	22.22	25.81	32.87	15.51	2.66	0.93
	Connecticut	48	0.00	25.00	41.67	31.25	2.08	0.00
	Maine	299	28.09	31.77	31.10	8.03	0.67	0.33
	Massachusetts	176	3.98	6.25	39.20	36.93	9.66	3.98
	New Hampshire	158	29.75	24.05	35.44	10.76	0.00	0.00
	Rhode Island	14	7.14	7.14	28.57	35.71	21.43	0.00
	Vermont	169	31.36	39.05	24.85	4.73	0.00	0.00
Middle Atlantic		1,518	2.83	13.18	31.03	42.82	8.04	2.11
	Delaware	49	0.00	6.12	18.37	44.90	26.53	4.08
	District of Columbia	0	0.00	0.00	0.00	0.00	0.00	0.00
	Maryland	193	2.59	8.29	22.80	51.30	11.92	3.11
	New Jersey	150	5.33	19.33	30.67	29.33	13.33	2.00
	New York	524	3.05	5.92	35.69	48.28	4.96	2.10
	Pennsylvania	602	2.33	20.10	30.73	38.54	6.64	1.66
Midwest		4,508	8.14	24.41	39.22	25.65	2.19	0.41
	Illinois	962	15.45	39.87	35.28	9.08	0.31	0.00
	Indiana	461	0.65	15.40	37.96	42.52	3.04	0.43
	Michigan	651	8.00	12.31	40.15	36.92	1.85	0.77
	Minnesota	698	7.33	29.64	37.60	21.53	2.96	0.94
	Ohio	982	2.16	12.85	44.50	35.97	4.01	0.51
	Wisconsin	754	11.94	31.17	38.73	16.84	1.33	0.00
West North Central		4,369	34.04	31.44	26.08	7.64	0.53	0.28
	Iowa	758	11.21	45.38	39.71	3.56	0.13	0.00
	Kansas	964	25.21	28.53	31.02	13.38	1.24	0.62
	Missouri	836	15.94	30.92	35.14	16.43	1.09	0.48
	Nebraska	861	57.13	26.27	14.13	2.36	0.00	0.12
	North Dakota	447	54.81	29.53	14.54	1.12	0.00	0.00
	South Dakota	503	57.77	27.29	11.55	2.99	0.20	0.20
South Atlantic		2,631	3.35	11.37	31.63	42.09	9.28	2.28
	Florida	312	0.32	3.22	14.15	51.45	24.44	6.43
	Georgia	348	0.00	6.03	25.00	47.13	16.95	4.89
	North Carolina	647	1.08	7.88	32.15	49.92	7.73	1.24
	South Carolina	295	1.02	11.53	35.93	45.76	4.07	1.69
	Virginia	561	4.99	10.34	35.83	39.75	7.49	1.60
	West Virginia	468	10.47	26.71	39.74	21.79	1.07	0.21
East South Central		1,649	2.73	13.41	33.37	41.44	7.77	1.27
	Alabama	374	2.14	9.09	33.69	42.51	11.23	1.34
	Kentucky	527	3.61	19.20	38.21	34.60	4.18	0.19
	Mississippi	370	0.54	7.03	29.19	48.92	12.16	2.16
	Tennessee	378	4.23	15.87	30.42	42.59	5.03	1.85
West South Central		2,986	13.57	30.36	35.25	17.43	2.65	0.74
	Arkansas	481	7.69	30.77	45.53	14.76	1.25	0.00
	Louisiana	329	0.30	11.89	39.33	43.90	3.66	0.91
	Oklahoma	800	29.79	37.92	25.78	6.26	0.25	0.00
	Texas	1,376	9.38	30.23	36.19	18.53	4.29	1.38
Mountain		2,147	42.49	23.82	20.12	11.61	1.36	0.61
	Arizona	157	23.38	22.73	28.57	24.03	1.30	0.00
	Colorado	390	29.43	29.69	27.60	12.50	0.52	0.26
	Idaho	246	18.37	31.43	33.88	16.33	0.00	0.00
	Montana	645	72.87	17.67	7.75	1.55	0.16	0.00
	Nevada	128	25.78	17.19	20.31	28.91	3.91	3.91
	New Mexico	223	30.49	34.98	18.83	14.35	1.35	0.00
	Utah	173	18.50	13.29	30.64	24.28	9.25	4.05
	Wyoming	185	60.00	24.86	14.05	1.08	0.00	0.00
Pacific		1,698	28.06	18.36	26.31	22.52	3.37	1.38
	Alaska	294	64.97	21.43	9.86	3.40	0.34	0.00
	California	715	21.96	14.93	25.62	29.28	6.00	2.20
	Hawaii	43	4.65	2.33	25.58	41.86	9.30	16.28
	Oregon	200	30.50	28.00	32.50	9.00	0.00	0.00
	Washington	446	14.06	18.82	35.60	29.02	2.27	0.23

SOURCE: U.S. Department of Education, National Center for Education Statistics, Common Core of Data Public School Universe, 1991–92.

Table 3-6.—Number and percentage distribution of school districts, by percentage of students attending rural schools: 1991-92

Percentage of students attending a rural school	Number of districts	Percentage of districts
None	6,503	43.3
1-24	913	6.1
25-49	391	2.6
50-74	249	1.6
75-99	209	1.4
100	6,764	45.0

SOURCE: U.S. Department of Education, National Center for Education Statistics, Merged file of Common Core of Data Public School Universe and Public Agency Universe, 1991-92.

Table 3-7.—Number and percentage distribution of districts, schools, students, and teachers, by rural or urban type of district: 1991-92

Indicator	Total number	Percent rural	Percent urban
Districts	15,029	46.4	53.6
Schools	79,876	21.8	78.2
Students	41.3 million	11.6	88.4
Teachers	2.2 million	13.1	86.9
Rural schools	22,370	76.6	23.4
Students attending rural schools	6.9 million	68.5	31.5
Teachers at rural schools	401,972	70.3	29.7

SOURCE: U.S. Department of Education, National Center for Education Statistics, Merged file of Common Core of Data Public School Universe and Public Agency Universe, 1991-92.

Table 3–8.—Number of rural and urban school districts and percentage by enrollment size, by division and state: 1991–92

Census division	State	Total number of districts	Percent rural districts	Percent urban districts	Rural — Number of rural districts	Rural — Percent under 300	Rural — Percent 300 to 2,500	Rural — Percent over 2,500	Urban — Number of urban districts	Urban — Percent under 300	Urban — Percent 300 to 2,500	Urban — Percent over 2,500
	United States	15,029	46.40	53.60	6,973	41.37	54.24	4.39	8,056	10.94	48.26	40.80
New England		1,173	35.04	64.96	411	68.37	29.93	1.70	762	8.92	62.47	28.61
	Connecticut	169	13.61	86.39	23	56.52	43.48	0.00	146	2.74	55.48	41.78
	Maine	229	54.59	45.41	125	61.60	37.60	0.80	104	13.46	68.27	18.27
	Massachusetts	326	8.59	91.41	28	28.57	57.14	14.29	298	8.72	57.72	33.56
	New Hampshire	163	44.79	55.21	73	61.64	38.36	0.00	90	12.22	70.00	17.78
	Rhode Island	37	8.11	91.89	3	33.33	0.00	66.67	34	0.00	38.24	61.76
	Vermont	249	63.86	36.14	159	86.16	13.84	0.00	90	14.44	84.44	1.11
Middle Atlantic		1,837	20.30	79.70	373	16.62	71.05	12.33	1,464	5.87	56.83	37.30
	Delaware	16	37.50	62.50	6	0.00	16.67	83.33	10	0.00	20.00	80.00
	District of Columbia	1	0.00	100.00	0	0.00	0.00	0.00	1	0.00	0.00	100.00
	Maryland	24	16.67	83.33	4	0.00	0.00	100.00	20	0.00	0.00	100.00
	New Jersey	555	11.89	88.11	66	45.45	53.03	1.52	489	12.07	63.60	24.34
	New York	741	27.13	72.87	201	15.42	76.62	7.96	540	4.81	58.89	36.30
	Pennsylvania	500	19.20	80.80	96	1.04	78.13	20.83	404	0.25	49.75	50.00
Midwest		3,334	42.59	57.41	1,420	19.15	77.39	3.45	1,914	7.84	56.01	36.15
	Illinois	942	38.22	61.78	360	31.94	67.78	0.28	582	9.97	66.49	23.54
	Indiana	295	35.59	64.41	105	2.86	93.33	3.81	190	0.00	47.37	52.63
	Michigan	615	34.31	65.69	211	20.38	73.46	6.16	404	11.88	48.27	39.85
	Minnesota	440	65.23	34.77	287	30.31	68.64	1.05	153	19.61	45.10	35.29
	Ohio	614	36.48	63.52	224	1.79	88.39	9.82	390	0.26	54.87	44.87
	Wisconsin	428	54.44	45.56	233	8.58	88.84	2.58	195	6.67	60.00	33.33
West North Central		2,483	74.02	25.98	1,838	53.65	45.05	1.31	645	32.40	45.43	22.17
	Iowa	425	69.41	30.59	295	25.08	74.92	0.00	130	0.00	76.15	23.85
	Kansas	304	81.25	18.75	247	25.10	68.83	6.07	57	3.51	70.18	26.32
	Missouri	539	66.42	33.58	358	37.71	60.34	1.96	181	13.81	51.38	34.81
	Nebraska	770	71.04	28.93	547	81.90	17.73	0.37	223	77.58	16.14	6.28
	North Dakota	272	90.81	9.19	247	77.73	22.27	0.00	25	24.00	40.00	36.00
	South Dakota	173	83.24	16.76	144	52.08	47.92	0.00	29	10.34	51.72	37.93
South Atlantic		666	29.73	70.27	198	1.01	66.67	32.32	468	0.21	14.96	84.83
	Florida	71	14.08	85.92	10	0.00	70.00	30.00	61	0.00	13.11	86.89
	Georgia	183	29.51	70.49	54	3.70	70.37	25.93	129	0.78	24.03	75.19

Table 3–8.—Number of rural and urban school districts and percentage by enrollment size, by division and state: 1991–92—Continued

Census division / State	Total number of districts	Percent rural districts	Percent urban districts	Rural				Urban			
				Number of rural districts	Percent under 300	Percent 300 to 2,500	Percent over 2,500	Number of urban districts	Percent under 300	Percent 300 to 2,500	Percent over 2,500
North Carolina	133	25.56	74.44	34	0.00	50.00	50.00	99	0.00	5.05	94.95
South Carolina	91	28.57	71.43	26	0.00	80.77	19.23	65	0.00	15.38	84.62
Virginia	133	39.10	60.90	52	0.00	63.46	36.54	81	0.00	18.52	81.48
West Virginia	55	40.00	60.00	22	0.00	72.73	27.27	33	0.00	3.03	96.97
East South Central	598	30.27	69.73	181	1.66	64.09	34.25	417	0.48	35.49	64.03
Alabama	129	17.05	82.95	22	4.55	31.82	63.64	107	0.00	28.97	71.03
Kentucky	176	35.23	64.77	62	1.61	66.13	32.26	114	0.88	42.98	56.14
Mississippi	155	43.87	56.13	68	1.47	66.18	32.35	87	0.00	39.08	60.92
Tennessee	138	21.01	78.99	29	0.00	79.31	20.69	109	0.92	31.19	67.89
West South Central	2,018	56.99	43.01	1,150	38.52	59.22	2.26	868	12.33	47.24	40.44
Arkansas	324	62.65	37.35	203	24.63	74.38	0.99	121	5.79	62.81	31.40
Louisiana	67	13.43	86.57	9	0.00	66.67	33.33	58	1.72	1.72	96.55
Oklahoma	578	64.01	35.99	370	51.62	47.84	0.54	208	27.88	55.77	16.35
Texas	1,049	54.15	45.85	568	35.56	61.09	3.35	481	8.52	45.11	46.36
Mountain	1,241	65.35	34.65	811	68.56	30.21	1.23	430	13.72	43.26	43.02
Arizona	217	40.09	59.91	87	59.77	39.08	1.15	130	17.69	43.85	38.46
Colorado	186	60.22	39.78	112	43.75	53.57	2.68	74	17.57	33.78	48.65
Idaho	113	63.72	36.28	72	34.72	65.28	0.00	41	0.00	43.90	56.10
Montana	529	84.88	15.12	449	89.98	10.02	0.00	80	25.00	63.75	11.25
Nevada	17	41.18	58.82	7	14.29	57.14	28.57	10	0.00	30.00	70.00
New Mexico	89	52.81	47.19	47	40.43	57.45	2.13	42	0.00	35.71	64.29
Utah	40	35.00	65.00	14	14.29	71.43	14.29	26	0.00	11.54	88.46
Wyoming	50	46.00	54.00	23	17.39	78.26	4.35	27	11.11	51.85	37.04
Pacific	1,679	35.20	64.80	591	47.38	49.58	3.05	1,088	18.29	36.86	44.85
Alaska	55	76.36	23.64	42	38.10	61.90	0.00	13	0.00	46.15	53.85
California	1,036	26.45	73.55	274	46.35	49.27	4.38	762	17.45	36.09	46.46
Hawaii	1	0.00	100.00	0	0.00	0.00	0.00	1	0.00	0.00	100.00
Oregon	291	36.08	63.92	105	68.57	30.48	0.95	186	27.96	46.24	25.81
Washington	296	57.43	42.57	170	38.24	58.82	2.94	126	11.11	26.98	61.90

NOTE: Rural districts are those where 75 percent of the students attend a regular public school in a rural locale.
SOURCE: Merged file of Common Core of Data Public School Universe and Public Agency Universe, 1991–92.

Table 3-9.—Selected population indicators, by metropolitan and nonmetropolitan county type

Code and characteristics	1990 population	Percent of 1990 population	Population per square mile	Percent population under 18 years old	Per capita income 1988
Totals	247,051,601	100.00	83	30.42	$16,290
0 Metro central counties, 1 million plus	69,662,368	28.20	981	40.60	$18,245
1 Metro, fringe counties, 1 million plus	43,714,038	17.69	469	27.40	$19,804
2 Metro, 250,000 to 1 million	54,994,615	22.26	248	25.64	$15,983
3 Metro, less than 250,000	22,589,641	9.14	127	25.91	$13,961
4 Nonmetro, 20,000 + urban, and adjacent	10,846,569	4.39	76	25.57	$13,727
5 Nonmetro, 20,000 + urban, and nonadjacent	8,807,724	3.57	36	26.81	$12,575
6 Nonmetro, 2,500 to 20K urban, and adjacent	15,098,923	6.11	36	26.85	$12,216
7 Nonmetro, 2,500 to 20K urban, and nonadjacent	14,962,484	6.06	17	27.09	$12,077
8 Nonmetro, completely rural, and adjacent	2,567,924	1.04	14	26.72	$11,990
9 Nonmetro, completely rural, and nonadjacent	3,807,315	1.54	7	26.60	$11,665

NOTE: Code designation determined by population size, urban concentrations, and adjacency to metropolitan county. Excludes Hawaii, Alaska, and outlying areas.

SOURCE: 1990 Census of Population and Housing. BEA Personal Income, and Economic Research Service county types.

Table 3–10.—Number and percentage of schools, rural schools, students, rural students, and density, by metropolitan and nonmetropolitan county type: 1989–90

Code and characteristics	Total number of schools	Percent of total schools	Number of rural schools	Percent of rural schools	Total number of students	Percent of total students	Number of rural students	Percent of rural students	Students per 100 sq. miles	Schools per 100 sq. miles
Totals	78,624	100.00	22,054	100.00	39,648,981	100.00	6,565,936	100.00	1,339	2.66
0 Metro central counties, 1 million plus	14,303	18.19	410	1.86	10,033,518	25.31	252,617	3.85	14,131	20.14
1 Metro, fringe counties, 1 million plus	11,501	14.63	1,339	6.07	6,657,515	16.79	609,890	9.29	7,145	12.34
2 Metro, 250,000 to 1 million	15,635	19.89	2,371	10.75	8,887,457	22.42	1,031,540	15.71	4,001	7.04
3 Metro, less than 250,000	7,520	9.56	1,667	7.56	3,805,202	9.60	582,114	8.87	2,137	4.22
4 Nonmetro, 20,000 + urban, and adjacent	4,193	5.33	1,360	6.17	1,846,038	4.66	438,361	6.68	1,292	2.94
5 Nonmetro, 20,000 + urban, and nonadjacent	3,850	4.90	1,471	6.67	1,593,265	4.02	416,105	6.34	648	1.56
6 Nonmetro, 2,500 to 20K urban, and adjacent	7.520	9.56	3,828	17.36	2,797,178	7.05	1,078,340	16.42	671	1.80
7 Nonmetro, 2,500 to 20K urban, and nonadjacent	8,991	11.44	4,654	21.10	2,836,614	7.15	1,010,354	15.39	324	1.03
8 Nonmetro, completely rural, and adjacent	1,622	2.06	1,556	7.06	481,108	1.21	459,985	7.01	269	0.91
9 Nonmetro, completely rural, and nonadjacent	3,489	4.44	3,398	15.41	711,086	1.79	686,630	10.46	133	0.65

NOTE: Code designation determined by population size, urban concentrations, and adjacency to metropolitan county. Excludes Hawaii, Alaska, and outlying areas.

SOURCE: Merged file of Common Core of Data Public School Universe, 1989-90 and Economic Research Service county types.

Table 3–11.—Number and percentage of schools by selected enrollment sizes, by metropolitan and nonmetropolitan county type: 1989–90

Code and characteristics	Number			Percentage		
	Under 100 students	Under 200 students	Under 400 students	Under 100 students	Under 200 students	Under 400 students
Totals	4,135	9,400	16,329	18.75%	42.62%	74.04%
0 Metro, central counties, 1 million plus	28	57	145	6.83	13.90	35.37
1 Metro, fringe counties, 1 million plus	56	231	659	4.18	17.25	49.22
2 Metro, 250,000 to 1 million	142	499	1,287	5.99	21.05	54.28
3 Metro, less than 250,000	172	506	1,109	10.32	30.35	66.53
4 Nonmetro, 20,000 + urban, and adjacent	141	441	957	10.37	32.43	70.37
5 Nonmetro, 20,000 + urban, and nonadjacent	282	643	1,135	19.17	43.71	77.16
6 Nonmetro, 2,500 to 20K urban, and adjacent	555	1,609	2,955	14.50	42.03	77.19
7 Nonmetro, 2,500 to 20K urban, and nonadjacent	1,289	2,673	3,998	27.70	57.43	85.90
8 Nonmetro, completely rural, and adjacent	268	639	1,145	17.22	41.07	73.59
9 Nonmetro, completely rural, and nonadjacent	1,202	2,102	2,939	35.37	61.86	86.49

NOTE: Code designation determined by population size, urban concentrations, and adjacency to metropolitan county. Excludes Hawaii, Alaska, and outlying areas.

SOURCE: Merged file of Common Core of Data Public School Universe, 1989-90 and Economic Research Service county types.

Table 3–12.—Selected population and education statistics, by nonmetropolitan county policy impact type

Indicators	Farm dependent	Manufacturing dependent	Mining dependent	Government dependent	Unclassified	Persistent poverty
Number of counties	511	54	124	347	519	240
1990 population	4,217,799	18,384,573	2,364,063	9,318,434	13,638,821	3,608,881
Percent of U.S. Population	1.71	7.44	0.96	3.77	5.52	1.46
Percentage change 1980-90	-4.01	2.46	-4.86	8.72	-0.10	0.45
Per capita income, 1988	$12,817	$12,343	$11,127	$11,838	$12,718	$9,442
Population per square mile	8.3	52.8	12.2	18.3	31.5	25.6
Number of public schools	4,252	7,889	1,448	4,532	7,823	1,739
Percent of U.S. public schools	5.41	10.03	1.84	5.76	9.95	2.21
Number of public schools students	826,792	3,352,250	494,265	1,673,540	2,495,521	706,411
Percent of U.S. students	2.09	8.45	1.25	4.22	6.29	1.78
Number of rural schools	3,334	3,542	809	2,307	4,157	1,213
Percent of rural schools	78.41	44.90	55.87	50.90	53.14	69.75
Number of rural students	508,004	1,206,672	218,824	604,042	945,896	425,646
Percent of rural students	61.44	36.00	44.27	36.09	37.90	60.25
Number of schools						
Under 100 students	1,400	282	122	544	1,011	133
Under 200 students	2,431	990	353	1,130	2,308	356
Under 400 students	3,157	2,363	649	1,790	3,570	771
Percent of schools						
Under 100 students	41.99	7.96	15.08	23.58	24.32	10.96
Under 200 students	72.92	27.95	43.63	48.98	55.52	29.35
Under 400 students	94.69	66.71	80.22	77.59	85.88	63.56
Total schools per 100 square miles	0.83	2.27	0.75	0.89	1.81	1.23
Total students per 100 square miles	162	963	256	329	576	502
Total student/teacher ratio	14.7	16.9	16.4	16.8	16.3	17.0
Rural student/teacher ratio	13.6	16.7	15.8	15.7	15.2	16.6

NOTE: Excludes Alaska, Hawaii and, outlying areas.

SOURCES: 1990 Census of Population and Housing, BEA Personal Income, Common Core of Data Public School Universe, 1989-90, and Economic Research Service Social-Economic county types.

Table 5–1.—Tactical objectives of the 1983 U.S. Department of Education's rural education and rural family education policy for the 1980s

- The Department will assist educators and administrators on all levels interested in developing outreach and volunteer programs with the active support and interaction of parents, teachers, civic groups, and the business community to improve the delivery of educational services to rural communities.

- The Department will work to expand the data base on the condition of education on rural areas, and will provide the necessary technologies to disseminate information relevant to curriculum, organization, personnel, and support services needed for educational institutions serving rural communities. *Data collection will focus on information relating to regional designations; goals of rural education and rural family education; surveys of rural curricula; test score comparisons; tax base/student ratios; characteristics of effective rural programs and institutions; and descriptions of intermediate service agency delivery systems. To disseminate information to educational institutions and programs serving rural communities, including rural school districts, the Department will utilize State Departments of Education; ERIC/CRESS; the National Rural Education Association; other professional and service organizations; national advisory councils; youth organizations; intermediate units; American Education Magazine; and county and local agencies.*

- The Department, *with appropriate control staff*, will closely monitor Education program regulations, eligibility and evaluation criteria, subregulatory directives, and administrative policies to insure equity for all LEAs regardless of size, location, or condition. *Monitoring will focus on reducing complexity of criteria for funding; reducing complexity of application and reporting procedures and forms; and reducing unrealistic requirements in general while insuring competent and enlightened staff monitoring.*

- The Department will assist in identifying and developing special programs available for handicapped individuals located in rural areas.

- The Department will provide personnel to coordinate the consolidation of available research on shortages and additional needs for analysis by the Secretary's Rural Education Committee. *Research will focus on effective practices and characteristics of effective rural programs and projects.*

- The Department will include rural institutions in demonstration and pilot projects and will involve cross sections of rural communities in educational technology planning.

- The Department will provide consultative and technical assistance to rural educational entities as a means to improve the quality of education in rural areas. *To facilitate communications, the Department will support initiatives such as an annual national forum; a monthly newsletter; and utilization of extension services and existing organizations for dissemination of information.*

- The Department will assist rural education in improving the achievement of black students, American Indian students, children of migrant workers, and other minorities. *To this end, the Department will focus on data concerning graduation from high school and college, including secondary and postsecondary vocational institutions and programs; gains in functional literacy, changes in college enrollment, and achievement in adult education.*

- The Department will assist individuals and families living in rural areas with family education programs and services through vocational home economics education, an established delivery system, as a means of improving the quality of rural family education.

SOURCE: U.S. Department of Education, *Rural Education and Rural Family Education Policy for the 80s.* Washington, DC: August 1983.

88

Table 5–2.—Percentage of public and private school students receiving publicly funded ECIA Chapter 1 services, by selected school characteristics: School year 1987–88

School characteristics	All schools Total	Public				Private			
		Total	Elementary	Secondary	Combined	Total	Elementary	Secondary	Combined
Total	10.2	11.1	14.8	4.9	12.1	3.3	3.7	(1)	4.3
Community type									
Rural/farming	12.1	12.4	16.8	4.6	11.7	5.1	4.0	(1)	(1)
Small city/town	9.3	9.9	13.2	4.2	12.2	3.1	3.4	(1)	(1)
Suburban	5.9	6.6	8.9	3.3	(1)	1.6	2.7	(1)	(1)
Urban	12.4	14.1	18.5	6.7	13.7	3.9	4.3	(1)	5.6
Other (2)	20.9	22.1	21.2	(1)	(1)	(1)	(1)	(1)	(1)
School size									
Less than 150	10.2	17.7	17.5	13.2	24.5	3.8	1.9	(1)	7.6
150–299	10.7	13.2	15.0	5.9	13.6	5.4	5.7	(1)	(1)
300–499	11.2	12.3	13.9	4.0	11.3	2.5	3.0	(1)	(1)
500–749	11.6	12.4	14.4	5.7	11.9	(1)	(1)	(1)	(1)
750 or more	8.2	8.7	16.4	4.6	9.1	(1)	(1)	(1)	(1)
Minority students									
Less than 5 percent	6.4	7.3	9.9	2.6	9.0	1.8	2.5	(1)	(1)
5 percent – 19 percent	6.3	7.0	9.4	3.2	10.2	1.8	2.5	(1)	(1)
20 percent – 49 percent	9.0	9.4	12.5	3.9	14.2	5.0	3.1	(1)	(1)
50 percent or more	20.4	21.2	26.7	10.8	18.1	9.6	9.0	(1)	(1)

NOTE: (1) Too few sample cases (fewer than 30) for a reliable estimate.
(2) Includes military bases and Indian reservations.

SOURCE: U.S. Department of Education, National Center for Education Statistics, Schools and Staffing Survey, 1987–88.

Table 5–3.—Ten largest providers of federal education funding for all levels of education: Fiscal year 1992

| Agency | FY 92 estimates | | Special programs targeted on rural, small school districts |
	Dollars (in billions)	Percent of total	
Total	61.4	100.0	
Department of Education	26.6	43.3	yes
Department of Health and Human Services	10.1	16.5	no
Department of Agriculture	7.5	12.3	yes
Department of Defense	4.0	6.4	no
Department of Energy	3.3	4.3	no
Department of Labor	2.8	4.5	no
National Science Foundation	2.1	3.4	no
National Aeronautics and Space Administration	1.5	2.4	no
Department of Veterans Affairs	1.0	1.7	no
Department of the Interior	.7	1.2	yes
All other federal agencies*	1.8	3.0	yes

* Includes Department of Commerce and the Appalachian Regional Commission

NOTE: Percentages based on unrounded numbers.

SOURCE: Hoffman, C. M. 1993. *Federal Support for Education: Fiscal Years 1980 to 1992.* Washington, DC: U.S. Department of Education, Office of Educational Research and Improvement. National Center for Education Statistics, 9.

Table 5-4.—Summary of basic strategies and tactics used by the states to enhance rural education: 1990

State strategy/tactics	Estimated extent of current state use
Promotion of structural change strategies	
• Mandated reorganization	limited
• Multi-district regional single-purpose schools	limited
• Multi-district comprehensive secondary schools	limited
Promotion of service delivery strategies	
• Single-purpose service centers	extensive
• Comprehensive service centers	moderate
• State-operated service centers	limited
• Multi-district sharing whole grades/staff	limited
• Distant learning technologies	moderate
• School-business partnerships	extensive
• State-operated instructional programs	moderate
Promotion of revenue enhancement strategies	
• Use of weighted student enrollment factor in state aid	extensive
• State aid based on program unit	limited
• State aid for capital outlay/debt service	extensive
• Regional general tax authority	limited
• Regional categorical tax authority	limited
Promotion of public choice theory strategies	
• Interdistrict parental choice	limited
• Privatization of public schools	limited
• Privatization of selected functions	moderate
Promotion of administrative tactics	
• Rural school coordinating unit in SEA	limited
• SEA task force on rural education	limited
• Education represented on state rural development group	moderate

NOTE: Extent of state use: limited = less than ten of the states
moderate = less than one-half the states
majority = more than one-half the states
extensive = more than three-quarters of the states

SOURCE: Stephens, Robert E., University of Maryland, College Park.

91

Table 6–1a.—Percentage distribution of rural and nonrural public school teachers, by sex and age: 1987–88

School setting	Sex		Age				Age range	
	Male	Female	Under 30 years	30–39 years	40–49 years	50 years or more	Under 40 years	40 years or more
Total	29.5	70.5	13.6	35.5	32.8	18.2	49.0	51.0
	(0.22)	(0.22)	(0.19)	(0.30)	(0.26)	(0.22)	(0.28)	(0.28)
Rural	30.3	69.7	16.2	39.8	29.3	14.7	56.0	44.0
	(0.51)	(0.51)	(0.42)	(0.63)	(0.60)	(0.38)	(0.58)	(0.58)
Nonrural	29.0	71.0	12.5	34.1	34.1	19.3	46.6	53.4
	(0.36)	(0.36)	(0.22)	(0.41)	(0.31)	(0.28)	(0.39)	(0.39)

NOTE: Standard errors in parentheses.

SOURCE: U.S. Department of Education, National Center for Education Statistics, Schools and Staffing Survey, 1987–88.

Table 6–1b.—Percentage distribution of rural and nonrural public school teachers, by years of full-time teaching experience: 1987–88

School setting	None	1–2	3–9	10–20	More than 20
Total	0.7	7.3	26.1	44.5	21.4
	(0.04)	(0.14)	(0.20)	(0.25)	(0.22)
Rural	0.9	8.8	29.5	43.4	17.4
	(0.10)	(0.36)	(0.45)	(0.59)	(0.41)
Nonrural	0.6	6.8	24.9	45.1	22.7
	(0.05)	(0.16)	(0.27)	(0.27)	(0.28)

NOTE: Standard errors in parentheses.

SOURCE: U.S. Department of Education, National Center for Education Statistics, Schools and Staffing Survey, 1987–88.

Table 6–2.—Percentage distribution of rural and nonrural public school teachers, by highest earned degree, sex, and level: 1987–88

Setting, level, and sex	No degree	A.A.	B.A.	M.A.	Ed. spec.	J.D./M.D./ Ph.D
Total	0.2	0.4	52.1	40.1	6.3	0.9
	(0.02)	(0.03)	(0.29)	(0.30)	(0.14)	(0.05)
Setting						
Rural	0.2	0.4	61.7	32.9	4.4	0.4
	(0.05)	(0.06)	(0.64)	(0.57)	(0.24)	(0.07)
Nonrural	0.2	0.5	48.9	42.6	6.7	1.0
	(0.02)	(0.04)	(0.35)	(0.37)	(0.15)	(0.07)
Level						
Rural						
Elementary	0.1	0.0	64.0	31.5	4.2	0.2
	(0.03)	(0.02)	(0.88)	(0.86)	(0.34)	(0.06)
Secondary	0.4	0.7	59.4	34.3	4.5	0.7
	(0.09)	(0.12)	(0.76)	(0.58)	(0.31)	(0.12)
Nonrural						
Elementary	0.0	0.0	54.4	39.1	5.9	0.6
	(0.01)	(0.01)	(0.55)	(0.56)	(0.24)	(0.08)
Secondary	0.4	0.9	43.2	46.4	7.6	1.5
	(0.05)	(0.09)	(0.53)	(0.51)	(0.20)	(0.11)
Sex						
Rural						
Male	0.5	1.0	56.6	36.3	4.9	0.7
	(0.12)	(0.17)	(1.02)	(0.83)	(0.42)	(0.15)
Female	0.1	0.1	63.9	31.4	4.1	0.3
	(0.04)	(0.04)	(0.74)	(0.70)	(0.27)	(0.08)
Nonrural						
Male	0.6	1.3	39.7	48.3	8.2	1.9
	(0.06)	(0.13)	(0.63)	(0.59)	(0.30)	(0.16)
Female	0.1	0.1	52.8	40.2	6.1	0.7
	(0.02)	(0.02)	(0.46)	(0.46)	(0.19)	(0.07)

NOTE: Standard errors in parentheses.

SOURCE: U.S. Department of Education, National Center for Education Statistics, Schools and Staffing Survey, 1987–88.

Table 6–3.—Percentage of rural and nonrural public schools whose districts offered certain benefits in teacher pay packages, by type of benefit: 1987–88

School setting	Medical insurance	Dental insurance	Life insurance	Pension	Trans- portation	Tuition	Other benefits
Total	94.5	65.1	72.0	67.5	9.2	35.7	21.6
	(0.28)	(0.48)	(0.52)	(0.51)	(0.31)	(0.55)	(0.43)
Rural	90.6	51.9	62.3	62.7	10.4	37.6	17.3
	(0.65)	(1.08)	(1.11)	(0.09)	(0.64)	(0.87)	(0.86)
Nonrural	96.6	72.2	77.3	70.1	8.5	34.7	24.0
	(0.22)	(0.46)	(0.62)	(0.61)	(0.41)	(0.64)	(0.62)

NOTE: Standard errors in parentheses.

SOURCE: U.S. Department of Education, National Center for Education Statistics, Schools and Staffing Survey, 1987–88.

Table 6–4.—Percentage of rural and nonrural public school teachers who had nonschool employment, by time of year employed outside school: 1987–88

School setting	Any nonschool employment	Time of year employed outside school		
		School year only	Summer only	Both school year and summer
Total	24.0	5.9	7.6	10.5
	(0.25)	(0.15)	(0.16)	(0.18)
Rural	24.9	5.6	8.8	10.5
	(0.46)	(0.25)	(0.29)	(0.33)
Nonrural	23.5	6.1	7.1	10.4
	(0.33)	(0.18)	(0.22)	(0.24)

NOTE: Standard errors in parentheses.

SOURCE: U.S. Department of Education, National Center for Education Statistics, Schools and Staffing Survey, 1987–88.

Table 6-5.—Percentage of rural and nonrural public schools whose districts used various criteria for teacher employment, by type of criteria: 1987–88

School setting	State certifi-cation	Graduation from teacher education program	Major or minor in assign-ment field	Pass district examin-ation	Pass state examin-ation	Pass National Teachers' Examin-ation
Total	78.3	67.6	63.7	7.9	40.3	28.2
	(0.47)	(0.46)	(0.60)	(0.30)	(0.42)	(0.37)
Rural	81.1	71.9	68.3	3.0	37.0	26.5
	(0.81)	(0.85)	(1.38)	(0.39)	(1.08)	(0.99)
Nonrural	76.8	65.3	61.2	10.6	42.1	29.1
	(0.65)	(0.61)	(0.69)	(0.40)	(0.45)	(0.52)

NOTE: Standard errors in parentheses.

SOURCE: U.S. Department of Education, National Center for Education Statistics, Schools and Staffing Survey, 1987–88.

Table 6-6.—Percentage of rural and nonrural public school principals who used various strategies to compensate for unfilled vacancies: 1987–88

School setting	Cancelled courses	Expanded class size	Increased teachers' course loads	Reassigned other teachers	Hired substitutes	Hired itinerants	Other
Total	5.0	8.8	6.2	16.1	36. 2	8.5	15.9
	(0.21)	(0.30)	(0.37)	(0.46)	(0.60)	(0.34)	(0.51)
Rural	7.0	8.9	7.4	19.0	26.1	8.6	16.9
	(0.48)	(0.63)	(0.65)	(0.90)	(1.07)	(0.63)	(1.01)
Nonrural	4.2	8.6	5.4	14.8	40.4	8.3	15.4
	(0.27)	(0.35)	(0.40)	(0.59)	(0.78)	(0.47)	(0.60)

NOTE: Standard errors in parentheses.

SOURCE: U.S. Department of Education, National Center for Education Statistics, Schools and Staffing Survey, 1987–88.

Table 6–7.—Percentage of rural and nonrural public school teachers who reported a high level of control over selected areas in their classrooms: 1987–88*

School setting	Homework	Teaching techniques	Discipline	Content, topics, skills to be taught	Textbooks, instructional materials
Total	86.8	85.3	69.5	58.8	54.1
	(0.21)	(0.17)	(0.26)	(0.31)	(0.33)
Rural	90.1	88.1	74.1	67.0	64.7
	(0.36)	(0.43)	(0.47)	(0.65)	(0.57)
Nonrural	85.9	84.6	68.3	56.0	50.6
	(0.27)	(0.28)	(0.35)	(0.39)	(0.43)

*Includes teachers who responded with a 5 or 6 on a scale of 1 to 6, where 1 represented "no control" and 6 represented "complete control."

NOTE: Standard errors in parentheses.

SOURCE: U.S. Department of Education, National Center for Education Statistics, Schools and Staffing Survey, 1987–88.

Table 6–8.—Percentage of rural and nonrural public school teachers who reported having a great deal of influence over school policy in various areas, by level: 1987–88*

Level	Discipline	Content of inservice programs	Grouping students in classes by ability	Curriculum
Total	34.8	31.1	28.1	35.0
	(0.39)	(0.33)	(0.35)	(0.35)
Rural				
Elementary	45.7	34.1	36.3	40.6
	(1.07)	(0.82)	(1.01)	(0.88)
Secondary	28.0	30.6	20.1	40.7
	(0.84)	(0.88)	(0.72)	(0.79)
Nonrural				
Elementary	44.9	33.7	35.7	30.5
	(0.78)	(0.71)	(0.62)	(0.50)
Secondary	23.5	27.7	20.4	35.7
	(0.55)	(0.59)	(0.53)	(0.58)

*Includes teachers who responded with a 5 or 6 on a scale of 1 to 6, where 1 represented "no influence" and 6 represented "a great deal of influence."

NOTE: Standard errors in parentheses.

SOURCE: U.S. Department of Education, National Center for Education Statistics, Schools and Staffing Survey, 1987–88.

Table 6–9.—Percentage of rural and nonrural public school teachers who were highly satisfied* with various aspects of their working conditions, by level: 1987–88

Setting and level	Overall view of of working conditions	Administrative support/ establish common goals	Buffering/ enforcement of rules	Collaborative norms/teacher participation in decision making	Adequacy of resources
Total	30.1	20.5	31.8	7.4	2.1
	(0.31)	(0.28)	(0.30)	(0.18)	(0.00)
School setting					
Rural	29.0	21.8	33.1	8.8	2.1
	(0.62)	(0.52)	(0.60)	(0.34)	(0.01)
Nonrural	30.7	20.3	31.4	6.9	2.1
	(0.41)	(0.33)	(0.41)	(0.21)	(0.00)
Level					
Rural					
Elementary	32.7	29.2	44.2	8.8	2.0
	(1.08)	(0.78)	(0.95)	(0.47)	(0.01)
Secondary	25.3	14.5	22.0	8.9	2.2
	(0.68)	(0.66)	(0.58)	(0.49)	(0.01)
Nonrural					
Elementary	37.2	27.5	42.1	7.2	2.0
	(0.62)	(0.58)	(0.59)	(0.31)	(0.01)
Secondary	23.8	12.7	20.1	6.6	2.2
	(0.44)	(0.32)	(0.49)	(0.29)	(0.01)

*Teachers responded to 23 questions concerning satisfaction with aspects of the working conditions in their schools. Through factor analysis these questions were reduced to four factors. A summary index of teachers' overall satisfaction was also computed. Teachers were defined as being "highly satisfied" if their scores on a factor ranged between 1.0 and 1.5 on a scale of 1 to 4, with 1 being the most satisfaction and 4 the least.

NOTE: Standard errors in parentheses.

SOURCE: U.S. Department of Education, National Center for Education Statistics, Schools and Staffing Survey, 1987–88.

Table 6–10.—Number of rural and nonrural public school principals, by sex and age: 1987–88

School setting	Total	Sex		Age				
		Male	Female	Under 40 years	40–44 years	45–49 years	50–54 years	55 years or over
Total	77,890	58,585	19,118	14,430	17,755	16,408	14,936	13,891
	(295.1)	(461.5)	(411.5)	(364.4)	(362.4)	(381.2)	(329.9)	(335.8)
Rural	25,382	21,033	4,286	6,297	6,245	4,959	4,322	3,454
	(416.0)	(356.3)	(256.1)	(280.1)	(256.2)	(260.2)	(196.7)	(218.1)
Nonrural	49,205	35,233	13,868	7,417	10,750	10,771	10,115	9,832
	(354.0)	(414.6)	(322.0)	(265.2)	(290.9)	(306.7)	(226.3)	(295.0)

NOTE: Standard errors in parentheses. Details may not add to totals because of rounding or missing values in cells with too few cases.

SOURCE: U.S. Department of Education, National Center for Education Statistics, Schools and Staffing Survey, 1987–88

Table 6–11.—Percentage distribution of rural and nonrural public school principals, by sex and age: 1987–88

School setting	Sex		Age				
	Male	Female	Under 40 years	40–44 years	45–49 years	50–54 years	55 years or over
Total	75.4	24.6	18.6	22.9	21.2	19.3	17.9
	(0.52)	(0.52)	(0.46)	(0.45)	(0.48)	(0.43)	(0.44)
Rural	83.1	16.9	24.9	24.7	19.6	17.1	13.7
	(0.89)	(0.89)	(1.00)	(0.96)	(0.92)	(0.79)	(0.83)
Nonrural	71.8	28.2	15.2	22.0	22.0	20.7	20.1
	(0.64)	(0.64)	(0.52)	(0.60)	(0.59)	(0.47)	(0.57)

NOTE: Standard errors in parentheses.

SOURCE: U.S. Department of Education, National Center for Education Statistics, Schools and Staffing Survey, 1987–88.

Table 6–12.—Percentage distribution of rural and nonrural public school principals, by race and ethnic origin: 1987–88

School setting	Race				Ethnic origin	
	Native American	Asian/Pacific Islander	Black	White	Hispanic	Non-Hispanic
Total	1.1	0.6	8.7	89.7	3.3	96.7
	(0.16)	(0.08)	(0.31)	(0.32)	(0.19)	(0.19)
Rural	1.6	0.3	3.6	94.5	1.7	98.3
	(0.37)	(0.07)	(0.33)	(0.41)	(0.31)	(0.31)
Nonrural	0.8	0.7	11.1	87.4	4.0	96.0
	(0.10)	(0.12)	(0.50)	(0.50)	(0.25)	(0.25)

NOTE: Standard errors in parentheses.

SOURCE: U.S. Department of Education, National Center for Education Statistics, Schools and Staffing Survey, 1987–88.

Table 6–13.—Percentage distribution of rural and nonrural public school principals, by highest degree earned, level, and sex: 1987–88

Setting, level, and sex	B.A. or less	M.A.	Education specialist	J.D./M.D./ Ph.D.
Total	2.5	53.4	35.1	8.9
	(0.26)	(0.51)	(0.49)	(0.35)
Setting				
Rural	5.4	53.5	36.1	5.0
	(0.62)	(1.04)	(0.89)	(0.52)
Nonrural	1.1	53.2	34.9	10.8
	(0.20)	(0.75)	(0.70)	(0.44)
Level				
Rural				
Elementary	6.2	54.1	34.7	5.0
	(0.91)	(1.37)	(1.29)	(0.80)
Secondary	2.5	52.3	40.3	4.9
	(0.44)	(1.74)	(1.70)	(0.78)
Combined	7.3	52.4	34.7	5.7
	(0.89)	(2.42)	(2.05)	(1.08)
Nonrural				
Elementary	1.1	54.4	34.3	10.2
	(0.24)	(1.04)	(0.97)	(0.58)
Secondary	0.8	50.3	36.4	12.6
	(0.24)	(1.02)	(0.94)	(0.66)
Combined	2.3	50.3	35.8	11.6
	(1.34)	(4.34)	(4.07)	(2.18)
Sex				
Rural				
Male	3.9	55.0	36.2	4.9
	(0.41)	(1.11)	(0.98)	(0.54)
Female	12.2	46.1	35.9	5.8
	(2.57)	(2.70)	(2.41)	(1.57)
Nonrural				
Male	0.8	55.8	33.5	9.9
	(0.19)	(0.79)	(0.82)	(0.46)
Female	1.8	46.7	38.3	13.3
	(0.39)	(1.35)	(1.31)	(0.94)

NOTE: Standard errors in parentheses.

SOURCE: U.S. Department of Education, National Center for Education Statistics, Schools and Staffing Survey, 1987–88.

Table 6–14.—Average years of experience of rural and nonrural public school principals, by type of experience and sex: 1987–88

Setting and sex	Principal	Other administrator	Teacher	Other elementary/ secondary	Outside elementary/ secondary
Total	10.0	2.6	9.8	1.2	1.0
	(0.09)	(0.04)	(0.06)	(0.04)	(0.03)
School setting					
Rural	9.6	2.1	9.5	0.9	1.1
	(0.19)	(0.10)	(0.14)	(0.08)	(0.06)
Nonrural	10.3	2.9	10.0	1.2	1.0
	(0.11)	(0.05)	(0.07)	(0.04)	(0.04)
Sex					
Rural					
Male	10.4	2.2	8.9	0.9	1.1
	(0.19)	(0.11)	(0.12)	(0.07)	(0.08)
Female	5.7	1.5	12.3	1.2	1.1
	(0.32)	(0.20)	(0.45)	(0.22)	(0.14)
Nonrural					
Male	11.8	2.8	9.1	1.1	1.0
	(0.12)	(0.06)	(0.08)	(0.05)	(0.04)
Female	6.3	2.9	12.4	1.6	0.9
	(0.19)	(0.09)	(0.17)	(0.10)	(0.06)

NOTE: Standard errors in parentheses.

SOURCE: U.S. Department of Education, National Center for Education Statistics, Schools and Staffing Survey, 1987–88.

Table 6–15.—Average annual salary of rural and nonrural public school principals, by length of work year and sex: 1987–88

Setting and sex	All	10–month	11–month	12–month
Total	$41,963	$38,726	$41,563	$44,326
	(103.0)	(235.4)	(216.9)	(139.5)
School setting				
Rural	36,208	32,978	36,258	38,692
	(215.1)	(468.8)	(259.7)	(253.6)
Nonrural	44,884	42,250	44,082	46,995
	(112.5)	(249.6)	(282.5)	(173.7)
Sex				
Rural				
Male	36,952	34,032	36,643	39,205
	(195.1)	(402.3)	(284.0)	(277.9)
Female	32,342	28,772	34,246	35,176
	(666.2)	(1244.3)	(819.6)	(868.4)
Nonrural				
Male	45,309	42,808	44,120	47,425
	(144.2)	(306.4)	(301.5)	(182.3)
Female	43,682	41,140	43,714	45,622
	(244.5)	(470.9)	(520.0)	(413.5)

NOTE: Standard errors in parentheses.

SOURCE: U.S. Department of Education, National Center for Education Statistics, Schools and Staffing Survey, 1987–88.

Table 6–16.—Percentage of rural and nonrural public school principals receiving various benefits: 1987–88

School setting	Housing	Meals	Tuition for self	Medical insurance	Dental insurance	Life insurance	Transportation	Pension	None
Total	1.0	1.8	9.4	85.3	60.6	66.6	35.0	58.5	4.9
	(0.10)	(0.15)	(0.33)	(0.45)	(0.44)	(0.54)	(0.57)	(0.67)	(0.29)
Rural	2.7	3.5	9.8	80.5	47.5	54.3	35.9	51.7	7.7
	(0.32)	(0.39)	(0.51)	(0.82)	(1.21)	(1.04)	(1.08)	(1.39)	(0.65)
Nonrural	0.2	0.9	9.2	88.0	67.1	73.1	35.1	61.5	3.3
	(0.07)	(0.12)	(0.44)	(0.53)	(0.46)	(0.72)	(0.59)	(0.74)	(0.32)

NOTE: Standard errors in parentheses.

SOURCE: U.S. Department of Education, National Center for Education Statistics, Schools and Staffing Survey, 1987–88.

Table 6–17.—Percentage of rural and nonrural public school principals who reported that various groups had a great deal of influence on different activities, by level: 1987–88

Setting and level	Curriculum development			Teacher hiring			Discipline policy		
	District	Prin-cipal	Teach-ers	District	Prin-cipal	Teach-ers	District	Prin-cipal	Teach-ers
Total	54.0	54.5	51.5	52.1	75.1	8.5	62.3	80.6	51.6
	(0.47)	(0.47)	(0.61)	(0.65)	(0.56)	(0.34)	(0.61)	(0.44)	(0.53)
School setting									
Rural	43.1	63.8	57.6	50.4	78.2	8.2	59.2	84.1	51.9
	(1.06)	(1.04)	(1.19)	(1.07)	(1.21)	(0.42)	(0.94)	(0.86)	(0.98)
Nonrural	59.6	49.5	48.7	52.9	73.5	8.9	63.4	78.8	51.9
	(0.60)	(0.66)	(0.73)	(0.89)	(0.74)	(0.44)	(0.79)	(0.53)	(0.61)
Level									
Rural									
Elementary	45.8	60.2	58.6	52.0	77.5	8.3	59.2	83.7	55.4
	(1.27)	(1.61)	(1.62)	(1.50)	(1.61)	(0.54)	(1.21)	(1.17)	(1.49)
Secondary	39.1	70.9	56.8	45.1	81.1	8.3	58.5	86.1	45.6
	(2.15)	(1.81)	(1.82)	(1.76)	(1.60)	(0.79)	(2.30)	(1.36)	(1.72)
Combined	36.7	67.4	53.2	53.7	75.8	7.6	60.5	81.2	45.8
	(2.50)	(2.39)	(2.33)	(1.97)	(2.04)	(1.44)	(2.22)	(1.99)	(2.12)
Nonrural									
Elementary	61.5	46.7	47.7	55.3	71.7	8.4	63.9	77.5	54.5
	(0.74)	(0.87)	(0.90)	(1.13)	(0.94)	(0.56)	(0.94)	(0.70)	(0.81)
Secondary	54.8	56.2	51.7	45.5	79.1	10.0	62.0	82.5	44.4
	(1.19)	(1.14)	(1.13)	(0.98)	(0.78)	(0.73)	(1.33)	(0.82)	(1.07)
Combined	51.6	61.9	50.4	54.6	73.7	10.6	64.5	79.7	47.6
	(4.30)	(3.19)	(3.34)	(3.05)	(3.72)	(2.46)	(2.90)	(2.54)	(3.91)

NOTE: Standard errors in parentheses.

SOURCE: U.S. Department of Education, National Center for Education Statistics, Schools and Staffing Survey, 1987–88.

Table 6–18.—Percentage of rural and nonrural public school principals who rated selected problems in their schools as "serious," by level: 1987–88

Level	Student								Teacher absenteeism
	Tardiness	Absenteeism	Cutting	Physical conflict	Vandalism	Pregnancy	Alcohol use	Drug use	
Total	4.7	7.0	1.3	2.4	0.9	2.0	3.6	1.8	0.8
	(0.22)	(0.27)	(0.10)	(0.21)	(0.11)	(0.15)	(0.20)	(0.14)	(0.11)
Rural									
Elementary	1.3	3.5	—	1.2	0.6	—	0.6	0.2	0.4
	(0.46)	(0.76)	—	(0.30)	(0.24)	—	(0.20)	(0.10)	(0.18)
Secondary	5.9	10.6	2.0	0.6	0.4	6.5	14.9	4.8	0.8
	(1.10)	(1.21)	(0.48)	(0.29)	(0.23)	(1.00)	(1.41)	(0.76)	(0.33)
Combined	3.3	7.6	—	1.0	0.7	3.0	8.8	3.0	0.8
	(0.62)	(1.36)	—	(0.52)	(0.37)	(0.91)	(1.48)	(0.89)	(0.46)
Nonrural									
Elementary	3.3	3.6	0.2	3.3	0.8	0.3	0.3	0.4	0.7
	(0.32)	(0.36)	(0.10)	(0.37)	(0.16)	(0.09)	(0.10)	(0.09)	(0.15)
Secondary	12.9	17.9	5.4	1.9	1.1	6.2	10.0	6.1	1.0
	(0.60)	(0.97)	(0.56)	(0.35)	(0.24)	(0.54)	(0.87)	(0.68)	(0.29)
Combined	5.5	15.2	3.3	5.9	2.4	6.6	4.4	4.8	6.5
	(1.49)	(2.79)	(1.17)	(1.82)	(1.16)	(1.63)	(1.46)	(1.04)	(1.57)

—Too few cases for a reliable estimate.
NOTE: Standard errors in parentheses.

SOURCE: U.S. Department of Education, National Center for Education Statistics, Schools and Staffing Survey, 1987–88.

Table 8–1.—Classification of major state basic education aid programs, by state: 1986–87

Full state funded	Foundation programs		Percentage equalization		Guaranteed tax base/ yield programs	Flat grant programs
	Requires local effort	Effort not required	Requires local effort	Effort not required		
California	Arkansas	Arizona	New York	Alaska	Colorado	Alabama
Hawaii	Florida	Illinois	Rhode Island	Kansas	Connecticut	Delaware
New Mexico	Georgia	Indiana		Pennsylvania	Michigan	Kentucky
Washington	Idaho	Maine			New Jersey	Nebraska
	Iowa	Massachusetts			South Dakota	North Carolina
	Louisiana	New Hampshire			Wisconsin	
	Maryland	Oregon				
	Minnesota	Texas				
	Mississippi					
	Missouri					
	Montana					
	Nevada					
	North Dakota					
	Ohio					
	Oklahoma					
	South Carolina					
	Tennessee					
	Utah					
	Vermont					
	Virginia					
	West Virginia					
	Wyoming					
Subtotal: 4	22	8	2	3	6	5
Total: Full state funded: 4	Foundation programs: 30		Percentage equalization: 5		Guaranteed tax base/yield programs: 6	Flat grant programs: 5

SOURCE: Salmon, Richard G., Virginia Polytechnic and State University, Blacksburg, Virginia, 1991.

State	State mean	Total percent variation	Nonmetro mean	Nonmetro percent variation	Metro mean	Metro percent variation
Texas	2167.37	22.7	2253.76	24.7	1807.73	14.1
Nebraska	2816.17	21.0	2865.16	21.8	1953.90	8.2
New Mexico	2604.62	19.8	2626.62	20.9	2274.59	2.6
Kansas	2715.53	18.4	2768.73	19.4	2070.42	6.7
Utah	2397.20	18.4	2473.13	20.7	1922.62	3.8
Nevada	2723.46	17.8	2805.41	19.3	2108.80	6.2
Oklahoma	2063.42	16.7	2130.64	17.4	1760.90	13.9
Idaho	1922.15	16.0	1928.07	16.3	1667.73	0
South Dakota	2124.81	15.9	2130.41	16.2	1766.39	0
Colorado	2700.93	15.7	2788.72	17.1	2235.68	8.6
Montana	2982.28	15.6	3004.91	16.1	2371.10	2.1
North Dakota	2559.92	14.3	2590.29	14.9	2187.99	7.2
Oregon	3156.68	13.9	3291.29	15.1	2685.54	9.7
Minnesota	2541.95	13.7	2601.29	14.3	2278.61	11.0
Michigan	2076.03	13.7	2028.96	13.9	2206.53	13.0
Missouri	1745.54	13.6	1746.06	14.0	1742.55	11.5
Maine	1887.43	12.8	1936.57	13.4	1674.49	10.5
Wisconsin	2175.98	12.4	2212.76	13.0	2077.22	10.8
Virginia	1926.11	12.3	1885.05	11.0	2000.19	13.7
Wyoming	3558.80	11.8	3579.48	12.4	3103.91	0
Tennessee	1334.73	11.5	1316.86	11.0	1382.17	12.9
Vermont	1987.23	11.4	2021.63	9.8	1780.83	21.2
California	2691.64	11.1	3022.30	17.2	2403.65	5.8
Illinois	2040.34	10.8	2074.88	10.7	1939.36	11.0
Iowa	2321.46	10.8	2332.51	10.9	2233.02	9.5
Louisiana	2067.22	10.8	2126.65	10.7	1926.47	11.0
Washington	2428.85	10.7	2473.93	12.9	2314.09	5.0
Pennsylvania	1988.54	10.7	1949.22	12.6	2029.04	8.8
Georgia	1531.18	10.5	1547.37	10.0	1479.63	12.1
Ohio	1975.72	10.2	1966.33	11.4	1989.28	8.5
Indiana	1780.63	10.2	1792.89	11.6	1755.30	7.1
New Hampshire	1900.02	10.1	2000.70	11.3	1665.09	7.2
Mississippi	1448.18	9.5	1467.45	9.5	1244.41	9.7
New York	2806.43	9.5	2749.76	9.0	2855.80	9.9
Massachusetts	2436.91	9.4	3025.28	17.4	2201.56	6.2
Kentucky	1454.22	8.8	1463.37	9.1	1405.56	7.1
South Carolina	1732.42	8.8	1753.25	8.7	1673.39	9.1
Delaware	2075.51	8.1	2149.91	12.2	1926.70	0
Alabama	1479.09	8.1	1513.70	8.3	1391.63	7.5
Maryland	2173.33	7.9	2245.86	8.3	2129.81	7.6
Arkansas	1644.04	7.8	1665.38	7.5	1505.38	9.8
West Virginia	2157.69	7.4	2165.74	7.7	2121.46	6.2
Arizona	2047.71	7.3	2085.21	8.4	1822.71	1.0
Florida	1996.92	7.2	2101.04	8.1	1876.00	6.3
North Carolina	1869.41	7.0	1909.64	7.0	1748.71	6.8
Connecticut	2198.79	6.9	2008.10	7.2	2262.35	6.8
New Jersey	2498.80	6.6	*	*	2498.80	6.6
Rhode Island	2270.85	4.8	2435.60	0	2229.67	6.0

* Not applicable

NOTE: Percent variation is measured using coefficient of dispersion from respective (State, State nonmetro, or State metro) mean expenditure per pupil. The presence of only one county of type metro or nonmetro results in 0 variation. Estimates of school enrollment by county were derived by multiplying the proportion of the population aged 7–18 years in 1980 in each county by county population in 1982. Estimates are biased to the extent that there are private school students and that there has been a change in the composition of the population of 7 to 18 years since 1980. Alaska and Hawaii are not included in the rankings because county boundaries and funding practices distort results.

SOURCE: Jansen, Anicca. "Rural Counties Lead Urban in Spending but is that Enough?" *Rural Development Perspectives* 7 (1) October 1990–January 1991.

Table 8–3.—Provisions in state funding formulas for additional revenue for rural school districts: 1989–90

State	No factor	Small	Sparsity/ isolated	Small & isolated	Combination	Other
Total	19	10	6	9	2	3
Alabama	X					
Alaska				X		
Arizona				X		
Arkansas					X	
California				X		
Colorado		X				
Connecticut	X					
Delaware	X					
Florida			X			
Georgia			X			
Hawaii						N/A
Idaho			X			
Illinois	X					
Indiana	X					
Iowa						X
Kansas		X				
Kentucky	X					
Louisiana		X				
Maine				X		
Maryland	X					
Massachusetts	X					
Michigan	X					
Minnesota				X		
Mississippi	X					
Missouri						X
Montana		X				
Nebraska			X			
Nevada		X				
New Hampshire	X					
New Jersey	X					
New Mexico		X				
New York	X					
North Carolina			X			
North Dakota		X				
Ohio		X				
Oklahoma		X				
Oregon				X		
Pennsylvania					X	
Rhode Island	X					
South Carolina	X					
South Dakota						X
Tennessee	X					
Texas				X		
Utah				X		
Vermont	X					
Virginia		X				
Washington				X		
West Virginia			X			
Wisconsin	X					
Wyoming	X					

SOURCE: Verstegen, D.A., *School Finance at a Glance*, Denver, CO: Education Commission of the States: 1990.

Table 9–1.—NAEP reading assessment: national and extreme rural mean proficiency levels, by age and year of assessment

Age and group		Year					
		1971	1975	1980	1984	1988	1990
9	Nation	208	210	216	211	212	209
	Rural	200	204	212	201	214	209
	Delta	* -8	* -6	-4	* -10	2	0
13	Nation	255	256	259	257	257	257
	Rural	247	249	255	255	262	251
	Delta	* -8	* -7	-4	-2	5	-6
17	Nation	285	286	286	289	290	290
	Rural	277	282	279	283	287	290
	Delta	* -8	-4	-7	-6	-3	0

* Negative rural difference at the $p \leq .05$ level.

NOTE: Delta is the difference between the national mean and the rural mean.

SOURCE: National Center for Education Statistics, *Trends in Academic Progress*, 1991; and special tabulations.

Table 9–2.—NAEP writing assessment: national and extreme rural mean proficiency levels, by grade and year of assessment

Grade and group		Year		
		1984	1988	1990
4	Nation	179	185	183
	Rural	154	185	186
	Delta	-25	0	3
8	Nation	207	203	197
	Rural	203	205	200
	Delta	-4	2	3
11	Nation	212	214	211
	Rural	206	215	211
	Delta	-6	1	0

NOTE: Delta is the difference between the national mean and the rural mean.

SOURCE: National Center for Education Statistics, *Trends in Academic Progress*, 1991; and special tabulations.

Table 9–3.—NAEP mathematics assessment: national and extreme rural mean proficiency levels, by age and year of assessment

Age and group		Year			
		1978	1982	1986	1990
9	Nation	218	219	221	230
	Rural	212	211	219	231
	Delta	-6	*-8	-2	1
13	Nation	264	268	269	270
	Rural	255	258	270	265
	Delta	*-9	*-10	1	-5
17	Nation	301	299	302	305
	Rural	295	293	305	304
	Delta	*-6	*-6	3	1

* Negative rural difference at the $p \leq .05$ level.

NOTE: Delta is the difference between the national mean and the rural mean.

SOURCE: National Center for Education Statistics, *Trends in Academic Progress,* 1991; and special tabulations.

Table 9–4.—NAEP science assessment: national and extreme rural mean proficiency levels, by age and year of assessment

Age and group		Year			
		1977	1982	1986	1990
9	Nation	220	221	225	229
	Rural	225	212	224	233
	Delta	5	-9	-1	4
13	Nation	247	250	252	255
	Rural	245	245	258	249
	Delta	-2	-5	6	-6
17	Nation	290	283	289	291
	Rural	289	283	296	294
	Delta	-1	0	7	3

NOTE: Delta is the difference between the national mean and the rural mean.

SOURCE: National Center for Education Statistics, *Trends in Academic Progress*, 1991; and special tabulations.

Table 9–5.—Recent NAEP assessments: national and extreme rural mean proficiency levels for six subject areas, by grade and year of assessment

		Subject					
		History	Writing	Civics	Reading	Math	Science
Grade and group		1988	1990	1988	1990	1990	1990
4	Nation	221	183	214	209	230	229
	Rural	220	186	215	209	231	233
	Delta	-1	3	1	0	1	4
8	Nation	264	197	260	257	270	255
	Rural	267	200	269	251	265	249
	Delta	3	3	*9	-6	-5	-6
12	Nation	295	211	296	290	305	291
	Rural	296	211	299	290	304	294
	Delta	1	0	3	0	-1	3

* Positive rural difference at the p≤ .05 level. The oldest students receiving the writing assessment were in the 11th grade. Students taking the reading, math, and science assessments were identified by age rather than grade. However, their ages, 9, 13, and 17, were those usually associated with the sequence of grades noted on this table.

NOTE: Delta is the difference between the national mean and the rural mean.

SOURCE: National Center for Education Statistics, *Trends in Academic Progress*, 1991; *The Civics Report Card*, 1990; *The U.S. History Report Card*, 1990; and special tabulations.

Table 9–6.—Recent NAEP assessments: disadvantaged urban and extreme rural mean proficiency levels for six subject areas, by grade and year of assessment

		Subject					
		History	Writing	Civics	Reading	Math	Science
Grade and group		1988	1990	1988	1990	1990	1990
4	Urban disadvantaged	198	159	193	186	214	209
	Rural	220	186	215	209	231	233
	Delta score	*22	*27	*22	*23	*17	*24
8	Urban disadvantaged	246	189	241	241	253	227
	Rural	267	200	269	251	265	249
	Delta score	*21	11	*29	10	*12	*22
12	Urban disadvantaged	274	196	274	273	285	254
	Rural	296	211	299	290	304	294
	Delta score	*22	*15	*25	*17	*19	*40

* Positive rural difference at the p≤ .05 level. The oldest students receiving the writing assessment were in the 11th grade. Students taking the reading, math, and science assessments were identified by age rather than grade. However, their ages, 9, 13, and 17, were those usually associated with the sequence of grades noted on this table.

NOTE: Delta is the difference between the national mean and the rural mean.

SOURCE: National Center for Education Statistics, *Trends in Academic Progress*, 1991; *The Civics Report Card*, 1990; *The U.S. History Report Card*, 1990; and special tabulations.

Table 9–7.—Recent NAEP assessments: advantaged urban and extreme rural mean proficiency levels for six subject areas, by grade and year of assessment

		Subject					
		History	Writing	Civics	Reading	Math	Science
Grade and group		1988	1990	1988	1990	1990	1990
4	Urban advantaged	236	195	226	227	244	241
	Rural	220	186	215	209	231	233
	Delta score	* -16	-9	* -11	* -18	* -13	-8
8	Urban advantaged	276	217	270	270	283	268
	Rural	267	200	269	251	265	249
	Delta score	* -9	* -17	-1	* -19	* -18	* -19
12	Urban advantaged	308	221	310	300	317	305
	Rural	296	211	299	290	304	294
	Delta score	* -12	-10	* -11	-10	* -13	-11

* Negative rural difference at the $p \leq .05$ level. The oldest students receiving the writing assessment were in the 11th grade. Students taking the reading, math and science assessments were identified by age rather than grade. However, their ages, 9, 13, and 17, were those usually associated with the sequence of grades noted on this table.

NOTE: Delta is the difference between the national mean and the rural mean.

SOURCE: National Center for Education Statistics, *Trends in Academic Progress*, 1991; *The Civics Report Card*, 1990; *The U.S. History Report Card*, 1990; and special tabulations.

Table 9–8.—NELS: 88 eighth-grade test scores in four subject areas, by urbanicity

	Subject			
Group	Science	Mathematics	Reading	History/ Government
National mean	9.87	15.95	10.31	15.11
Delta				
Rural	+.14	-.43	-.23	-.28
Urban	-1.05	* -1.73	* -.72	* -1.02
Suburban	* +.49	* +1.29	* +.58	* +.77

* Significant at the $p \leq 0.5$ level.

NOTE: Delta is the difference between the national mean and the community type.

SOURCE: U.S. Department of Education, National Center for Education Statistics, *The Tested Achievement of the National Education Longitudinal Study of 1988 Eighth Grade Class.*

Table 9–9.—Percentage of 1988 eighth graders with one or more risk factors, by urbanicity

Community type	Risk factors		
	None	One	Two or more
Total	54.40	25.67	19.92
Standard Error	0.648	0.366	0.514
Unweighted N	22,651	22,651	22,651
Weighted (1,000s)	2,816	2,816	2,816
Rural	52.13	26.07	21.79
Standard Error	1.078	0.610	0.899
Unweighted N	6,423	6,423	6,423
Weighted (1,000s)	902	902	902
Urban	47.20	26.74	26.06
Standard Error	1.352	0.717	1.084
Unweighted N	6,859	6,859	6,859
Weighted (1,000s)	689	689	689
Suburban	60.13	24.78	15.09
Standard Error	0.953	0.585	0.716
Unweighted N	9,369	9,369	9,369
Weighted (1,000s)	1,224	1,224	1,224

NOTE: Risk factors include single-parent family, low parent education, limited English, low family income, sibling dropout, and more than 3 hours home alone.

SOURCE: U.S. Department of Education, National Center for Education Statistics, National Education Longitudinal Study of 1988: Base Year Student Survey.

Table 9-10.—Percentage of 1988 eighth graders with various risk factors, by urbanicity

							Risk factors						
Urbanicity	Parent is single		Parents have no h.s. diploma		Limited English proficiency		Income less than $15,000		Has a sibling who dropped out		Home alone more than three hours	
	yes	no	yes	no	yes	no	yes	no	yes	no	yes	no
Total	21.66	78.34	10.23	89.77	2.07	97.93	21.13	78.87	6.39	93.61	13.49	86.51
Standard error	0.441	0.441	0.422	0.422	0.281	0.281	0.574	0.574	0.208	0.208	0.269	0.269
Unweighted	22,433	22,433	22,626	22,626	22,409	22,409	21,594	21,594	21,967	21,967	22,219	22,219
Weighted (1,000s)	2,790	2,790	2,813	2,813	2,785	2,785	2,689	2,689	2,735	2,735	2,761	2,2761
Urban	28.73	71.27	12.08	87.92	2.83	97.17	26.86	73.14	6.90	93.10	14.80	85.20
Standard error	1.048	1.048	0.833	0.833	0.465	0.465	1.215	1.215	0.413	0.413	0.539	0.539
Unweighted	6,774	6,774	6,844	6,844	6,772	6,772	6,509	6,509	6,623	6,623	6,697	6,697
Weighted (1,000s)	681	681	688	688	679	679	655	655	665	665	671	671
Suburban	18.82	81.18	8.10	91.90	1.65	98.35	14.47	85.53	5.61	94.39	12.62	87.38
Standard error	0.577	0.577	0.630	0.630	0.262	0.262	0.788	0.788	0.315	0.315	0.429	0.429
Unweighted	9,284	9,284	9,363	9,363	9,271	9,271	8,925	8,925	9,094	9,094	9,206	9,206
Weighted (1,000s)	1,213	1,213	1,224	1,224	1,211	1,211	1,168	1,168	1,191	1,191	1,203	1,203
Rural	20.16	79.84	11.72	88.28	2.06	97.94	25.79	74.71	7.06	92.94	13.69	86.31
Standard error	0.669	0.669	0.774	0.774	0.720	0.720	0.966	0.966	0.374	0.374	0.442	0.442
Unweighted	6,375	6,375	6,419	6,419	6,366	6,366	6,160	6,160	6,250	6,250	6,316	6,316
Weighted (1,000s)	896	896	902	902	894	894	865	865	879	879	887	887

SOURCE: U.S. Department of Education, National Center for Education Statistics, National Education Longitudinal Study of 1988: Base Year Student Survey.

Table 9–11a.—Percentage of schools offering levels of mathematics courses, by graduating class size: 1980

Course	Graduating class size						
	(<25)	(25-49)	(50-99)	(100-199)	(200-299)	(300-399)	(>400)
Base:	80.7	100.0	87.8	87.7	90.8	85.8	80.8
Advanced:							
At least 1 + base	72.3	100.0	85.4	87.8	90.8	85.8	80.8
At least 2 + base	59.9	94.0	83.4	87.0	89.3	85.5	80.8
At least 3 + base	34.8	61.0	64.1	80.7	81.5	76.7	76.5
Alternative:							
At least 1	74.4	95.9	90.8	94.9	96.6	93.4	96.8
At least 2	29.9	47.4	59.5	80.8	93.3	88.9	83.6
At least 3	19.5	2.4	38.3	50.9	78.3	76.7	73.0
At least 4	–	–	22.1	28.7	51.2	49.7	43.5
Weighted N	1,541	1,844	2,650	2,611	1,435	821	674
Unweighted N	14	18	52	103	106	84	104

SOURCE: Haller, Emil J. et al. "School Size and Program Comprehensiveness." *Educational Evaluation and Policy Analysis* 12(2), 109–116.

Table 9–11b.—Percentage of schools offering levels of science courses, by graduating class size: 1980

Course	Graduating class size						
	(<25)	(25-49)	(50-99)	(100-199)	(200-299)	(300-399)	(>400)
Base:	56.4	67.2	57.4	69.1	82.4	71.5	77.5
Advanced:							
At least 1 + base	45.4	67.2	55.6	68.9	80.8	70.6	75.9
At least 2 + base	26.5	38.2	49.8	66.9	76.5	70.6	74.3
At least 3 + base	10.9	34.1	45.3	51.0	68.1	67.0	71.7
Alternative:							
At least 1	52.4	33.1	61.7	64.7	71.8	71.2	76.4
At least 2	11.0	4.7	26.4	21.9	26.9	39.6	45.0
At least 3	11.0	–	3.7	7.3	6.0	20.9	17.4
At least 4	–	–	–	2.0	–	2.9	2.8
Weighted N	1,541	1,844	2,650	2,611	1,435	821	674
Unweighted N	14	18	52	103	106	84	104

SOURCE: Haller, Emil J. et al. "School Size and Program Comprehensiveness." *Educational Evaluation and Policy Analysis* 12(2), 109–116.

Table 9–11c.—Percentage of schools offering levels of foreign language courses, by graduating class size: 1980

Course	Graduating class size						
	(<25)	(25-49)	(50-99)	(100-199)	(200-299)	(300-399)	(>400)
Base:	36.8	54.0	77.9	93.5	97.0	90.5	96.8
Advanced:							
At least 1+base	25.9	41.4	71.4	92.3	94.7	90.5	96.0
At least 2+base	9.1	17.7	39.8	79.4	93.2	89.6	96.0
At least 3+base	9.1	—	23.7	59.7	82.0	88.3	94.3
Alternative:							
At least 1	—	—	5.0	2.6	11.7	16.4	19.0
At least 2	—	—	—	0.9	3.4	4.6	5.2
At least 3	—	—	—	—	1.5	2.7	—
At least 4	—	—	—	—	—	—	—
Weighted N	1,541	1,844	2,650	2,611	1,435	821	674
Unweighted N	14	18	52	103	106	84	104

SOURCE: Haller, Emil J. et al. "School Size and Program Comprehensiveness." *Educational Evaluation and Policy Analysis* 12(2), 109–116.

Table 9–11d.—Percentage of schools offering different foreign language courses, by graduating class size: 1980

Number of languages offered	Graduating class size						
	(<25)	(25-49)	(50-99)	(100-199)	(200-299)	(300-399)	(>400)
0	63.2	46.0	22.1	6.5	3.0	9.5	3.2
1	29.7	48.1	54.8	26.9	2.2	1.6	1.1
2	7.1	5.9	20.2	48.2	31.5	11.1	7.1
3	—	—	2.9	12.8	39.4	40.0	35.6
4	—	—	—	4.8	14.8	36.0	40.1
5	—	—	—	0.8	4.6	1.0	9.8
6	—	—	—	—	3.0	—	3.1
7	—	—	—	—	1.5	0.2	—
Weighted N	1,541	1,844	2,650	2,611	1,435	821	674
Unweighted N	14	18	52	103	106	84	104

SOURCE: Haller, Emil J. et al. "School Size and Program Comprehensiveness." *Educational Evaluation and Policy Analysis* 12(2), 109–116.

Table 9–12.—NELS:88 eighth-grade test scores in four subject areas, by school size

Group	Subject			
	Science	Mathematics	Reading	History/Government
National Mean	9.87	15.95	10.31	15.11
Delta				
Size < 500	* +.39	* +.75	* +.53	* +.71
500 – 999	-.11	-.26	-.21	- .31
> 1000	* -.54	* -.85	* -.48	* -.63

* Significant at the p≤ .05 level.

NOTE: Delta is the difference between the mean for a group and the nation.

SOURCE: U.S. Department of Education, National Center for Education Statistics, *The Tested Achievement of the National Education Longitudinal Study of 1988 Eighth Grade Class*, 1991.

Table 10–1.—Jobs 1980 nonrural and rural high school seniors reported they expected to have by age 30

Job	Percentage	
	Nonrural	Rural
Clerical	11.3	11.6
Craftsman	5.9	9.3
Farmer	0.5	3.5
Housewife	1.2	3.4
Laborer	0.7	2.7
Manager/administrator	7.6	5.3
Military	2.5	2.6
Operative	1.9	3.9
Professional (lower)	29.1	24.2
Professional (higher)	15.2	9.0
Proprietor/owner	2.9	3.3
Protective services	1.7	1.7
Sales	1.8	1.8
School teacher	3.5	4.2
Service	3.3	4.1
Technical	9.7	8.1
Not working	1.3	1.5

SOURCE: Cobb, R.A., W.G. McIntire, and P.A. Pratt. 1989. Vocational and Educational Aspirations of High School Students: A Problem for Rural America. *Research in Rural Education* 6 (2): 11–16.

Table 10–2.—Educational expectations of the high school class of 1980, by location

Expectation	Location		
	Urban	Suburban	Rural
	Percent		
Less than high school	0.7	0.3	0.8
High school graduate only	14.1	13.7	22.8
Less than 2 years at business or vocational school	5.8	6.4	10.2
Two years or more at business or vocational school	11.9	10.3	12.8
Less than 2 years college	3.2	2.8	2.8
Two or more years of college with associate's degree	12.3	12.6	12.6
Finish college with bachelor's	26.1	27.8	22.6
Master's or equivalent	13.1	14.2	9.0
Ph.D., M.D. or equivalent	12.9	11.8	6.3

SOURCE: Cobb, R.A., W.G. McIntire, and P.A. Pratt. 1989. Vocational and Educational Aspirations of High School Students: A Problem for Rural America. *Research in Rural Education* 6 (2): 11–16.

Table 10–3.—Lowest acceptable level of education expressed by the high school class of 1980, by location

Level	Location		
	Urban	Suburban	Rural
	Percent		
Less than high school	1.8	1.1	1.9
High school graduate only	24.1	25.5	37.3
Less than 2 years at business or vocational school	5.5	5.7	8.8
Two years or more at business or vocational school	10.0	9.0	10.7
Less than 2 years college	6.4	5.7	5.2
Two or more years of college with associate's degree	18.4	18.3	14.6
B.S./B.A. degree	22.6	24.9	18.1
Master's degree	7.2	6.1	3.2
Ph.D. degree	4.2	3.7	2.1

SOURCE: Cobb, R.A., W.G. McIntire, and P.A. Pratt. 1989. *Vocational and Educational Aspirations of High School Students: A Problem for Rural America. Research in Rural Education* 6 (2): 11–16.

Table 10–4.—Postsecondary educational plans of 1980 high school seniors, by SES quartile and location

Plans	Total*			Lowest quartile			Second quartile			Third quartile			Highest quartile		
	Urban	Suburb	Rural	Urban	Suburb	Rural	Urban	Suburb	Rural	Urban	Suburb	Rural	Urban	Suburb	Rural
Total N	1,792	4,470	2846	549	792	863	414	1,032	812	423	1,186	634	352	1,397	509
								Percentage							
No plans	16.9	15.7	23.8	24.7	33.6	38.9	18.9	21.7	25.1	13.9	11.0	13.4	3.5	4.1	8.1
Vocational-tech.	18.1	18.1	22.1	24.6	23.4	26.9	20.5	25.2	27.7	16.1	20.7	19.9	8.0	7.7	7.7
Less than 4-year degree	13.8	15.9	15.4	13.6	17.4	14.1	13.9	17.3	18.2	16.0	16.6	17.5	11.0	13.0	11.4
BA/BS degree	27.7	26.5	23.5	20.3	15.0	13.7	29.5	21.7	17.2	31.4	30.3	33.7	34.8	33.6	38.0
Advanced degree	23.5	23.8	15.1	16.8	9.6	6.5	17.3	14.0	11.7	22.6	21.4	15.5	42.7	41.6	34.8

*The total sample is slightly larger than the sum of the quartile samples because of missing values on the SES quartile variable.

SOURCE: U.S. Department of Education, National Center for Education Statistics, High School and Beyond, 1980–1986.

Table 10–5.—1980 high school program type, by SES quartile and location

Type	Total*			Lowest quartile			Second quartile			Third quartile			Highest quartile		
	Urban	Suburb	Rural	Urban	Suburb	Rural	Urban	Suburb	Rural	Urban	Suburb	Rural	Urban	Suburb	Rural
Total N	1,804	4,532	2,889	537	792	868	419	1,032	821	426	1,211	642	355	1,428	511
							Percentage								
General	33.1	33.5	42.5	34.4	43.2	46.3	34.1	37.2	44.7	34.4	33.0	44.8	28.3	25.8	29.5
Academic	39.1	43.5	32.5	28.0	22.8	17.7	37.6	33.9	26.8	38.7	44.3	37.8	62.4	61.9	61.9
Vocational	27.8	23.1	25.0	37.6	34.0	36.1	28.3	29.0	28.5	26.9	22.7	17.4	9.4	12.3	8.6

*The total sample is slightly larger than the sum of the quartile samples because of missing values on the SES quartile variable.

SOURCE: U.S. Department of Education, National Center for Education Statistics, High School and Beyond, 1980–1986.

121

Table 10–6.—Parental expectations of children's post-high school experience as reported by nonrural and rural students

Expectation	Father		Mother	
	Nonrural	Rural	Nonrural	Rural
	Percent			
College	57.9	49.2	72.3	60.0
Full-time job	8.5	14.1	9.2	14.1
Trade school	6.0	9.5	7.7	11.5
Military	3.1	4.1	2.9	3.2
They don't care	2.5	3.9	1.6	3.1
I don't know	8.8	9.9	3.8	5.7
Does not apply	13.2	9.3	2.4	2.3

SOURCE: Cobb, R.A., W.G. McIntire, and P.A. Pratt. 1989. Vocational and Educational Aspirations of High School Students: A Problem for Rural America. *Research in Rural Education* 6 (2): 11–16.

Table 10–7.—Persistence in postsecondary education by members of the high school class of 1980 who had entered college between 1980 and 1984, by location

Years in college	Rural		Suburban		Urban	
	Number	Percent	Number	Percent	Number	Percent
1 year or less	511	28.3	778	23.0	323	25.0
2 years	315	17.5	668	19.8	271	20.9
3 years	320	17.8	594	17.6	220	17.0
4 years	656	36.4	1,337	39.6	479	37.0

SOURCE: U.S. Department of Education, National Center for Education Statistics, High School and Beyond, 1980–1986.

Table 10–8.—Education aspirations and attainment of rural, suburban, and urban youth: 1980–86

Aspiration and attainment	Rural stayers[*]	Rural leavers[*]	Suburban	Urban
		Percentage		
Total N	966	1,961	4,597	1,848
Aspirations				
Post-secondary (1980)				
No college	28	16	16	17
Some college	26	24	21	21
College degree	46	61	63	62
Post-secondary (1986)				
No college	2	1	1	1
Some college	28	17	19	20
College degree	70	82	81	79
		Months		
Attainment				
Mean months of college (1980–84)				
All subjects	12.8	18.4	18.6	17.1
Mean months of college (1980–84)				
Subjects with college	21.6	25.1	24.2	23.5
		Percentage		
Attainment (1986)				
No college	64	56	59	64
Some college	20	20	19	19
College degree	16	24	23	18
Post-secondary attainment as a function of educational aspirations (1980)				
More college	5	3	3	2
Less college	49	54	56	60

[*]"Stayers" were 1980 rural seniors who were still living in rural areas in 1986, whereas "leavers" were those 1980 rural seniors who were not living in rural communities in 1986.

SOURCE: McIntire, W.G., D.A. Mirochnik, P.A. Pratt, and R.A. Cobb. 1992. Choosing to Stay or Leave: A Continuing Dilemma for Rural Youth. Presented at the *Creating the Quality School* Conference, Norman, OK.

Table 10–9.—Percentage of adults[1] who have completed 4 or more years of high school, by year, race, and community type

Year	Race	Community type	
		Nonmetro	Metro
1970	Black	18.4	34.5
	Hispanic	26.5	33.2
	White	48.7	57.9
1977	Black	31.1	45.5
	Hispanic[2]	36.0	43.1
	White	60.7	70.3
1987	Black	48.6	66.5
	Hispanic	42.9	51.5
	White	70.7	78.9
1991	Black	49.3	70.2
	Hispanic	46.5	51.7
	White	73.9	81.7

[1] Persons 25 years and older.
[2] Data are for 1979.

SOURCE: U.S. Bureau of the Census. Current Population Reports. Series P–20, No. 356; Series P–23, No. 75; Series P–20, No. 428.

Table 10–10.—Percentage of adults[1] who have completed fewer than 5 years of elementary school, by year, race, and community type

Year	Race	Community type	
		Nonmetro	Metro
1970	Black	26.2	11.0
	Hispanic	26.7	18.2
	White	5.2	3.9
1977	Black	18.7	7.1
	Hispanic[2]	26.1	16.2
	White	3.7	2.7
1987	Black	10.3	3.9
	Hispanic	15.0	8.5
	White	2.2	2.0
1991	Black	8.2	4.0
	Hispanic	14.8	12.3
	White	1.9	2.0

[1] Persons 25 years and older.
[2] Data are for 1979.

SOURCE: U.S. Bureau of the Census. Current Population Reports. Series P–20, No. 356; Series P–23, No. 75; Series P–20, No. 428.

Table 10–11.—Status dropout rate ages 16–24, by region and metropolitan status: selected years, October 1975–October 1990

Region and status	October				
	1975	1980	1985	1989	1990
	Percentage				
Total	13.9	14.1	12.6	12.6	12.1
	(0.26)	(0.26)	(0.27)	(0.31)	(0.30)
Region					
Northeast	11.3	10.4	9.9	9.3	8.7
	(0.51)	(0.49)	(0.53)	(0.60)	(0.59)
Midwest	10.9	11.5	9.8	9.0	9.1
	(0.45)	(0.45)	(0.48)	(0.53)	(0.54)
South	18.9	18.2	15.2	15.1	14.5
	(0.53)	(0.50)	(0.51)	(0.57)	(0.56)
West	13.0	14.9	14.6	16.2	14.7
	(0.61)	(0.61)	(0.66)	(0.76)	(0.72)
Metropolitan status					
Central city	15.7	16.9	15.3	15.4	15.5
	(0.50)	(0.52)	(0.56)	(0.59)	(0.59)
Suburban	10.2	11.1	10.0	10.7	9.9
	(0.37)	(0.37)	(0.38)	(0.42)	(0.41)
Nonmetropolitan	16.8	15.3	13.6	12.6	11.7
	(0.51)	(0.48)	(0.51)	(0.67)	(0.65)

NOTE: Standard errors in parentheses

SOURCE: U.S. Department of Commerce, Bureau of the Census, "School Enrollment-Social and Economic Characteristics of Students," October (various years), Current Population Reports, Series P–20, and unpublished tabulations.

Table 10–12.—Educational attainment of 25–44-year-olds, by county type: selected years

Item	1971	1975	1979	1983	1987
Completed high school					
			Percentage		
Metro	73.7	79.6	83.2	85.7	87.1
Nonmetro	65.6	70.7	77.8	80.8	82.7
			Percentage points		
Nonmetro gap	8.1	8.9	5.4	4.9	4.4
Completed 1 or more years of college					
			Percentage		
Metro	31.9	38.9	44.2	47.9	49.1
Nonmetro	21.2	25.9	34.3	35.3	34.2
			Percentage points		
Nonmetro gap	10.7	13.0	9.9	12.6	14.9
Completed 4 or more years of college					
			Percentage		
Metro	17.0	21.4	24.0	26.8	27.5
Nonmetro	10.8	13.8	17.5	18.0	16.2
			Percentage points		
Nonmetro gap	6.2	6.6	6.5	8.8	11.3

SOURCE: U.S. Department of Commerce, Bureau of the Census. Current Population Reports, Series P–20, various issues.

Table 10–13.—Share of counties with one or more colleges and universities: 1986

Type of school	Total	Metro	Nonmetro		
			Total	Adjacent	Non-adjacent
			Percentage		
Public					
University	2.2	7.9	0.6	0.5	0.6
4–year college	13.1	33.7	6.9	6.6	7.1
Any 4–year college					
or university	15.0	40.0	7.5	7.1	7.7
2–year college	23.5	50.7	15.3	17.2	14.2
Any public college					
or university	31.4	64.5	21.5	22.3	20.9
Private					
University	1.0	4.1	0	.1	0
4–year college	17.8	47.2	9.0	13.0	6.4
Any 4–year college					
or university	17.9	47.5	9.0	13.0	6.4

SOURCE: U.S. Department of Health and Human Services, Bureau of Health Professionals, Area Resources File: 1988.

Table 10–14.—Educational attainment by rural youth in the high school class of 1980, by census division: 1986

Census division	High school diploma*		License or 2–3 year vocational		BS/BA or advanced degree **	
	Number	Percent	Number	Percent	Number	Percent
New England	119	48.1	55	22.0	74	29.9
Mid-Atlantic	189	63.3	60	20.2	49	16.5
East North Central	271	60.3	85	18.9	94	20.8
West North Central	249	52.6	117	24.8	107	22.6
South Atlantic	324	63.4	91	17.9	96	18.7
East South Central	176	72.6	33	13.5	34	13.9
West South Central	222	67.5	65	19.9	42	12.7
Mountain	151	74.5	37	18.1	15	7.4
Pacific	105	60.6	43	24.9	25	14.5

* Includes those students who did not complete high school (approximately 0.2%).
** This category includes those students with an advanced degree (approximately 0.5%).

SOURCE: U.S. Department of Education, National Center for Education Statistics, High School and Beyond, 1980–1986.

B. Statistical Data Sources and Methodology

Sources and Comparability of Data

The information presented in this report was obtained mainly from federal sources. The data were collected using many research methods, including surveys of a universe (such as school districts) or of a sample, compilations of administrative records, and statistical projections. Users of this report should take particular care when comparing data from different sources. Differences in procedures, timing, phrasing of questions, interviewer training, and so forth mean that the results from the different sources may not be strictly comparable. Following are general descriptions of the information sources and data collection methods, grouped by sponsoring organization.

Accuracy of Data

The accuracy of any statistic is determined by the joint effects of sampling and nonsampling errors. Estimates based on a sample will differ somewhat from the figures that would have been obtained if a complete census had been taken using the same survey instruments, instructions, and procedures. In addition to such sampling errors, all surveys, universe and sample, are subject to design, reporting, and processing errors and errors due to nonresponse. To the extent possible, these nonsampling errors are kept to a minimum by methods built into the survey procedures.

Chapter 2

Employment and earnings data

Data on nonmetro employment, unemployment and earnings come from the monthly Current Population Survey (CPS), conducted by the Bureau of the Census for the U.S. Department of Labor. It provides detailed information on the labor force, employment, unemployment, and demographic characteristics of the metro and nonmetro population. CPS derives estimates based on a national sample of about 58,000 households that are representative of the U.S. civilian noninstitutional population 16 years of age and over. Labor force information is based on respondents' activity during 1 week each month. The labor force participation rate describes civilian labor as a percentage of the civilian noninstitutional population age 16 and older.

Metro areas. Metropolitan Statistical Areas (MSAs), as defined by the Office of Management and Budget, include core counties containing a city of 50,000 or more people and a total area population of at least 100,000. Additional contiguous counties are included in the MSA if they are economically and socially integrated with the core county. Metro areas are divided into central cities and areas outside central cities (suburbs).

Throughout this chapter "urban" and "metro" have been used interchangeably to refer to people and places within MSAs.

Nonmetro areas. These are counties outside metro area boundaries. Throughout this chapter, "rural" and "nonmetro" are used interchangeably to refer to people and places outside of MSAs.

Chapter 3

Common Core of Data

The National Center for Education Statistics (NCES) uses the Common Core of Data (CCD) survey to acquire and maintain statistical data on the 50 states, the District of Columbia, and the outlying areas from the universe of state-level education agencies. Information about staff and students is collected annually at the school, local education agency (LEA) or school district), and state levels. Information about revenues and expenditures is also collected at the state level.

Data are collected for a particular school year (July 1–June 30) via survey instruments sent to the states by October 15 of the subsequent school year. States have 2 years to modify the data originally submitted.

Since the CCD is a universe survey, CCD information presented in this report is not subject to sampling errors. However, nonsampling errors could come from two sources—nonreturn and inaccurate reporting. Almost all of the states return the CCD survey instruments each year, but submissions are sometimes incomplete or too late for publication.

Understandably, when 57 education agencies compile and submit data for more than 85,000 public schools and about 15,000 local school districts, misreporting can occur. Typically, this results from varying interpretations of NCES definitions and differing record-keeping systems. NCES attempts to minimize these errors by working closely with the Council of Chief State School Officers and its Committee on Evaluation and Information Systems.

The state education agencies report data to NCES from data collected and edited in their regular reporting cycles. NCES encourages the agencies to incorporate into their own survey systems the NCES items they do not already collect so that those items will also be available for the subsequent CCD survey. Over time, this has meant fewer missing data cells in each state's response, reducing the need to impute data.

NCES subjects data from the education agencies to a comprehensive edit. Where data are determined to be inconsistent, missing, or out of range, NCES contacts the education agencies for verification. NCES-prepared state summary forms are returned to the state education agencies for verification. States are also given an opportunity to revise their state-level aggregates from the previous survey cycle. Questions concerning the CCD can be directed to:

John Sietsema
Elementary and Secondary
   Education Statistics Division
National Center for Education
   Statistics
555 New Jersey Avenue NW
Washington, DC 20208–5651

Methodology: The discussion about rural schools and districts, however, and the types of counties within which they are situated is dependent upon the linking and analysis of several different data files, no one of which contains all the basic descriptors needed. Because the analysis is data driven, and because *locale codes* are relatively new, a review of the data files and how they were used is provided below.

Schools file. The CCD schools file contains a record of information for each public elementary and secondary school in the country as reported to NCES by state education agencies.

Locale codes. Beginning in 1987–88, one of seven codes was assigned to each school in the CCD file based on geographic information from a set of Bureau of the Census files (Frank Johnson. *Assigning Type of Locale Codes to the 1987–88 CCD Public School Universe.* Technical Report CS 89–194. Washington, DC: U.S. Department of Education, National Center for Education Statistics, 1989). The codes used are as follows:

Large City: Central city of a Metropolitan Statistical Area (MSA) with the city having a population greater than or equal to 400,000 or a population density greater than or equal to 6,000 people per square mile.

Mid-Size City: Central city of an MSA, with the city having a population less than 400,000 and a population density less than 6,000 people per square mile.

Urban Fringe of Large City: Place within an MSA of a large city and defined as urban by the Bureau of the Census.

Urban Fringe of Mid-Size City: Place within an MSA of mid-size city and

defined as urban by the Bureau of the Census.

Large Town: Town not within an MSA with a population greater than or equal to 25,000.

Small Town: Town not within an MSA with a population less than 25,000 and greater than or equal to 2,500 people.

Rural: A place with less than 2,500 people or a place having a ZIP code designated rural by the Bureau of the Census.

Johnson's locale codes use the Bureau of the Census definitions of metropolitan-nonmetropolitan counties and urban-rural places. The Johnson codes can be summarized into four classes: *Central Cities, Urban Fringes, Towns,* and *Rural.* The first three are urban locales. In terms of metropolitan status, *Central Cities* and *Urban Fringes* are conceptually entirely metropolitan, *Towns* is conceptually entirely nonmetropolitan, and *Rural* can be located within both metropolitan and nonmetropolitan counties.

An advantage of the use of the Census definition of rural in the locale codes is that because schools are linked to places rather than only counties, it is possible to examine the distribution of rural schools across the different types of counties within which they are situated—including metropolitan areas.

Another advantage is locale codes are part of a data file that includes basic information about most U.S. public schools. The 1989–90 CCD schools file included records for 85,029 public schools in the 50 states, District of Columbia, and five outlying areas. To simplify comparisons, only regular public schools (81,029) were included for this analysis. Also, because locale codes were not calculated for the out-codes were not calculated for the outlying areas, only schools from the 50 states and District of Columbia were included, resulting in a file of 79,307 regular public schools. Data elements included identification codes, total number of students, total classroom teacher FTE (full-time equivalent), school size class based on student enrollment, and school grade type (primary, secondary or other) based on the enrollment by grade.

Local education agency file.
In addition to the schools file, the U.S. Department of Education maintains a CCD public education agency file. The 1989–90 agency file includes records for 16,967 public school districts in the United States. Among the variables included on the district file, but not included on the schools file, is the county in which the district is located. For this analysis, records from the CCD district file, including county codes and a few other select variables, were merged to the schools file. The district identification codes on the school file and the codes on the district file matched exactly. This linkage between school and district files was done to assign each regular public school to a U.S. county, based on the county in which its district office is located.

In some instances, schools are not located in the same county as their district offices. To assess the extent of possible incorrect assignments, schools were also matched to U.S. counties based upon the ZIP code of the school's mailing address using a U.S. Postal Service file. A comparison of the county assigned to a school record based on ZIP code and the county assigned based on the school's district showed less than a 4 percent difference nationally.

Counties file.
A file of selected U.S. county statistics was created for this study by merging data elements from the 1990 Census of Population Public Law 94–171 file (the only national 1990 Census file available at the time), the 1988 Bureau of Economic Analysis personal income series, the 1980 Census of Population and Housing, and a file of county types from the Economic Research Service, U.S. Department of Agriculture. From the CCD files, selected characteristics of regular public schools were summarized by county and merged to the counties file. Thus, the distribution of rural schools and rural districts can be summarized by type of U.S. counties with associated population and income characteristics. Because, as mentioned above, some schools are not actually located in the same county as their district office, the county link is not an exact match for all 79,307 schools. Consequently, a number of schools with *urban* locale codes appear in counties that are classified as entirely *rural*. However, the magnitude of this problem appears to be only about 4 or 5 percent and is not a serious limitation for the purposes of this analysis.

Districts file.
The schools file described above contains one record for each regular public school in the 1989–90 universe, including a locale code that indicates if the school is in a rural area. Unlike the schools file, the CCD agency file does not include locale information. Therefore, for this study the schools file was summarized by district identifier carrying forward counts of the total number of schools, the total number of students enrolled, the total number of classroom teacher FTE, the number of rural schools, the number of students attending rural schools, and the number of classroom teacher FTE.

In addition, counts of the number of rural schools by enrollment size were accumulated and the percentage of the district's total enrollment at rural schools calculated.

The resulting file included a record for each school district that administered at least one regular public school in 1989–90. If rural school enrollment was 75 percent or more of total enrollment, then the district was designated a rural district in this analysis. This is a conservative estimate of the number of rural districts. Consequently, the proportion of rural schools, rural students, and rural teachers in urban districts may be slightly overstated in the analysis. In any case, the difference is relatively slight because most districts are entirely rural or urban, and a broader breakpoint (say, 50 percent) would affect only 246 (1.6 percent) out of 15,133 districts.

Emerging typologies and expanding rural data sources.
Stephens provides a useful summary of efforts to develop more educationally meaningful typologies of rural school districts (E.R. Stephens. *The Changing Context of Education in a Rural Setting*. Occasional Paper No. 26. Charleston, WV: Appalachia Educational Laboratory). Work to further refine such typologies is continuing. This work is bound to be stimulated by the greatly expanded level of detail about rural areas that is part of the 1990 Census of Population and Housing. The 1990 Census will be available for very small levels on geography (blocks) even in rural areas. In addition, 1990 Census products include files that will make computerized mapping and spatial analysis of small areas such as school districts commonplace. Indeed, a cooperative federal and state project

to digitally map the boundaries of all U.S. school districts will be accessible on CD-ROM shortly. Thus the next few years should yield a much clearer picture of the conditions of schooling in Rural America.

(Prepared by William L. Elder, University of Missouri)

Chapter 6

Schools and Staffing Survey

The Schools and Staffing Survey (SASS) data were collected through a sample survey of school districts, schools, school administrators, and teachers. The surveys of schools and school principals were based on the 9,317 public and 3,513 private schools in the school samples. In addition, 56,242 public school teachers and 11,529 private school teachers participated in the teacher survey.

The public school sample was selected from the Quality Education Data (QED) file of public schools. All public schools in the file were stratified by state and by three grade levels (elementary, secondary, and combined). Within each stratum, the schools were sorted by urbanicity, ZIP code, highest grade in the school, and the enrollment. For each stratum within each state, sample schools were selected by systematic sampling with probability proportional to the square root of the number of teachers within a school.

The private school sample was selected primarily from the QED file of private schools. To improve coverage, two additional steps were taken. The first step was to update the QED file with current lists of schools from 17 private school associations. All private schools in the file were stratified by state and then by three grade levels (elementary, secondary, and com-

bined) and 13 affiliation groups. Within each stratum, the schools were sorted by urbanicity, ZIP code, highest grade in the school, and the enrollment. For each stratum within each state, sample schools were selected by systematic sampling with probability proportional to the square root of the number of teachers within a school. The second step was to include an area-frame sample, contained in 75 Primary Sampling Units (PSU), each PSU consisting of a county or group of counties. Within each PSU, an attempt was made to find all eligible private schools. A telephone search was made, using such sources as yellow pages, religious institutions, local education agencies, chambers of commerce, local government offices, commercial milk companies, and real estate offices. The PSUs were stratified by Census geographic region, MSA status, and private school enrollment. These PSUs were selected from the universe of 2,497 PSUs with probability proportional to the square root of the PSU population. All schools not on the QED file or the lists from private school associations were eligible to be selected for the area-frame sample. Schools in the area frame that could be contacted were sampled with probability proportional to the square root of the number of teachers. A systematic equal probability sample was then drawn from the schools in the area frame that could not be contacted.

The School Administrator Questionnaire was mailed to the administrator of each sampled school in February 1988. Weighted response rates for the School Administrator Questionnaire were 94.4 percent for public school administrators and 79.3 percent for private school administrators. There was no explicit imputation for item nonresponse and for a small number of schools found to be missing from the QED lists of public schools. The na-

tional estimate for public school principals is underestimated because of missing schools.

For more information about this survey, contact:

Dan Kasprzyk
Elementary and Secondary
    Education Statistics Division
National Center for Education
    Statistics
555 New Jersey Avenue NW
Washington, DC 20208–5651

Methodology: For this chapter, the base year SASS (1987–88 academic year) was used. The data from the following four SASS surveys were employed: Public School Teachers Questionnaire; School Administrator Questionnaire; Public School Questionnaire; and Teacher Demand and Shortage Questionnaire for Public School Districts.

The respondents were classified for purposes of analysis as rural or non-rural according to an item on the Public School Questionnaire filled out by the principal. Respondents could select among the following community types to describe where the school was located: (1) rural or farming community; (2) small city or town of fewer than 50,000 people that is not a suburb of a larger city; (3) medium-sized city (50,000 to 100,000 people); (4) suburb of a medium-sized city; (5) large city (100,000 to 500,000 people); (6) suburb of a large city; (7) very large city (more than 500,000 people); (8) suburb of a very large city; (9) military base or station; or (10) an Indian reservation.

In this chapter, if the respondents indicated the school was located in "a rural or farming community" or "an Indian reservation," it was classified as *rural* for purposes of analysis and all other categories were considered *nonrural*.

The items contained in the Public School Teachers Questionnaire focused on the characteristics of the respondents and the conditions in the schools. Of the approximately 65,000 public school teachers sampled, 86.4 percent (56,242) returned the questionnaire. Respondents were classified for analyses as elementary if the lowest grade was six and the highest grade eight, and as secondary if the school included any grade eight.

The School Administrator Questionnaire solicited information from school principals about the conditions in the schools. The questionnaire was distributed to approximately 9,300 public school principals and was returned by 94.4 percent.

For a complete explanation of the procedures and design for SASS, the reader is referred to S. Kaufman, 1991, *Technical Report: 1988 Schools and Staffing Survey Sample Design and Estimation* (NCES 91–127). Washington, DC: U.S. Department of Education, National Center for Education Statistics.

Chapter 9

National Assessment of Educational Progress

The National Assessment of Educational Progress (NAEP) is a cross-sectional study designed and initially implemented in 1969. NAEP has gathered information about selected levels of educational achievement across the country. NAEP has surveyed the educational attainments of 9-, 13-, and 17-year-olds and young adults (ages 25–35) in 10 learning areas. Different learning areas have been assessed periodically, and all areas have been reassessed to measure possible changes in educational achievement.

The assessment data presented in this publication were derived from tests designed and conducted by the Education Commission of the States (1969–1983) and by the Educational Testing Service (1983 to present). Three-stage probability samples have been used. The PSUs have been stratified by region and, within region, by state, size of community, and, for the two smaller sizes of community strata, by socioeconomic level. The first stage of sampling entails defining and selecting PSUs. For each age/grade level (3, 7, and 11), the second stage entails enumerating, stratifying, and randomly selecting schools, public and private, within each PSU selected at the first stage. The third stage involves randomly selecting students within a school for participation in NAEP. Assessment exercises have been administered either to individuals or to small groups of students by specially trained personnel.

After NAEP data are scored, they are weighted in accordance with the population structure and adjusted for nonresponse. Analyses include computing the percentage of students giving various responses and using Item Response Theory (IRT) technology to estimate levels of achievement for the nation and various subpopulations. IRT technology enables the assessment of a sample of students in a learning area or subarea on a single scale even if different students have been administered different exercises. The underlying principle is that when a number of items require similar skills, the regularities observed across patterns of response can often be used to characterize respondents and tasks in terms of a relatively small number of variables. When aggregated through appropriate mathematical formulas, these variables capture the dominant features of the data.

Sample sizes for the reading proficiency portion of the 1989–90 NAEP study were 4,268 for the 9-year-olds, 4,609 for the 13-year-olds, and 2,689 for the 17-year-olds. Response rates were 93 percent, 90 percent, and 82 percent, respectively. Response rates for earlier years (1970–71, 1974–75, and 1979–80) were generally lower. For example, the lowest response rate for the 9-year-olds was 88 percent in 1974–75, and the lowest response rate overall was 70 percent for the 17-year-olds in 1974–75.

The 1987–88 U.S. history assessment data in this report are based on a nationally representative sample of 3,950 4th graders, 6,462 8th graders, and 5,507 12th graders. The response rates were: 93 percent for 4th graders, 88 percent for 8th graders, and 78 percent for 12th graders.

The 1987–88 U.S. civics assessment trend data in this report are based on a nationally representative sample of 1,938 13-year-olds and 1,786 17-year-olds. The response rates were 90 percent for the 8th graders and 79 percent for the 17-year-olds in 1987–88. Sample sizes for the earlier years were much larger with 19,952 13-year-olds and 17,866 17-year-olds in 1976 and 7,268 13-year-olds and 6,751 17-year-olds in 1982. The 1987–88 analyses for 4th, 8th, and 12th graders were based on a somewhat different 1987–88 sample. The sample sizes were 1,974 4th graders, 4,487 8th graders, and 4,275 12th graders. The response rates were: 93 percent for 4th graders, 88 percent for 8th graders, and 78 percent for 12th graders.

The 1983–84 NAEP writing assessment used a stratified, three-stage sampling design. The first stage was counties (or aggregates of counties). The second stage was schools, and the third stage involved selecting students within the schools at random. The 1983–84 assessment included 24,437 students at age 9; 26,228 students at age 13; and 28,992 students at age 17. Student response rates for the 1989–90 writing assessment were 93 percent for the 9-year-olds, 90 percent for the 13-year-olds, and 82 percent for the 17-year-olds. Sample sizes varied depending on the test items and the scoring method used.

The 1989–90 NAEP mathematics and science assessments were administered to 6,235 students age 9; 6,649 students age 13; and 4,411 students still in school at age 17. The response rates were 93 percent for the 9-year-olds, 90 percent for the 13-year-olds, and 82 percent for the 17-year-olds.

The 1987–88 geography assessment was administered to 3,030 high school students. The response rate for the assessment was 77 percent. The National Geographic Society provided support for conducting the assessment.

The literacy assessment data used in this report are based on a nationally representative household sample of 21- to 25-year-olds. Blacks and Hispanics were oversampled to allow samples of sufficient size for reliable results. A total of 38,400 households were screened to locate 4,494 potential respondents. (No more than one person was surveyed from any one household.) Of the potential respondents, 3,618 young adults participated, resulting in a response rate of 80 percent.

The 1989–90 NAEP assessed reading, writing, science, and mathematics. Data were collected from a national

probability sample of more than 45,000 students per age/grade or a total of about 146,000 students in nearly 2,100 schools. Data were also collected for the assessed students' principals and a sample of their teachers. Representative state-level data were produced for mathematics at the eighth-grade level. This was the first time NAEP had produced data on a state-by-state level.

Information from NAEP is subject to nonsampling and sampling error. Two possible sources of nonsampling error are nonparticipation and instrumentation. Certain populations have been oversampled to assure samples of sufficient size for analysis. Instrumentation nonsampling error could result from failure of the test instruments to measure what is being taught and, in turn, what is being learned by the students.

For further information on NAEP, contact:

Gary W. Phillips
Education Assessment Division
National Center for Education
    Statistics
555 New Jersey Avenue NW
Washington, DC 20208–5653

National Education Longitudinal Study of 1988

The National Education Longitudinal Study of 1988 (NELS:88) is the third major longitudinal study sponsored by the National Center for Education Statistics. The two studies that preceded NELS:88, the National Longitudinal Study of the High School Class of 1972 (NLS–72) and High School and Beyond (HS&B), surveyed high school seniors (and sophomores in HS&B)

through high school, postsecondary education, and work and family formation experiences. Unlike its predecessors, NELS:88 begins with a cohort of eighth-grade students. In 1988, some 25,000 eigth graders, their parents, their teachers, and their school principals were surveyed.

NELS:88 is designed to provide trend data about critical transitions experienced by young people as they develop, attend school, and embark on their careers. It will complement and strengthen state and local efforts by furnishing new information on how school policies, teacher practices, and family involvement affect student educational outcomes (i.e., academic achievement, persistence in school, and participation in postsecondary education). For the base year, NELS:88 consists of a multifaceted study questionnaire and four cognitive tests, a parent questionnaire, a teacher questionnaire, and a school questionnaire.

Designed to ensure that private schools, rural schools, and schools with high minority membership were adequately represented, sampling was first conducted at the school level and then at the student level within schools. Additionally, oversamples of students with Hispanic and Asian or Pacific Island heritage were drawn. The data represented in this report are drawn from a nationally representative sample of 1,000 schools (800 public schools; and 200 private schools, including parochial institutions). Within this school sample, 26,000 eighth-grade students were selected at random. Followups to this survey are to be conducted every 2 years.

Further information about the survey can be obtained from:

Jeffrey A. Owings
Elementary and Secondary
    Education Division
National Center for Education
    Statistics
555 New Jersey Avenue NW
Washington, DC 20208–5651

Chapter 10

High School and Beyond

High School and Beyond (HS&B) is a national longitudinal survey of 1980 high school sophomores and seniors. The base-year survey was a probability sample of 1,015 high schools with a target number of 36 sophomores and 36 seniors in each of the schools. A total of 58,270 students participated in the base-year survey. Substitutions were made for noncooperating schools—but not for students—in those strata where it was possible. Overall, 1,122 schools were selected in the original sample and 811 of these schools participated in the survey. An additional 204 schools were drawn in a replacement sample. Student refusals and student absences resulted in an 82 percent completion rate for the survey.

Several small groups in the population were oversampled to allow for special study of certain types of schools and students. Students completed questionnaires and took a battery of cognitive tests. In addition, a sample of parents of sophomores and seniors (about 3,600 for each cohort) was surveyed.

HS&B first followup activities took place in the spring of 1982. The sample design of the first followup survey called for the selection of about 30,000 persons who were sophomores in 1980. The completion rate for sophomores eligible for on-campus survey administration was about 96 percent. About 89 percent of the students who left school between the base year and first followup surveys (dropouts, transfer students, and early graduates) completed the first followup sophomore questionnaire.

As part of the first followup survey, transcripts were requested in fall 1982 for an 18,152-member subsample of the sophomore cohort. Of the 15,941 transcripts actually obtained, 1,969 were excluded because the students had dropped out of school before graduation, 799 were excluded because they were incomplete, and 1,057 were excluded because the student graduated before 1982 or the transcript indicated neither a dropout status nor graduation. Thus 12,116 transcripts were used for the overall curriculum analysis presented in this publication. All courses in each transcript were assigned a six-digit code based on *A Classification of Secondary School Courses* (developed by Evaluation Technologies, Inc. under contract with NCES). Credits earned in each course were expressed in Carnegie units. (The Carnegie unit is a standard of measurement that represents one credit for the completion of a 1-year course. To receive credit for a course, the student must have received a passing grade— "pass," "D," or higher.) Students who transferred from public to private schools or from private to public schools between their sophomore and senior years were eliminated from public/private analyses.

In designing the senior cohort first followup survey, one goal was to reduce the size of the retained sample, while still keeping sufficient numbers of minorities to allow important policy analyses. A total of 11,227 (94 percent) of the 11,995 persons subsampled completed the questionnaire. Information was obtained about the respon-dents' school and employment experiences, family status, attitudes, and plans.

The sample for the second followup, which took place in spring 1984, consisted of about 12,000 members of the senior cohort and about 15,000 members of the sophomore cohort. The completion rate for the senior cohort was 91 percent, and the completion rate for the sophomore cohort was 92 percent.

HS&B third followup data collection activities were performed in spring of 1986. The sophomore and senior cohort samples for this round of data collection were the same as those used for the second followup survey. The completion rates for the sophomore and senior cohort samples were 91 percent and 88 percent, respectively.

Further information on the HS&B survey may be obtained from:

Aurora D'Amico
Postsecondary Education Statistics Division
National Center for Education Statistics
555 New Jersey Avenue, NW
Washington, DC 20208-5652

Methodology: As reported in this chapter, the variables were either drawn directly from the HS&B data set or were composites formed by combining multiple HS&B variables.

Demographic variables. HS&B used the U.S. Census classification for Context to determine if students and schools were in rural (N=1,849), suburban (N=4,597), or urban (N=2,927) environments. Division was another HS&B demographic variable derived directly from the U.S. Census Bureau's classification of the nine census divisions in the United

States as follows: (1) New England (N=575), (2) Mid-Atlantic (N=1,335), (3) East-North Central (N=1,756), (4) West-North Central (N=746), (5) South Atlantic (N=1,301), (6) East-South Central (N=481), (7) West-South Central (N=772), (8) Mountain (N=380), and (9) Pacific (958).

Socioeconomic status is an HS&B-created composite based on five components: (1) father's occupation, (2) father's education, (3) mother's education (4) family income, and (5) material possessions in the household (i.e., personal calculator, 50 or more books, place to study, etc.). The socioeconomic composite is the simple average of the non-missing components from the 1980 survey, after each of the five scores has been standardized.

Academic Variables. Standardized achievement is a HS&B-created composite that includes a 21-item vocabulary test, a 19-item reading test, and a 28-item math test. High school grades were students' self-reports of their average grades in high school. Values ranged from a score of 1 (mostly D's or less than 60 percent) to 8 (mostly A's or 90–100 percent).

Two variables were used to assess educational aspirations. The first was postsecondary educational plans (PSEPLANS)—taken from a single 1980 item "As things stand now, how far in school do you think you will get?" Choices ranged from "less than high school graduation" to "Ph.D, M.D., or other advanced professional degree." The second educational aspirations variable was a composite formed combining the standardized scores of the following items: whether or not the respondent's closest friend was planning to attend college, whether or not the student was planning to attend college, whether or not the respondent would be disappointed

if he or she did not graduate from college, and expected educational plans, similar to PSEPLANS above. The standardized score was then transformed into a T-score, with a mean of 50 and a standard deviation of 10 (Cronbach's alpha = .88).

The education attainment variable was drawn from the 1986 survey and reflects the highest level of education achieved by the respondent. Choices are similar to those for the PSEPLANS variable described above. Academic orientation was a composite computed from standardized scores of variables such as time spent on homework, school work habits, satisfaction with education, interest in school, and academic habits of peers (Cronbach's alpha = .66).

Persistence in postsecondary education was a computed variable based on college attendance patterns assessed on the 1986 HS&B third followup survey. Respondents were asked whether they were: in a public or private institution, enrolled in 2- or 4-year college, attending postsecondary school as a part-time or full-time student, or if they were not currently in school. They were asked to respond to this item for eight different times—from October 1980 through February 1984. The composite variable was created by giving 2 points for full-time attendance, 1 point for part-time attendance, and 0 points for not being enrolled in school. Therefore, a maximum value of 16 points would be computed for a student who had been enrolled full-time during all eight semesters.

Vocational and Career Variables. HS&B data base contains a substantial amounts of information on the labor market experiences of the 1980 Sophomore cohort. Composite measures derived from the second

(1984) and third (1986) followup surveys are described below:

Salary. Dropouts and graduates were asked to report their current salaries at the time of the third followup survey in 1986. All reported wages were converted to an hourly scale. To eliminate obvious misreports and errors, these hourly wages were compared with individual's occupations, and implausible salaries were eliminated.

Periods of unemployment. Respondents to the second and third followup surveys were asked to report their employment status for each month from June 1982 to July 1986. A composite variable was constructed that reflects the total number of months unemployment was reported. A high score on the measure (scale of 0 to 43) reflects more periods of unemployment.

Number of jobs. Respondents to the second and third followup surveys also were asked to indicate the number of jobs they held between June 1982 and March 1986 (up to eight jobs). A high value on this variable reflects a greater number of jobs during this period.

Work satisfaction. Participants were asked in the third followup survey (1986) to rate their satisfaction with 12 aspects of the most recent job. These items pertained to the pay and fringe benefits, importance and challenge, working conditions, opportunity for advancement with the employer, opportunity for advancement with the job, opportunity to use past training, security and permanence, satisfaction with supervisor, opportunity to develop new skills, job-related respect from family and friends, relationship with co-workers, and the job as a whole. Respondents rated these items on a Likert scale of satisfaction (1-4) and the standard scores of these items were summed to form the composite measure (Cronbach's alpha = .89).

(Prepared by Scott Marion, University of Maine, Orono)

Bureau of the Census: Current Population Survey

Current estimates of school enrollment, as well as social and economic characteristics of students, are based on data collected in the Census Bureau's monthly household survey of about 60,000 households. The monthly Current Population Survey (CPS) sample consists of 729 areas comprising 1,973 counties, independent cities, and minor civil divisions throughout the 50 states and the District of Columbia. The sample was initially selected from the 1980 census files and is periodically updated to reflect new housing construction.

The monthly CPS deals primarily with labor force data for the civilian noninstitutional population (i.e., excluding military personnel and their families living on post and inmates of institutions). In addition, in October of each year, supplemental questions are asked about highest grade completed, level and grade of current enrollment, attendance status, number and type of courses, degree or certificate objective, and type of organization offering instruction for each member of the household. In March of each year, supplemental questions on income are asked. The responses to these questions are combined with answers to two questions on educational attainment: highest grade of school ever attended, and whether that grade was completed.

The estimation procedure employed for the monthly CPS data involves inflating weighted sample results to independent estimates of characteristics of the civilian noninstitutional population in the United states by age, sex, and race. These independent estimates are based on statistics from decennial censuses; statistics on births, deaths, immigration, and emigration; and statistics on the population in the armed services. Generalized standard error tables are provided in the *Current Population Reports*. The data are subject to nonsampling and sampling errors.

School enrollment. Each October, CPS includes supplemental questions on the enrollment status of the population 3 years old and over. Annual reports documenting school enrollment of the population have been produced by the Bureau of the Census since 1946. They are the October *Current Population Reports, School Enrollment—Social and Economic Characteristics of Students.*

Educational attainment. Data on years of school completed are derived from two questions on the CPS instrument. Formal reports documenting educational attainment are produced by the Bureau of the Census using March CPS results. The reports are entitled *Educational Attainment in the United States* and are available from the Government Printing Office.

Beginning with the data for March 1980, tabulations have been controlled to the 1980 census. The figures shown in the table hold for total or white population estimates only. The variability in estimates for subgroups (region, household relationships, etc.) can be estimated using the tables presented in *Current Population Reports*.

Further information is available in the *Current Population Reports*, Series P–20, or by contacting:

Education and Social Stratification Branch
Population Division
Bureau of the Census
U.S. Department of Commerce
Washington, DC 20233

Acknowledgments

This document was prepared in the Office of Educational Research and Improvement (OERI) by Joyce D. Stern, OERI rural education coordinator, in her capacity as project director and editor. Overall direction was provided by David P. Mack, director of the Educational Networks Division, Programs for the Improvement of Practice, within OERI.

An Editorial Advisory Board composed of rural researchers and others intimately acquainted with rural education issues guided the project from its inception. Members were Toni Haas, consultant, and former deputy director, Mid-continent Regional Educational Laboratory (McREL); Michael Mayo, associate director, Regional Laboratory for Educational Improvement of the Northeast and Islands (NE-I); Steven Nelson, director, Rural Education Program, Northwest Regional Education Laboratory (NWREL); Charlene Popham Rudolf, past president, National Rural Education Association; J. Norman Reid, director, Strategy Development Staff, Rural Development Administration, U.S. Department of Agriculture (USDA); E. Robert Stephens, professor, Department of Education Policy, Planning, and Administration, College of Education, University of Maryland, College Park; and Todd Strohmenger, consultant and former co-director, ERIC Clearinghouse on Rural Education and Small Schools and director, Rural, Small Schools Program, Appalachia Educational Laboratory, Inc.(AEL).

Commissioned background papers provided the foundation for specific chapters. The authors and where their material was primarily used in whole or in part are: Toni Haas, chapter 1;

Norman Reid, chapter 2; William L. Elder (University of Missouri), chapter 3; Susan R. Raftery (Southeastern Educational Improvement Laboratory, now with Auburn University, Auburn, Alabama), chapter 4; Robert Stephens, chapter 5; Joyce Stern and William A. Matthes (University of Iowa), chapter 6; one paper by Marianne Vaughan and another one by Deborah Jolly and Patricia Deloney, Southwest Educational Development Laboratory (SEDL), chapter 7; Richard G. Salmon (Virginia Polytechnic and State University, Blacksburg) and Joyce Stern, chapter 8; Wayne Welch (University of Minnesota), chapter 9; Scott F. Marion, Denise A. Mirochnik, Edward J. McCaul, and Walter McIntire (University of Maine, Orono), chapter 10; and Paul Nachtigal, chapter 11. A paper on rural school operations by Jerry G. Horn (East Texas State University) informed several portions of this report. Material from these papers was updated as necessary and augmented by the editor in the process of final manuscript preparation. The editor takes full responsibility for any errors of fact or interpretation in the final report.

Several individuals with broad knowledge in rural education issues provided valuable advice as invited external peer reviewers of the final draft manuscript. They were Thomas W. Bonnett, senior staff associate, Council of Governors Policy Advisors, Washington, DC, and former member, Vermont House of Representatives; Edward W. Chance, director, Center for the Study of Small/Rural Schools, University of Oklahoma, Norman; David Dodson, executive vice president, MDC, Inc., Chapel Hill, North Carolina; David Leo-Nyquist, school teacher (rural) of

English and journalism, Weott, California, and editor, *The Country Teacher*; David H. Monk, professor of educational administration, College of Agriculture and Life Sciences, Cornell University, Ithaca, New York; and Paul G. Theobald, rural historian and assistant professor of education, South Dakota State University, Brookings, South Dakota.

Many others deserve recognition for their contributions. Ullik Rouk of the Council for Educational Development and Research (CEDaR), Washington, DC, helped guide the development of background papers funded by CEDaR (those by William Elder, Robert Stephens, Wayne Welch, and Jerry Horn). Sharon A. Bobbitt of the National Center for Education Statistics (NCES) arranged for the special tabulations from the Schools and Staffing Survey for chapter 6 and Susan P. Choy of MPR Associates produced them. For chapter 9, analyses of National Assessment of Educational Progress data, originally designed by Wayne Welch, were updated by the editor with guidance by Doug Wright of NCES and with statistical functions carried out by Brian Taylor of Pinkerton Associates. Statistical analyses of the NELS:88 data set were conducted by Bruce Daniels of Pinkerton. Special thanks go to other NCES staff for their help at critical junctures of data preparation, analysis, or review: Nabeel Alsalam, Robert Burton, William Fowler, Charlene Hoffman, Frank Johnson, Laura Lippman, Celeste Loar, Brenda Wade, and Jerry West.

The rural education coordinators at the regional educational laboratories made important content and editing suggestions. They are Jack Sanders, deputy executive director, AEL, Charleston, West Virginia; Stanley Chow, director, Center for School Improvement and Policy Support, Far West Laboratory for Educational Research and Development (FWL), San Francisco, California; Paul Nachtigal, director, Rural Initiative, McREL, Aurora, Colorado; Joseph D'Amico, rural program director, North Central Regional Educational Laboratory (NCREL), Oak Brook, Illinois; Steve Nelson, director, Rural Education Program, NWREL, Portland, Oregon; Jim Brough, resident scholar, Pacific Regional Educational Laboratory (PREL), Honolulu, Hawaii; Wyllys Terry, rural program coordinator, NE-I, Andover, Massachusetts; John Connolly, deputy director, Research for Better Schools (RBS), Philadelphia, Pennsylvania and co-director, Rural Education Project, and Robert Bhaerman, co-director, Rural Education Project; Elliott Wolf, director, Special Programs and Operations, Southeastern Regional Vision for Education (SERVE), Greensboro, North Carolina; and Deborah Jolly, vice-president, Services for School Improvement, SEDL, Austin, Texas. Other laboratory reviewers were Wendy McCloskey, research program manager, SERVE; Michael Sullivan, research associate, SEDL,

and Gary Huang, assistant director, ERIC Clearinghouse on Rural Education and Small Schools. Donna Bronson of NCREL helped type supporting tables.

Several individuals were invited to critique early drafts of certain chapters and provided valuable counsel. They were Bruce Miller, rural education specialist, NWREL; Richard Reeder, senior economist, Economic Research Service (ERS), USDA; Anicca Jansen, economist, ERS, USDA; Jacqueline Spears, co-director of the Rural Clearinghouse for Lifelong Education and Development, Kansas State University, Manhattan; Janet Poley, director, Communication, Information, and Technology, Extension Service, USDA; and Theodore Coladarci, editor, *The Journal of Research in Rural Education*, University of Maine, Orono.

Within the U.S. Department of Education, reviews were conducted by Tom Landess, Office of the Secretary; Alan Ginsburg, Robert Barnes, and Daphne Hardcastle, Office of Policy and Planning; Doreen Torgerson and Ronn Hunt, Office of Intergovernmental and Interagency Affairs; Nguyen Ngoc Bich and Terry Sullivan, Office of Bilingual Education and Minority Lan-

guages Affairs; Walter Steidle, Office of Elementary and Secondary Education; Thaine McCormick and Larry Case, Office of Vocational and Adult Education; Kathleen G. Johnson, Office of Private Education; William Wolf, Office of Special Education and Rehabilitative Services; and Maris Vinovskis, Office of the Assistant Secretary for Educational Research and Improvement. From the Education Networks Division, OERI, in-depth manuscript reviews were provided by Charles Stalford, as laboratory team leader, and Hunter Moorman, as networks development team leader. Typing assistance on tables was provided by Betty Welch, Annie Thompson, and Melvin Rogers. Paige Johnson formatted all tables consistently across chapters. Adria White provided critical copyediting review. From the OERI Publications Unit, Nancy Floyd served as copyeditor, while Phil Carr designed the publication's format and presentation. Donna DiToto typeset the text.

Finally, a special debt of gratitude is owed Craig Howley, director of the ERIC Clearinghouse on Rural Education and Small Schools, for the depth of knowledge and the editing skills he generously and skillfully applied to several chapters of this report.

ED/OERI 92–16